100 THINGS JETS FANS SHOULD KNOW & DO BEFORE THEY DIE

Jon Waldman

Library of Congress Cataloging-in-Publication Data

Waldman, Jon.
100 things Jets fans should know & do before they die / Jon Waldman.
pages cm
One hundred things Jets fans should know and do before they die
ISBN 978-1-62937-100-9
1. Winnipeg Jets (Hockey team)—Anecdotes. 2. Winnipeg Jets (Hockey team)—History. I. Title. II. Title: One hundred things Jets fans should know and do before they die.
GV956.N37W35 2015
796.332'64097471—dc23

2015009334

This book is available in quantity at special discounts for your group or organization. For further information, contact:

Triumph Books LLC
814 North Franklin Street
Chicago, Illinois 60610
(312) 337-0747
www.triumphbooks.com

Printed in U.S.A.
ISBN: 978-1-62937-100-9
Design by Patricia Frey
Photos courtesy of Jon Waldman unless otherwise indicated

This book is dedicated to my daughter,
Kaia Maielle Waldman, the Jets' youngest fan.
Hope you enjoy Daddy's book.

Contents

Foreword

The night before the NHL draft in June 1980 was a sleepless one, not because of the nightlife in Montreal but because it would be a life changer the next morning when young men's dreams were realized as their names were announced by one of the NHL teams that selected them. That morning I was selected second by the Winnipeg Jets. It could've been Montreal, Chicago, L.A., and only knowing Winnipeg by the heyday of the WHA and as a struggling new NHL team, it didn't matter. I was going to have a chance to play in the NHL and it was all good with me.

After the draft, for most first-round picks the teams would bring the player into town to formally sign a contract, meet the press, and highlight the city. At the press conference John Ferguson asked me, "What number would you like?" I said I've always had 21, but if someone had it, I would take whatever was available. He said there was a guy in the minors, but I could have it. I declined as I didn't want to start pissing possible teammates off already. Fergie went up to the mike and was asked what number I would wear, and he said, "Well, he's probably twice as good as I was, so let's give him 44." It was the first time in the NHL someone had worn the number, and it stuck with me my whole career. After that we talked about the next season with Tommy McVie, Bill Sutherland, and Fergie.

Tommy asked, "Are you excited about playing for us next season?" I said, "I just hope I make the team." They all laughed and said, "If you don't make the team we are all fu__ing fired." Needless to say I was relieved and became part of a city and organization that was very proud of its past and was excited about the future by adding players like Dale Hawerchuk, Serge Savard, Paul MacLean, and Teemu Selanne just to name a few. All this was to start building the NHL team to try to mirror the success of the WHA Avco Cup teams with the likes of Hull, Hedberg, and Nilsson leading the way.

I do miss Winnipeg in a lot of ways, from figuring out what a social was to the culinary genius of Goldeye and Pickerel cheeks to wearing a fur coat (Moe Mantha and myself bought them when we were 19 years old because it was so cold), just to name a few. There are so many fond memories with the Jets and stories (100 to be exact) that any Jets fan or hockey enthusiast will enjoy. The stories, good and bad, can be told in this book, but if you see an old Jet alumnus somewhere and want the stories to get even better, buy him a beer—the stories get better with age. These stories are definitely some of the best times of our lives. Enjoy!

—Dave Babych

Introduction

There are few seats that are better anywhere in the hockey world than one of the 15,000 or so in the Winnipeg Arena or the MTS Centre.

Looking at the action unfolding in front of you and sharing in the revelry of Winnipeg Jets hockey is an experience unlike any other. Through three distinct eras—the WHA, Jets 1.0, and Jets 2.0—the club has entertained generations of fans. Grandparents, parents, and kids will each stake claim to theirs being the greatest and will argue it to the hilt.

It's what we do in Winnipeg. We have immense pride in our boys, no matter their success on the ice. Sure, we'll call into radio shows and blast this coach's decision or harp on the indecision of that general manager, but we do it because we genuinely love our hockey. Let's face it—in an environment where -10 Celsius is considered a balmy winter day worthy of T-shirts, we are truly the heart of hockey.

That's why this book had to be written. As much a tribute to the people of Winnipeg as the players who called Winnipeg home, there are so many intricacies of life with (and without) the Jets that have made them such a compelling story. That's why it's the fans, not a player or a particular roster, that gained the No. 1 spot on this list.

Over the course of 100 chapters and a series of sidebars, you'll learn about some of the ins and outs of one of hockey's unique hotbeds. From 1972 to modern day—and yes, that's IHL and AHL inclusive—Winnipeg has maintained a love affair with the game. It's why the NHL came back. Without that passion, the Winnipeg Jets would not have been reborn.

Naturally, just as those generational arguments will be made, so too will debates come on the rankings of some items on the list.

This, unapologetically, is one person's list. Though I had consults with Winnipeg hockey faithful, ultimately the numerical order fell on my shoulders, and I'm ready to pay the piper; and truly, I look forward to debating the rankings down the road, be it through Twitter (@jonwaldman) or whichever medium succeeds it.

I thank you for picking up this copy of *100 Things Jets Fans Should Know & Do Before They Die* and look forward to starting conversations.

Go Jets Go!

1 Celebrate a Jets Moment at Portage and Main

"Portage and Main is famous across North America, so why not?"
—Barry Shenkarow, former owner, Winnipeg Jets

While you'll find that almost every other moment listed has to do with one of the three Jets eras, there is only one that unites them all, and unquestionably it's the one thing any Jets fan, hockey fan, or simply a citizen of Winnipeg absolutely must do before they die—be part of a celebration at Portage and Main.

Colloquially known as the "Wind Tunnel," Portage and Main is one of the busiest intersections in Winnipeg. It's been called the coldest spot in the city, and urban legend will tell you that the speed of gusts that blow through this area make it the testing ground for car companies.

By ordinary day, Portage and Main is a hub of activity from financial to tourist. Depending on which direction you head toward, you'll see a wide landscape unfold in front of your eyes. Stay too long in one spot, though, and you'll get honked at (albeit very politely). In the summer it's the hub for hot dog carts, and in winter...okay not much happens on the deepest of deep-freeze days, but there is still a mystique at this spot.

But by hockey night, Portage and Main becomes the central gathering ground for Winnipeg's faithful. Whether it's the local Jets or national team (namely during the Olympics), Portage and Main becomes the single biggest hotbed for shinny. Hoot, holler, grab your stick, and get ready for the best street fest known to mankind.

It's hard to say what was the most important event that took place at the famed intersection—contract signings, Avco Cup celebrations, Save the Jets campaigns, the impromptu celebration when Stephen Brunt's famous *Globe and Mail* article was published—yeah, there've been a few special moments at this one spot in the city of 750,000 frozen chosen individuals.

The popularity of the spot started with that moment that has been shown time and time again in any Jets retrospective—Bobby Hull in the background of a jubilant Ben Hatskin, holding aloft the contract that the Golden Jet had just signed. Just a couple short years later, the same intersection became the celebration ground for the Jets as they brought the Avco Cup to Winnipeg. Staging was set up at the intersection for a massive street party.

Years later, the signing of the Jets first (and thankfully only) No. 1 overall draft pick was to take place in the River City. Barry Shenkarow reflected on picking the location, noting that the first signing at the spot had started a trend. "Benny Hatskin signed Bobby Hull first at Portage and Main, and that made the WHA and put Winnipeg on the hockey map," he said. "I guess when we signed Hawerchuk, we thought he was the next foundation of the hockey team so that would be the...I wouldn't say the tradition, but you could call it that."

In years following, there wasn't much to celebrate at the corner at least for local hockey, but it was a regional hotspot for national hockey. In both 2002 and 2010, Canada came away from the Winter Olympics with the gold medal, and the good citizens of Winnipeg feted the feat at the famed corner, as they did in 2014; but those moments didn't compare to 2012, first with the Stephen Brunt–ignited celebration then as the secondary spot during the official announcement that the Jets were coming home.

Once the team was back, however, there was one celebration waiting to happen, and on the night of April 9, 2015, it took place, as Jets fans gathered to toast Winnipeg returning to the NHL playoffs for the first time in 19 years. Only a Stanley Cup victory parade, whenever that happens, will be able to rival the emotion that night at Portage and Main.

2 $1 Million for Hull

There are few times that an exorbitant salary given to an NHL player will be deemed "worth it," especially as salaries escalate to ungodly levels.

But if $7 million signings in the NHL today cause jaws to drop in amazement, imagine what the hockey community felt in 1972 when Bobby Hull signed with the Winnipeg Jets for $1 million.

The signing gave the Jets—and the WHA as a whole—instant credibility and a face to be marketed around. Hull quickly became the face of the league, even being the subject of a table hockey game.

But the negotiation to bring the Golden Jet (and yes, the nickname pre-dates his time with the Jets) wasn't an easy deal—after all, Hull was the spotlight player for the Chicago Blackhawks (or Black Hawks, as the team name was spelled at that time). To this point in his career, Hull was a three-time Art Ross Trophy winner, a two-time Hart Trophy winner, a Stanley Cup champ, and one of the marquee names of the tried and true NHL.

And yet, there was Hatskin making a bold declaration of an offer for the Golden Jet.

"How would you like to see Bobby Hull play in Winnipeg?" Hatskin told the *Winnipeg Free Press* in a November 3, 1971, article, just a short time after Hull was in town with the Hawks for an exhibition game. "Don't laugh. It's not beyond the realm of possibility. You remember a few years ago the late Jim Norris of Chicago offered the Toronto Maple Leafs $1 million for Frank Mahovlich? Well, I'm prepared to give Bobby Hull $1 million if he'll sign a five-year contract with the Jets."

The deal soon evolved, though. To bring Hull to Winnipeg Hatskin had to have that cool mil upfront while additional dollars were to be worked out for the length of the contract.

Of course, a million wasn't easy to come by, and it meant that the teams of the WHA would have to pool their resources a bit. The opportunity, however, was one they couldn't pass up, and there may have been no simpler declaration of the hope that the entire league held of landing one of the NHL's marquee superstars than a simple quote that appeared in the May 17, 1972, edition of the *Winnipeg Free Press*.

"We think we have a good chance to sign Hull," WHA President Gary Davidson told Reyn Davis.

Just a few days later the Associated Press cornered Hull, who spilled the beans a bit. "I've made a verbal deal with Winnipeg. And if they make good on it, I'm gone."

It all came down to dollars and sense for Hull, as he told Davis. "I have financial security staring me in the face," Hull said in an article published May 20, 1992. "More and more I've been establishing ties to Chicago, but I can see myself moving for this job."

But Hull wasn't the only player in wait, and in the coming days the likes of Ernie Wakely and Bob Woytowich signed with the Jets.

Owner Ben Hatskin had to make several trips out to Chateau Bobby, a journey that he told *Free Press* columnist Maurice Smith was wearing on him. "I certainly hope a decision is made one way or another," Hatskin was quoted as saying in Smith's June 15, 1972, article. "I'm tired. I want to rest and get away from hockey for a while. You know I can't sleep at nights. So many things are turning over in my brain."

The date of that first report was key—it was before Hatskin left Winnipeg to meet Hull in Chicago for a two-day round of negotiations. *Free Press* reporter Reyn Davis spoke with Hatskin again upon his return to Winnipeg, and progress had been made. "I feel the signs are definitely good that Hull is coming to play in Winnipeg," Hatskin said. "Before I left, I felt I was 99 per cent sure of him coming here. Now I have to say I'm 99.99 per cent sure he's coming here."

That extra 0.01 per cent came less than two weeks later—June 27, 1972, to be exact, as Hull stood at Portage and Main with Hatskin. The agreement amounted to $2.7 million and included a $1 million signing bonus. The image of Hatskin holding a novelty cheque above his head with a smiling Golden Jet looking on remains one of the most iconic photos in Jets history.

Hull, of course, went on to be the centrepiece of the Jets WHA years. He was the league's MVP twice, a postseason All-Star five times, and led the Jets to three Avco Cups. His No. 9 was the first to be raised to the rafters of the Winnipeg Arena, and to this day he draws unparalleled crowds for autograph sessions and speaking engagements.

3 True North Acquires the Thrashers

"It all happened pretty quick. There was a little bit of talk throughout the year, but a lot of it was about Phoenix and Winnipeg and didn't really have to do with Atlanta, then in a two-week span, it was, 'Okay, maybe it is Atlanta,' and then it was, 'Yup, it is Atlanta.' For us, it happened really quick, and it was a shock for everyone."

—Andrew Ladd, captain, Atlanta Thrashers/Winnipeg Jets

Of all the teams that were speculated to be coming to Winnipeg over the years, the Atlanta Thrashers weren't on the list. Phoenix Coyotes? Definitely. Nashville Predators? Yup. Pittsburgh Penguins? At one point.

But the Atlanta Thrashers?

Let's take a trip back through the process, starting in 1999, where Atlanta was facing ownership unrest, and rumours had the team moving to Hamilton, fuelled by reports in regional news coverage.

But Winnipeg speculation also grew amidst the ever-present rumours that the Phoenix Coyotes would be the team coming to Winnipeg. On February 17, 2010, the *Winnipeg Sun*'s Ken Wiebe published an article that included comments from NHL Deputy Commissioner Bill Daly addressing the rumours. "There has been absolutely zero discussion at the league level of Thrashers to Winnipeg," Daly said. "There is no truth whatsoever to these rumours."

Fast forward through the 2010–11 season, where the Thrashers averaged 13,649 fans per game, a far cry from the 16,000-plus in 2006–07. Ownership was even worse of a mess. In late April, Darren Dreger of TSN provided an update on the move rumours.

"The future of the Atlanta Thrashers hangs in the balance," Dreger said after talking about efforts to keep the Phoenix Coyotes in Atlanta. "Sources say Atlanta is waiting patiently for the league [NHL] to determine the fate of the Phoenix Coyotes. If a deal is salvaged, and the Coyotes stay in Glendale, there's a possibility the Thrashers will move quickly into negotiations with True North to move their team to Winnipeg."

May 2011 was the breaking time for Winnipeg hockey fans. After months of speculation and more eyeballs on Glendale municipal politics than there probably had been in history, the bid to bring the Coyotes—the former Jets—to the River City was dead;

Fans at The Forks in Winnipeg celebrate the return of the Jets.

and in the wake came speculation that another team was going to be relocating—the Atlanta Thrashers.

Now here's where a little more story needs to be told. Just because the Thrashers were going to be packing up their operations and moving, didn't mean that they were going to be making a beeline for the MTS Centre. In fact, as owner Mark Chipman points out, it was a man who was vilified by Winnipeg hockey fans—and even larger Canadian hockey fans as a whole—who was one of the keys to Winnipeg getting the consideration it received as the new destination for the Thrashers franchise.

"If people boo Gary Bettman, they have no understanding how or why our team came back here because if it wasn't for Gary Bettman, the team wouldn't be here," Chipman explained. "It would have been easy for him to dismiss us at any point along the road, but he never did. He always took us seriously.

"We weren't the only option for relocation," Chipman continued. "If he decided to have gone down a different path, there were other cities out there that—with arenas and potential ownership—were very capable of hosting an NHL team. When I asked him the question why he thought we were the right place for Phoenix or Atlanta, he thought it was an opportunity to right a wrong. It bothered him deeply that the team had ever left here. It's something he wasn't proud of at all."

Of course, these conversations all led to one moment, but even before the formal announcement couple be made, word broke on May 19 courtesy of one of Canada's most respected journalists, *Globe and Mail* scribe Stephen Brunt. "An agreement to sell the National Hockey League's Atlanta Thrashers to a Winnipeg group which plans to relocate the franchise to the Manitoba capital is done," Brunt wrote. "Sources confirmed Thursday night that preparations are being made for an announcement Tuesday, confirming the sale and transfer of the Thrashers to True North Sports and Entertainment, which owns and operates the Manitoba Moose of the American Hockey League and the MTS Centre arena, which would become the NHL team's new home."

The proclamation by Brunt set off an immediate street party in Winnipeg, appropriately at Portage and Main. Fans decked out in retro jerseys and T-shirts, carried hockey sticks, and chanted the all too familiar "Go Jets Go" call to arms, something they had waited to do for 15 years.

Though NHL Commissioner Gary Bettman tried to deny the claim, the reality was soon to unfold.

Fast forward to May 31, 2011. Speculation that had once cooled off a bit ignited into the single biggest street party in Winnipeg. The Forks, long heralded as the heart of Winnipeg, saw a gathering of thousands. Hundreds more met at Portage and Main. Business went on hold for the day, schools tuned in, and nearly every television was set to show the landmark press conference emanating from the MTS Centre.

Mark Chipman, flanked by partner David Thomson, NHL commissioner Gary Bettman, and a bevy of officials, touched off the biggest celebration in Winnipeg history with a declaration that resonates in the hearts and minds of everyone who bore witness on this incredible day.

"Today, on behalf of my family, our partner David Thomson, and our entire organization, I am excited beyond words to announce our purchase of the Atlanta Thrashers."

4 First Goals

The first "anything" is always something to be celebrated, and with three distinct eras of top-tier hockey in Winnipeg, there are three players who had the honours of tallying the first goals for their respective iterations of the Winnipeg Jets.

Through three eras—the WHA years, Jets 1.0, and Jets 2.0—Winnipeg hockey fans have had these magical firsts to celebrate. Here's a look at the three players behind those momentous tallies.

Ab McDonald—WHA

The first captain of the Winnipeg Jets was also the first to tally a goal for the team, making the marker at arguably the world's most famous arena, Madison Square Garden. The goal came in a contest against the short-lived New York Raiders, the first of several scored that night en route to a 6–4 victory.

Funny thing about that goal—its scorer, Ab McDonald, didn't think too much of it. "I didn't really think the goal was extra special; I had scored lots of goals before that," McDonald said in a 2012 interview with Metro. "But it was the first goal.... Somebody has to score the first goal, and it just happened to be me."

Alvin McDonald, a native Winnipegger, was picked up by the Jets and made their team captain. Bringing with him a boatload of experience, McDonald won two Stanley Cups with the Montreal Canadiens and another with the Chicago Black Hawks. He was also the first captain in the illustrious history of the Pittsburgh Penguins after they picked him up in the 1967 NHL Expansion Draft.

When the opportunity came to play professional hockey, McDonald jumped at it. As recorded by the Manitoba Sports Hall of Fame, who inducted Ab into its ranks in 1996, McDonald, whose NHL career already spanned 14 seasons, knew his time left on the ice was short but felt proud to be among the first to play for the WHA Jets.

The Emerson Goal

There have been some memorable goals throughout Winnipeg Jets history from the likes of Dave Ellett and Teemu Selanne, but there's one goal that lives on for reasons that aren't, shall we say, positive.

It was October 16, 1993, and the Jets were embroiled in a fierce battle with the Chicago Blackhawks. In a game that went to overtime, it seemed that anyone could take home the win. Midway through extra time, the Jets were literally handed victory by Nelson Emerson, who scooped up a puck behind the Hawks net and tossed it into the cage. Ed Belfour and co. were understandably hot, but the goal stood.

"I saw the puck two inches inside the goal line," referee Denis Morel told *Chicago Tribune* reporter Mike Kiley. "I didn't see any player direct the puck in the net with his hand."

"I know I won't play long," he said. "But I saw this as an opportunity to help bring major league hockey to the city."

Ab played two seasons in Winnipeg and was instrumental in the team's run to the WHA finals that first year. In total, he suited up for 147 Jets games, tallying 70 points (including 29 goals).

Oh, and you can't really blame Ab for a passé attitude when it comes to the goal—it was also the same day his daughter, Kristina, was born.

Morris Lukowich—Jets 1.0

It's appropriate that "Luke" would score the first goal in the Jets' NHL history. After all, he was one of two skaters protected by Winnipeg when the WHA was absorbed into the league.

Destined for hockey greatness, Lukowich was initially a member of the Houston Aeros after being picked by the club in the 1976 WHA Amateur Draft. That same year, he was picked by the NHL's Pittsburgh Penguins but chose to go to the WHA for the opportunity to play with his hero, Gordie Howe.

After the Aeros folded in 1978, Luke moved on to Winnipeg where he increased his already impressive offensive output, tallying 99 points, including 65 goals, in the final WHA season. He also counted eight goals and 15 points in the Jets' march to the Avco Cup.

Upon entry to the NHL, Luke again showed his prowess. Along with that first goal, Lukowich tallied 34 others and counted 74 points total across 78 games. His output put him atop the Jets scoring leaders, far ahead of the 59 points from Peter Sullivan. He would go on to play several more seasons for the Jets before being dealt to the Boston Bruins partway through the 1984–85 season. Eventually, Luke finished his hockey career in Europe. Today, he trains the future stars of hockey at Maximum Goal Scoring.

Nikolai Antropov—Jets 2.0

In a nationally broadcast game with the eyes of the hockey world on him, Nik Antropov planted himself in front of the Montreal Canadiens net, put home a rebound off a Mark Stuart shot, and gave himself the first goal in the new history of the Winnipeg Jets.

The moment was somewhat special to Antropov, but as so many team-focused players would do, Antro brushed off the honour. "From the personal side it's great, but it doesn't matter for me," he said. "It's a team game and we were going out there to get two points and we didn't. We came up short. So it's disappointing," Antropov told Ed Tait of the *Winnipeg Free Press* following the game, one that the Jets lost. "We want to give our fans a good day and end it with a win, but unfortunately, it didn't happen. They've been waiting for this day for the last few months."

Antropov's arrival to the Jets came after he started his career with the Toronto Maple Leafs. One of few players from Kazakhstan

Nik Antropov scored the first goal in the Jets' second history.

to play in the NHL, Antropov was drafted 10th overall in the 1998 Entry Draft. After a year with Dynamo Moscow, Antropov arrived on North American soil, splitting his first few years between Toronto and their AHL squad in St. John's. Eventually, he would gain a starting role with the Maple Leafs that made him attractive to other teams, first for the New York Rangers where he went in a trade before the Atlanta Thrashers picked him up via free agency.

Antropov's career in the NHL now appears to be over. During the 2012–13 NHL lockout, Antropov kept his skills sharp in the KHL and ended up moving to the Russian league in time for the 2013–14 season.

Incidentally, Antropov's time with the Jets wasn't his first experience in Winnipeg. In 1999, Antropov was a member of the Khazak team that played in the World Junior Hockey Championship at the Winnipeg Arena.

5 Three Avco Cups

"They all have a special spot in my heart."

—Joe Daley, Winnipeg Jets goaltender, three-time Avco World Trophy winner

Younger Jets fans, pay attention to this chapter—we had championship hockey squads in Winnipeg.

I know. Sounds amazing, huh?

Before you were born, Winnipeg had one of the most dominant teams in hockey. It beat NHL teams, international teams like the powerful Soviets, and ruled the second major league of hockey—the World Hockey Association.

Born in 1972, the WHA was an ambitious project headed up by Gary Davidson and Dennis Murphy, the latter of whom was no stranger to founding rebel sports leagues after helping establish the American Basketball Association.

Immediately, the Winnipeg Jets became one of the marquee teams thanks to the signing of Bobby Hull. The team made it to the Avco World Trophy championship series that first year before being defeated by the New England Whalers 4–1. The only other Finals loss by the squad came at the hands of the Quebec Nordiques in 1976–77, and it was a close one—4–3 in favor of the Nords.

Though it was three years before the Jets would make it back to the Avco Cup Finals, when they did return they did so with one of the strongest squads in professional hockey history. Just one year prior, the great import of Anders Hedberg, Ulf Nilsson, Veli-Pekka Ketola, and other European stars took place, while Peter Sullivan and Willy Lindstrom played their rookie seasons of pro hockey. Add veteran import Ted Green, longtime Jet leader Norm Beaudin, stalwart netminder Joe Daley and, of course, Bobby Hull, and you had one of the most potent teams that North American hockey had ever seen. It's no surprise, thus, that the Jets finished tied for first in the WHA overall standings. Moreover, the Jets lost only one game through three playoff series as they steamrolled through Edmonton, Calgary, and finally Houston.

The memory of this team was a favorite of Mike Ford, who was part of the Jets' first two championship squads. "The first Avco Cup. That, for me, was the nicest of the two," Ford told Reyn Davis in the December 21, 1986, edition of *The Jets Magazine.*

As good as this squad was though, the 1977–78 team may have been even better. Finishing the regular season with 50 victories in 80 games, the Jets outpaced their closest of seven fellow WHA teams handily. The arrival of Kent Nilsson and his 107 points (including 40 goals) provided the Jets with strength beyond the

See the Avco World Trophy

As the final team to win the Avco World Trophy, the Winnipeg Jets were given the right to keep the championship in their possession. Since then, a version has almost always been in Winnipeg, most often as part of displays at the Manitoba Sports Hall of Fame. Of course, a version of the Trophy also sits in the Hockey Hall of Fame.

If you do get a chance to see it, you'll notice almost immediately that there are 10 plaque spots on the trophy. Of course, not all of them were filled.

Those looking to add a replica version of the Avco World Trophy to their own shrines to the sport, however, will be hard pressed to find one. From time to time, miniature versions once given to players will pop up in auction houses, including Larry Hillman's from the 1975–76 championship team. The miniature trophy sold in Classic Auctions' Spring 2014 auction for nearly $4,500.

Hot Line, while Gary Bromley coming in as the 1a goalie alongside Daley helped solidify action between the pipes.

It was for this reason that Curtis Walker believes that the team outpaces the 1975–76 team and perhaps would have stood up well against NHL squad. "The '75–76 team was very strong as well, but the '77–78 team had considerably more depth," Walker said, noting that conversations he had with Hedberg pointed in the same direction. "That is the one team I would have liked to see take on the best the other league could offer. It's doubtful the Jets would have won, but you never know."

The Jets' road to the Avco Cup had only two stops in the unique structure for the season—each of the six qualifying playoff teams competed in the first round with the Jets squaring off with the Birmingham Bulls. By winning their series, the Jets earned a bye to the championship round (the highest ranking team left standing after the quarter finals garnered that privilege) where they met the New England Whalers. For the second time, the Jets swept their Finals opponents and earned the Avco Cup. Robert

Guindon, with eight goals and 13 points in nine postseason games, was named playoff MVP.

The last victory came after a tumultuous off-season for the Jets when multiple player losses put the team's on-ice performance in jeopardy. Heck, it's probably the last way you'd ever expect a team to repeat as champs.

Fortune, however, shone on the team's new ownership group, led by Barry Shenkarow. As he explained, another WHA team was (shockingly) facing financial fall-apart, which made it—and its stars—ripe for plucking.

"It was a great win at the time," Shenkarow said with a laugh. "The year before, we had a great loss of Hedberg and Nilsson to the New York Rangers, and we had bought the Houston Aeros so we could get the guys off their team and maintain a very competitive team."

The Aeros team was indeed a strong crew. Among its players were Terry Ruskowski, Rich Preston, Morris Lukowich, and Scott Campbell. By the end of the 1978–79 season, Ruskowski, Preston, and Lukowich ranked among the top six scorers on the Jets in the regular season with none scoring less than 60 points or 20 goals. Additionally, all three players scored at more than a point-per-game pace in the playoffs.

And yet, there was doubt as to whether the Jets could get it done. This was a team that wasn't nearly as dominant as its predecessors, finishing third in the league during the regular season, well back of the rival Edmonton Oilers who featured a young centre by the name of Wayne Gretzky; and yet come playoff time, the team was as strong as ever, beating the second ranked Quebec Nordiques before overtaking the Oilers in the final series ever played for the WHA, four games to two.

"The last one was kind of out of the blue," Daley said. "I don't think that that team really was as good as the previous two winners, but we were the best team at the right time, and that was against Edmonton. They had a pretty formidable team at that time."

The Avco World Trophy was retired that summer and remained with the Jets, marking them as both the final WHA champs and the winningest franchise in the history of the Rebel League.

6 The Original Jet—Norm Beaudin

When you start a franchise, there are many firsts that come with it, and for trivia's sake, there's probably none that mean more to fans than knowing who their first hockey hero will be. Regardless of whether they are a superstar, a plugger, or simply a bus-rider, that first player has an instant cache that accompanies them for the remainder of their career.

For the Winnipeg Jets, the player was Norm Beaudin.

On the surface, Beaudin may have seemed like an unassuming prospect. Like most WHA'ers, Beaudin's first elite-level hockey experience was not in the Rebel League but instead in the NHL. Originally, Beaudin was a draft pick of the Detroit Red Wings in 1963, but it took a selection by the St. Louis Blues in the '67 Expansion Draft before Beaudin saw NHL ice. That year saw the Montmartre, SK, native play in 13 games and collect his first NHL goal and assist.

Unfortunately, the next few years were unkind to Beaudin. Despite playing at-or-above point-per-game hockey in the AHL, Beaudin didn't get another crack at the big league until he was wearing the uniform of the Minnesota North Stars three seasons later, and this too was a brief stint—12 games, just one assist.

After one more season toiling in the AHL, the WHA was a godsend for Beaudin, who was picked up by the Jets in the 1972 General Player Draft. Just a few months later, Beaudin was signed by the Jets. Though the announcement of his signing came after those of goalies Ernie Wakely and Joe Daley, it was in fact Beaudin who was the first to have the ink dry on his contract.

At the time of the announcement, Beaudin shared much jubilation in the formation of the "Rebel League."

"The WHA is the best thing to happen to hockey players," Beaudin said to Reyn Davis of the *Winnipeg Free Press* in May 1972. "I've got the best contract I ever had."

The investment made proved wise for Winnipeg, which placed Beaudin with Bobby Hull and Christian Bordeleau on the "Luxury Line." The result? A 38-goal, 103-point season for Beaudin.

Beaudin's time as a central figure in the Jets' lineup, however, was short lived. Shrewd management brought Ulf Nilsson and Anders Hedberg to Winnipeg, forming the Hot Line alongside Hull, leaving Beaudin and Bordeleau out of the spotlight.

Beaudin stayed on with the Jets for two additional seasons. In total, he counted 252 points in 309 games in Winnipeg, including 97 goals, and earned one Avco Cup ring along the way.

Following two seasons of play in Switzerland, Beaudin retired and today owns two hockey stores in Florida.

Though his time in Winnipeg may not have been the longest, the impact Norm Beaudin made on the Winnipeg community was incredible, so much so that his family returned to the River City in 1998 to stage a benefit game for his daughter, Carrie. The "Pond Kings," as the Beaudin family was called, took on Jets alumni in the benefit game, bringing much needed support for Carrie. "It was great to see all the fans support us," Norm said later. "Our daughter had a brain aneurism and she's paralyzed. She's in a wheelchair and needs a lot of support. Seeing all my friends and the players helping us out with the event made it so special to try and give our daughter a good life through all her trials and tribulations."

Truly, Beaudin remains one of the most popular names from the Jets' WHA days, and with a continued relationship with the city he called home for four years, "The Original One" will never be forgotten.

7 Origin of the Jets Name

There are a lot of differing tales as to how the Jets name came about, but the most popular one that people like to speak of is due to the relationship between Ben Hatskin and the New York Jets.

Michael Kovacs, scribe for lastwordonsports.com, put the story fairly succinctly. "The WCHL team's owner, Ben Hatskin, was a fan of the New York Jets, and umm, 'borrowed' the name for his hockey club."

Simple. Done.

Right?

Not so fast. There are other legends for us to consider.

The notion that the name indeed came from Hatskin's affinity for the New York football club gels with another popular theory, one summed up in the book, *Yankees to Fighting Irish: What's Behind Your Favorite Team's Name*. Author Michael Leo Donovan summed up some discussion in talking about the Jets (well, really as background when discussing the Phoenix Coyotes but still...).

So first, Donovan dispelled one of the other popular rumours, that being around Bobby Hull, a.k.a. the Golden Jet. "Though it sounds like he lent his nickname to the club from Winnipeg, that's not the official story," Donovan wrote.

Instead, Donovan stated, "He originally picked the name to mirror Sonny Werblin's New York Jets of the National Football League fame. Hatskin also said the nickname was chosen because of the city's growing air transport business."

This isn't the first time that Werblin's name has been linked to Mr. Hatskin. Another popular story that's made the rounds is that the two were friends and Hatskin picked the name in tribute to the New York club, first asking permission from Werblin.

So here we have two different stories, but they're still tied to the New York Jets. There's yet another story that refutes the connection to the gridiron. For this one, let's take a look, again online, to what was revealed by Jetz Aviation Inc.'s blog. "Legend has it that the name came to Jets founder Ben Hatskin while flying on a plane—he maintained that it had nothing to do with the football team, the New York Jets. Regardless of its origin, the name is sure to generate interest in the local aviation industry, which is a great thing."

Okay, admittedly the last may be more tongue-in-cheek than actual theory, but no matter what way you slice it, there's a bit of mystique to how the name came about.

The "Junior" Jets

Before the Winnipeg Jets became the first pro hockey team in the Manitoba capital, the moniker was being used by Ben Hatskin's WCHL team. Following the 1972–73 season, when both the WHA club and junior team used the nickname, the team was rechristened the Winnipeg Clubs and later the Winnipeg Monarchs. By 1977, the team moved to Calgary and today are the Lethbridge Hurricanes of the WHL.

The Jets were just about as successful as the first NHL team—that is, very limited. In six seasons, the Jets couldn't advance past the semifinals, only twice making it out of the quarterfinal round in the junior league. They did, however, graduate several players to the NHL, the most noteworthy being 1980s Black Hawks netminder Murray Bannerman. Also among their ranks were future big league Jets including Barry Legge, Jim Hargreaves, Mike Ford, Brian Cadle, and Milt Black.

But the original name only tells part of the story. While the first incarnation of the Jets name was a carte-blanche selection by Hatskin, the name selection process that faced Mark Chipman square in the eye was different. With a legacy of the Jets in Winnipeg, Chipman faced a difficult decision—create a new brand that would separate the two Winnipeg NHL eras, or continue on the same path?

The situation, on both sides, had precedence. In 1996, the NFL's Cleveland Browns moved to Baltimore and returned in 1999 as an expansion team with the moniker intact, while the Washington baseball club, once known as the Senators, chose the nickname Nationals.

For Chipman, there was a bit of a division. There was no question in his mind that had the Coyotes been the relocated franchise, there was only one name that would be appropriate; but with the Thrashers came a bit more of a clean sheet.

"When it looked as though we were going to be bringing the Jets back [from Phoenix] that was the logical way to go—that was the logical name," Chipman explained. "When it turned to the Thrashers, our organization had a different feeling, which we ought to consider putting our own stake in the ground, whether we keep our current team name [the Manitoba Moose] or do something new."

In the days and weeks following the announcement on May 31 of the Thrashers relocating, the unofficial game of "name the team" took hold across news broadcasts, social media, and every conversation in Winnipeg. Names that were thrown around in media or under consideration by TNSE included retaining the Manitoba Moose, using Falcons as a nod to the historic Olympic gold medal–winning team, or going in a new direction such as the Wolves. One that Chipman talked about being a distinct possibility was "Bears," using a polar bear image in the logos. "The thinking behind it was that the future of the prosperity of our province, a lot of it was going to come from the north," he explained. "It's an incredible, iconic image that's unique to the province."

The overwhelming feeling, though, was that the Jets name should be resurrected. "In Winnipeg, NHL equals Jets and vise versa. Every article printed said, 'bring the Jets back.' It didn't matter what team, it was bring back the Jets," Chipman said. "It wasn't really surprising that people took this really strong position behind the name change, so we took that into account and we decided that was the correct name."

8 The Memorial in '95

"This is it. This is the funeral. The body is being laid to rest today."

These were the first words uttered by Scott Oake during CBC's *24 Hours* special edition broadcast of the Jets' memorial on May 6, 1995, just days after the team had seemingly played its final game—a 2–1 loss to the Los Angeles Kings. The contest itself was meaningless for Winnipeg—it had been eliminated from playoff spot contention by the Chicago Blackhawks already.

Though the Jets 1.0's extinction officially came following the 1995–96 season, the team truly passed on following the 1994–95 campaign.

By all admissions, the 1995–96 season was lame duck. The overwhelming knowledge was that the team was going to be moving to Phoenix, Arizona. The reality of the new NHL, where high salaries ruled the day and the Canadian dollar left the small-market Jets unable to compete with larger metropolises, dictated the move much the same way that the Nordiques were forced to abandon Quebec City.

The last hope for the Jets came in the form of a consortium of the Manitoba Entertainment Complex, and when the announcement came that the group's proposal was going to be pulled, there was nothing left to do but count down to the inevitable move. Initially, the thought was the team was going to be heading just a few hours south to Minnesota, where only two years prior the North Stars had abandoned the "State of Hockey" for the green (pun intended) pastures of Dallas, Texas.

The 15,000+ assembled at the Winnipeg Arena weren't ready, however, to let their team roll over and die. Screams of "Save Our Jets," a popular rally cry during the preceding months, echoed throughout the old barn, one of the loudest in the history of hockey. And though there were boisterous moments, the celebratory mood in the Arena hid a wall of sorrow. No longer would Winnipeg be on the hockey map. No "Go Jets Go" chants, no challenges between generations of fans for who was the best player in the team's history.

On that day, Oake was a reporter for CBC's Winnipeg region, but now as a member of the *Hockey Night in Canada* team, the day has still been with him, through Stanley Cup championships, Olympic coverage, and other events that most fans and journalists only dream about. "As a person who made a substantial part of his living covering NHL hockey, to see it go affected me and a lot of other people in a big way.

"Sometimes I can't remember the score of a hockey game two minutes after it's over, but I have very vivid memories of that day."

Among the speakers at the event was honourary Winnipegger Don Cherry, one of the most ardent supporters of hockey in Winnipeg, as Jets fans would especially learn in the weeks and months leading up to the team's return. After sounding off on the supposed sale to a Minnesota group (this is Don Cherry after all), Grapes gave a quick few words to the assembled masses.

"I want to thank you all for the sea of white, for how good you've treated all of us at *Hockey Night in Canada*," Cherry said during his address. "They might've taken your franchise, but they didn't take your heart and soul. You're the greatest."

After a couple other brief speeches, the players were introduced one last time on Winnipeg Arena ice. Each player, starting with No. 2 Neil Wilkinson through No. 35 Nikolai Khabibulin, were given a standing and boisterous ovation, before a couple players had their chance to say thank you to the fans. Among them was Ed Olczyk, who had two tours of duty with the Jets.

"Any player that's gone through this organization has had nothing but great things to say about the people, and the city, and the love and support that you people have shown, along with the people on these benches here, the people standing right here (referring to Jets staff including management and trainers) is what the city of Winnipeg is all about."

The accolades for the assembled masses and the city as the ceremony continued and other players gave their remarks, before a banner was raised, retiring the Jets logo. Following this, Thomas Steen's No. 25 was retired in an adjunct ceremony, fitting for a personality whose entire NHL career was spent in Winnipeg.

The ceremony then closed with emcee Bob Irving's last words. "Ladies and gentlemen, on behalf of the Winnipeg Jets hockey club, thanks for your support over the years, thanks for coming out today, and this will always be the home of the Winnipeg Jets. Thank you very much."

9 Taking Aim at the Queen

If there was any polarizing aspect of the Winnipeg Arena (well, save for the trough), it was the portrait of Queen Elizabeth II.

Check that, the *gigantic* portrait of Queen Elizabeth II.

At 5 x 7 metres, the portrait was the single biggest rendition of the reigning Queen of the British Empire. Painted by Gilbert Burch, the portrait, painted on sheets of plywood, was unveiled in the first season of Winnipeg Jets NHL play and remained hanging throughout their entire tenure in the NHL and the early years of the Manitoba Moose.

The hanging image of the Queen became a unique aspect of Winnipeg hockey, but to say that it was widely accepted, celebrated, and loved would be a bit of a misnomer. Leaving aside the political aspect of Winnipeggers not all wanting to remain part of the monarchy, the portrait was seen by some as an eyesore; and yet, it stayed hanging for years, puck marks and all.

You see, Her Royal Highness became the object not of admiration and respect by members of the various hockey clubs but instead a bull's-eye. Across generations, from the WHA Jets to the AHL Moose, the portrait became a target like one you would see at a carnival's shooting gallery. Dave Babych tells the story of hitting the Queen right in her visage, as will other players, quite willingly.

But it wasn't just team players who took aim at the smiling face of Her Majesty; their kids did, too. Witness, for example, what one future NHL Hall of Famer said in his autobiography:

"The Winnipeg Arena was my playground," wrote Brett Hull in his autobiography, *Brett: His Own Story*. "When the team finished practice, the Hulls would begin. We would get in line with those staying around for extra work. I liked to line up pucks at centre ice and try to hit that god-awful, ugly portrait of Queen Elizabeth hanging on the arena wall. Dad said I could shoot like an NHL player when I was 10, but I was never good enough to nail the Queen."

The story of the Queen in Winnipeg ended in 1999 when the portrait was removed. Even when the MTS Centre opened, the Queen couldn't find new life in the city that the royal family has visited several times within the last several years, including Her Royal Highness.

So what happened to the Queen, then, in 1999? Essentially, nothing special. It has primarily been in storage after originally being bound for Souris and their hockey arena. In 2010, the *Winnipeg Sun*'s Paul Turenne reported that the Camp X Historical Society in Toronto was going to take hold of it, but the destination museum never came to be. Instead, it ended up in a storage facility in Whitby, Ontario.

Since then, caretakers weren't able to find a permanent home for it. "We've had offers to hang her in a few places, but everybody wants it for nothing," Anya Wilson told the *Toronto Star* in late 2011.

At the time of the interview, the word had been that the painting would be going on the auction block, but there has been no word since of this supposed auction actually taking place.

That's not to say, though, that Her Royal Highness hasn't graced the MTS Centre with her presence. Nay, a more, shall we say, lively tribute has taken shape in Winnipeg in the form of Jets superfan Matthew Janzen. Janzen and his friends (now the Royal Guard) were talking about traditions that would emerge with the birth of the new team. By this time, of course, the Queen's portrait was long departed from Winnipeg. It was then that Janzen got a stroke of inspiration.

"We suggested to continue the presence of QEII, as it was one of the few notable features of the old Winnipeg Arena and Jets 1.0

era. We predicted that fans would dress in various themes of aircraft and pilots...but to us this lacked acknowledgement of traditions past and the struggle which the city and fan base had endured. The Jets were back...better than before...never to leave again! We demanded a tribute that embodied that sentiment."

And so, Janzen set out to find the appropriate regal attire required and has made quite the living tribute to the Queen and Jets heritage. Before one season, he and his friends were even spotted on Portage Avenue, escorted in a horse-drawn carriage to the MTS Centre for opening night.

The tribute has not only been met with adoration from the Winnipeg faithful but Jets players themselves. "Blake Wheeler has been the most frequent recipient of the Queen's affection. He has been knighted and given the distinguished title of 'The Duke of Robbinsdale,'" Janzen said. "Young Blake has acknowledged this attention on social media [Twitter] and during an interview with Hustler on TSN 1290. I believe he called it 'an honour' to be recognized by the Queen. I believe members of the GST line [perhaps Slater or Glass] also made reference to seeing the Queen on Twitter."

While Janzen's tribute was filling a gap and keeping the homage alive, there were still fans who called for the return of the portrait to Winnipeg, and at long last, in late February 2015, word broke that the painting would return. News broke that CN executives Jamie Boychuk and Michael Cory had purchased the portrait and were indeed having it delivered back to the Manitoba capital. "It means so many memories for me—of the old arena, of being a young kid in the '80s, going to hockey games with my father," Boychuk told the *CBC*.

Though the location had not been confirmed (and the MTS Centre likely not a destination), it didn't seem to matter—Her Royal Majesty was going to be coming back to her loyal subjects in Winnipeg.

10 The 2015 Playoff Push

"That's what we come to work for every year—to make the playoffs and make the push. I think everyone pictures making the playoffs, and that's what you shoot for."

—Dustin Byfuglien

We never thought it was possible.

The idea of the Winnipeg Jets making the playoffs during the 2014–15 season seemed like an impossibility. Any pundit or fan would have told you there was no chance in hell that the campaign would end with the Jets making the postseason.

Yet there the Jets were for Game No. 82, the final game of the regular season, with a playoff spot already secured. On this day, with white jerseys and T-shirts peppering the stands, the Jets were playing a meaningless game in front of a boisterous, celebrating crowd at the MTS Centre, concluding one of the most remarkable seasons in Winnipeg hockey history. Finishing with 99 points, the Jets claimed a Winnipeg/Atlanta franchise record for points in a season.

The start of the season, though, didn't give any allusion to this being probable, thanks to a tough Central Division that included St. Louis, Chicago, Nashville, and Minnesota, along with a Colorado team that one season prior got into the playoffs on the strength of a surprising corp. Things looked even bleaker when the team went 1–4–0 in their first five games, including being shut out twice; but the Jets quickly regrouped, so much so that midway through the campaign, the Jets had positioned themselves in the playoff hunt. The team as a whole was clicking. People started to believe that a playoff push was possible and that the early season run could be sustained, unlike in past years where the Jets had

The First Playoffs

Following the 2014–15 regular season, the Jets, after 19 years, made their return to the NHL playoffs; and although they were swept 4–0 in the series by the Anaheim Ducks, you wouldn't know by talking to fans that anyone was upset about the quick departure.

Following two games in Anaheim, the series shifted to Winnipeg where the White Out was reborn. Fans, whether they were fortunate to get tickets to the games or not, were decked out in white shirts, jerseys, or more. Car flags flew not only on civilian vehicles but on fire trucks and police cruisers as well. Truly, this was a city united.

Inside the MTS Centre, it was the biggest party you could've ever seen. The White Out was in full effect with a boisterous crowd that rivaled noise in any sports venue in history. Chants of "Katy Perry" directed at Anaheim superstar Corey Perry were deafening, as were the traditional "Go Jets Go" shout-outs.

After the final whistle blew in the third period, the Jets did their now traditional handshake among their own team before meeting the Ducks at centre ice. Once Anaheim cleared the ice, the Jets saluted their fans who continued to chant "Go Jets Go," escorting the team to the locker room and capping the most amazing season in Jets 2.0 history.

faltered. Something seemed different—being in the locker room you could feel a palpable difference in the players' attitudes.

"The main thing is we go out there every night and we know how we need to play to win hockey games. Everyone in this room understands that," Jim Slater said in a *Winnipeg Men Magazine* interview around the NHL All-Star Break. "Everyone knows their roles and what they can do to help this team win. It's been a good start for us. We've got a ways to go, but we like where we're at right now, and we're going to try to get better every single day and make a push."

Getting to that point wasn't easy by any stretch of the imagination, especially when you consider the number of total games the Jets lost to injury. At times, it seemed like there were more injured players than starters in the Jets lineup. Consider that of the top 10 scorers, only five had played at or around the 80-game mark and only two among them, Mark Scheifele and Michael Frolik, played all 82 games. Injuries got so bad at various junctures that it felt like there were more Ice Caps players in the lineup than Jets.

On top of that, the Jets had to deal with the distraction of Evander Kane. Still considered a future leader of the team, Kane was showing all signs of being a dissatisfied player. Well before the NHL Trade Deadline, Kevin Cheveldayoff finally pulled the trigger, swapping Kane and crowd favourite Zach Bogosian and a prospect for Tyler Myers, Drew Stafford, a draft pick, and a couple prospects. The move couldn't have been better for the Jets, who now had a presence that matched Jacob Trouba on the blue line and a strong, dependable forward that legitimately wanted to play in the Manitoba capital. Later additions Jiri Tlusty and Lee Stempniak, along with earlier pickup Jay Harrison, smoothly transitioned into the Jets locker room.

The difference maker on ice, however, was the goaltending. Going into the season, Ondrej Pavelec had as many doubters as supporters. With Michael Hutchinson playing well in a small audition at the end of the 2013–14 season, many felt he would be a capable backup if not replacement. Hutch did exactly that, going 21–10–5 and at times having the best save percentage in all the NHL. But Pav, who had been talked about as having remarkable off-season conditioning, kept plugging as either the starter or shared starting role without complaining. By season's end, he had gone on a three-game shutout streak.

By the time Game No. 81 was done, the Jets had 97 points and were four up on the Stanley Cup Champion Los Angeles Kings. With a Flames victory coming mere minutes after the Jets lost a shootout to the Avalanche, the Jets had secured the coveted spot.

"It was tough. I was watching the out-of-town scores all game from the bench," said Michael Hutchinson, who was the backup goalie that night against Colorado. "The L.A.-Calgary game was the last they showed, and it seemed like it took 10 minutes to get to it, so every time it came close I held my breath and hoped for the best. It was a great relief when we couldn't get that extra point and clinch, coming into the dressing room, and seeing that Calgary pulled through for us. It was a great feeling."

Twitter was ablaze, Portage and Main was quickly packed, and for the first time since 1996, playoff hockey was coming back to Winnipeg. A simple message—Our Team, Our Tradition—let fans know that the White Out would be returning.

And when the season was all said and done, there was no question that there was one man above all others who was responsible for what had been a 15-point increase in the Jets performance—head coach Paul Maurice. Maurice, who had been hired midway through the 2013–14 season, taking over for Claude Noel, had guided the Jets through their injury woes, through their goaltending battle, and through games against tough divisional opponents.

And yet, it was the humble Maurice, who almost a year to the day that the Jets qualified for the postseason, had signed a four-year contract extension with the club, who gave all the credit to the boys on the ice.

"The players took on the things they were responsible for. It started with how they came to training camp and...came back in far better shape than when we left at the end of the year, and did all the things they needed to do based on leadership," Maurice said in the post-game press conference following that final game. "They took care of things that hockey players and hockey teams need to take care of. We defined what we do, this is the way we're going to play, these are the things we think best suit the players in our locker room."

11 Halls of Fame

There are some NHL teams loaded with Hall of Fame talents and others who are lacking in those names that receive hockey's ultimate honour.

For the Winnipeg Jets, the roster of Hall of Famers, as of the Class of 2015, sat at four players, and the names won't be surprising to even the most casual hockey fan…well, at least two of them.

The first is possibly the most obvious name to ever have played hockey in Winnipeg—Bobby Hull. The Golden Jet was a hockey hero for all time in Winnipeg. Delivering three Avco Cups to Winnipeg and unparalleled excitement, the Golden Jet was the marquee name the Jets needed to become the powerhouse darlings of the WHA. Hull also spent a short period with the Jets in the NHL.

The second obvious name is Dale Hawerchuk. Though he never reached the Stanley Cup, Hawerchuk did deliver exciting hockey in Winnipeg, gaining a following unlike almost any other player in the 1980s while being heralded as one of the top players in the NHL. Ducky registered six 100-point seasons and helped the Jets reach the playoffs in all but one of his seasons in the River City.

The third name that occupies the Jets wing of the Hockey Hall of Fame is Serge Savard. Better known for his days in Montreal, Savard spent a couple seasons in Winnipeg plying his trade after first retiring as a member of the *bleu, blanc, et rouge*. It was those seasons in Winnipeg that stymie fans from time to time.

The fourth—and most recent—was Phil Housley, who was inducted in 2015. Though he's better known for his time in Buffalo, where he plied his trade straight out of high school, Housley spent three years with the Jets and was a perpetual NHL All-Star. He peaked in 1992–93 when he tallied a career-high 97 points. Housley also was an international star suiting up for the United States, winning the gold medal at the 1996 World Cup of Hockey.

Now these are the members of the Jets that are in the Hockey Hall of Fame, and no one would ever question that they deserve to be there; but how about the players who have gained entry into *other* hallowed halls?

For starters, look at the WHA Hall of Fame. The virtual home of the immortals twice opened its doors to voting that recognized the best on-ice performers and personalities who helped shape the game, and perhaps not surprisingly, there are a number of Jets who gained entry into this league-specific brotherhood.

Of course, Bobby Hull was one of the honoured members, but several other names were part of the honoured legacy. They include:

Christian Bordeleau—Bordeleau was considered one of the top signings by the Jets out of the gate and showed he was worth his weighty expectations as he put together back-to-back 100-point seasons. His time in Winnipeg was all too brief before he moved to the Québec Nordiques where he won an Avco Cup. Bordeleau also captured the Stanley Cup with the Montreal Canadiens.

Joe Daley—The local goalie made his debut in the NHL and shifted between Pittsburgh, Buffalo, and Detroit before being one of the first players to sign on with the Jets. He often ranked among the league leaders in netminding categories, was a two-time postseason All-Star, and remains one of the most visible alumni in Winnipeg.

Ted Green—Green was a standout with the Boston Bruins, known as much as a bruiser as he was a scorer, before coming to the WHA with the New England Whalers. Along with winning the Memorial Cup with the Winnipeg Braves, Green was part of all three Jets Avco Cup wins before retiring among the all-time WHA leaders in games. Green won two Stanley Cups as a player and five as a member of the Edmonton Oilers coaching staff.

Anders Hedberg—As one of the premier names of the Jets in their WHA days, Hedberg was a lock for the Hall as soon as the ballots were announced. Hedberg was a first- or second-team post-season All-Star each year he was in the league, won two Avco Cups with the Jets, and was the Rookie of the Year, on top of never going lower than 100 points in a season and twice eclipsing the 60-goal mark, numbers that are rarely seen in the NHL by one player.

Ben Hatskin—The founding father of the Winnipeg Jets was one of the biggest reasons the WHA was able to get off the ground and challenge the NHL, not just by signing Bobby Hull but by pushing other NHL'ers to make the leap of faith. So revered by the league was Hatskin that it's award for the best goalie was named in his honour. Hatskin continues to be one of the most revered names in WHA history.

Kent Nilsson—Nilsson played only two years in the WHA, but man did he make the most of his time in the league. In his inaugural campaign, "Mr. Magic" was named Rookie of the Year on the strength of a 42-goal, 107-point campaign. One season later he again hit the 107-point mark, and was named the most gentlemanly player in the league while helping the Jets gain the Avco Cup. Nilsson went on to score at more than a point-per-game pace in the NHL and won a Stanley Cup with the Edmonton Oilers.

Ulf Nilsson—Nilsson played four seasons with the Jets and was instrumental in two Avco Cup victories. A member of the famed Hot Line, Nilsson, known as "Lill-Projsarn" in Sweden, never went below the assist-per-game pace over four seasons, let alone points where his lowest was 114 in his sophomore campaign. A three-time postseason All-Star, Nilsson was playoff MVP in 1976, the first of three Avco Cup championship runs for the Jets.

Lars-Erik Sjoberg—Alongside Hedberg and Nilsson, Sjoberg joined the Jets in the 1974–75 season and maintained his standing as one of the best defensemen in the WHA throughout his time in North America. Known as the "Little General," Sjoberg was a leader in the locker room and on the ice, four times tallying 40 or more points. In 1977–78, Sjoberg was named the WHA's Defenseman of the Year. Though he was limited to nine regular season games in 1978–79, Sjoberg returned in time for the playoffs to get his third Avco Cup ring. Sjoberg made the trip to the NHL with the Jets and was the first non–North American born and bred player to captain a squad.

Terry Ruskowski—Ruskowski played all of one season in Winnipeg but made it memorable. He was one of the team's leaders in the 1978–79 final WHA season, putting together an 86-point, 211-PIM regular season before counting 13 points in eight playoff games to help the Jets claim their third Avco Cup. Ruskowski, unfortunately, was a victim of the dispersal draft, left unprotected by the Jets, and was picked up by the team that originally drafted him, the Chicago Black Hawks.

Ernie Wakely—Wakely played more games and had more shutouts than any netminder in WHA history. The Flin Flon native played three seasons in Winnipeg in tandem with fellow Manitoban Joe Daley and was a star in the league, but ultimately found more success with the San Diego Mariners, reaching a lofty 35 wins in 1975–76. Wakely retired at the age of 39 when the WHA folded, finishing his career, unfortunately, without an Avco Cup ring, but he did accumulate two Stanley Cup victories with the Montreal Canadiens.

Additionally, four Jets have been honoured by the IIHF in its Hall of Fame. In addition to the aforementioned Hedberg and Kent Nilsson, inductees include:

Teppo Numminen—A cornerstone of the '90s era of the Jets, Numminen was a 1986 second-round pick who gained a permanent roster spot as soon as he came over to the NHL in time for the 1988–89 season. Numminen became a fan favorite as he maintained a point-per-two-game pace for most of his time in Winnipeg. Along with being captain of the Phoenix Coyotes and a multi-time All-Star, Numminen has three medals from the Olympics, including two silver and a bronze.

12 52, 53, 54—Bossy's Record Is No More

There have been some spectacular rookie seasons in NHL history, and then there are those that blow all others out of the water.

Dale Hawerchuk was one of those spectaculars, with 45 goals and 103 points; but his team record wasn't enough to pass Mike Bossy's rookie goal scoring record (53) or Peter Stastny's points mark (109).

For nearly a decade, other Winnipeg rookies (and those on other teams in the NHL, to be fair) attempted to reach the peaks set by the Islanders and Nordiques freshmen and ultimately follow in their skate strides. Both Stastny and Bossy, of course, went on to be stars of the '80s and ultimately Hockey Hall of Fame honoured members.

The rookie to finally break into that vaunted territory was a Finnish import drafted by the Jets in 1988—Teemu Selanne.

Somewhat overage by the standards of his rookie brethren, Selanne was 22 when he skated in his first NHL game. Already, he had been an SM-liiga scoring champ and served in the Finnish army.

Bringing Selanne to the Winnipeg Arena had one obstacle. By the time the Jets felt Selanne was ready, he had already become a restricted free agent, and old rival Calgary had stepped in with an offer sheet to young Teemu. Agent Don Baizley spoke with nhl.com's Tal Pinchevsky before his passing about the Flames' bid.

"The offer sheet had come in at about $1.5 million higher than what the Jets had offered, so there was a lot of angst in Winnipeg about, was any player worth this kind of money?" Baizley said. "I think he [Selanne] was really determined coming over under that sort of pressure. He was going to prove to people that he was a good player. It wasn't the offer sheet so much as the reaction to the offer sheet."

Selanne's debut finally came in the 1992–93 NHL season. The same year that the league was celebrating the Stanley Cup's centennial, scoring was at a peak. It seemed like every club had at least one 50-goal scorer and/or 100 point-getter. Who knew that the lone Jet to achieve both statistical milestones would be a rookie?

But the determination Baizley spoke of was that which drove Selanne to the greatest rookie season in NHL—if not all pro sports—history. In his first game, Selanne tallied two assists, and two nights later, he had his first two goals against the recently born San Jose Sharks.

By the time of the NHL All-Star Game, Selanne was gaining huge momentum and was named to the mid-season showcase. Though his Campbell Conference team was soundly defeated 16–6, Selanne used the opportunity to display his talents with the league-wide audience, tallying a goal and an assist.

When the season resumed, Selanne was well on his way to breaking both Bossy and Stastny's records, and it didn't take long for either to fall.

The first came in a home game against the Quebec Nordiques. With the Jets soon to embark on a road trip, Winnipeg faithful were hoping to see the history-making moment live and in-person. Sitting at 51 goals, the chances seemed a bit beyond reach; however, in the space of the game, Selanne did just that. The breaker came on a long outlet from Tie Domi, putting the Finnish Flash on a partial breakaway. An errant stab at the open puck by goalie Stephane Fiset gave Selanne the simple touch to guide the puck into the net and ignite a celebration in one of the loudest buildings in all of hockey, led by Teemu throwing his glove up in the air and "firing" at it with his stick.

"I wasn't planning to do that, but I was so pumped and it just came into my mind," Selanne said years later about the celebration.

"I had done it once before back home when my team won the Finnish championship and I scored the winning goal."

Just a short time later, on March 23, Selanne broke Stastny's point record. Again, the moment came on home ice, this time against the Toronto Maple Leafs. The moment is less celebrated but possibly even more impressive.

By season's end, Selanne had tallied 76 goals, tying him for the league lead with Buffalo's Alexander Mogilny, and tied for fifth in scoring with 132 points in the 84-game season. The marks gave Teemu the Calder Memorial Trophy as best rookie and a rare-for-a-freshman berth on the first NHL All-Star Team.

Selanne's stellar play was buoyed by a Jets squadron that was now benefiting from the Dale Hawerchuk trade to Buffalo. Phil Housley was playing the best hockey of his career and finished the campaign with 97 points, good for the league lead among rear-guards. Keith Tkachuk, who was drafted in the Sabres' position, counted 28 goals and 51 points. Alexei Zhamnov and Thomas Steen also passed the 20 goal and 70 point plateaus.

Selanne wouldn't hit those highs again in his career (no one can blame him for that), but did count three more seasons of 100-point hockey (one being a partial with the Jets) and two 50-goal seasons. Overall, Selanne's career finished with better than one point per game (1,457 points vs. 1,451 games) and 684 goals. Though he would win a Stanley Cup in Anaheim and collect other awards south of the border, it is this rookie campaign that is perhaps the most well-remembered and acknowledged of his stellar NHL career.

13 The 1984–85 Season

"We felt we had a real opportunity that year."

—Laurie Boschman

If there was ever a season that the Jets seemed to have everything going their way, it was 1984–85. It seemed that all the stars were aligning just right. Dale Hawerchuk, now a three-year veteran of the NHL, was named team captain after Lucien DeBlois was traded in the off-season. Barry Long, who had previously filled in as interim head coach, was retained, and the team truly seemed to have gelled and arguably had the most firepower in the history of the franchise.

The season started out fairly strong for the Jets, as they went 4–4–2 through the first 10 games. By their 30th game, the Jets were showing marked improvement, thrice going on streaks of at least three contests where they garnered at least one point (and more often than not they were wins). But before the midway point of the campaign things slowed for the franchise, and at the midway point of the season, the Jets were sitting on a seven-game winless skid.

As the second half started, however, the Jets began to show promise again. They reeled off two more runs of three-plus games with at least a tie, before putting on one of the most impressive rushes to the postseason in NHL history. From March 8, 1985, forward, the Jets didn't lose a single game, going 10–0–3 in this stretch, including a nine-game winning streak. The point total at season's end was 96 points, a new club standard, while also placing it second in the Smythe Division, setting up a playoff encounter with the Calgary Flames, only this time with the Jets having the home advantage.

The team statistics tell only part of the story of this remarkable year:

- The Jets counted six players with at least 30 goals: Dale Hawerchuk, Paul MacLean, Laurie Boschman, Brian Mullen, Doug Smail, and Thomas Steen.
- Hawerchuk and MacLean both cracked the 100-point plateau, while Mullen, limited to 69 games, also tallied at better than a point-per-game pace.
- Two defensemen—Dave Babych and Randy Carlyle—hit the 50 point mark.

A ticket stub from the 1985 game that ended in a 5–5 tie, part of a 13-game Jets streak without a loss.

- Brian Hayward, who appeared in 61 games, came away with 33 wins.

All this while trading away Morris Lukowich, long regarded as one of the premier players on the Jets roster.

As the playoffs started, the Jets seemed to be firmly in control of their rivals from Cowtown, as they topped the Flames in Game 1 and Game 2 at the Winnipeg Arena; but it was in the third contest of that opening round where everything came crashing down around the Jets when Jamie Macoun put Hawerchuk out of action with a cross check that resulted in a rib injury to the team's leader. The Flames went on to win that game.

The Jets, however, rebounded in Game 4 and put out the Flames with a 5–3 victory. It was the first time the club had ever won a playoff series.

And had it not been for Macoun, who knows what would've happened—maybe the Jets would've been able to put the Oilers on their heels instead of being swept aside without a victory, as they had been the past two years by Edmonton; but the injury derailed Winnipeg and put aside any hope of beating the impossible rival.

"I was very young at the time—and optimistic and idealistic and hadn't had my heart ripped out of me enough times to not believe that maybe there was a chance—but the loss of Dale Hawerchuk in that series really did prove the doom of the Jets," TSN1290 Radio host Andrew Paterson recalled. "They had a really solid team that year, but when you think about what they had to go through, this was not an average team—this was the Edmonton Oilers. Still to this day I have a hate on for Jamie Macoun."

14 Ben Hatskin

"Working with Benny and getting to know him was certainly a thrill for me. The man took a giant step in regards to pro hockey in Winnipeg. Without him and his efforts to get Bobby here, we may not be as excited as we are today. I really feel strongly that Benny did a great service to the people of Winnipeg."

—Joe Daley, former goaltender, Winnipeg Jets

Ben Hatskin was the principal owner of the Winnipeg Jets when they entered the WHA, and though his stake in the team lasted only but a couple years—he sold the club to a community group in 1974—Hatskin was largely responsible for the WHA's rise to prominence and its ability to stand up against the imposing figure of the NHL.

Hatskin's time in sport pre-dates his entry into the hockey world. Long before he got involved in shinny on the business end of things, Hatskin was a member of the Winnipeg Blue Bombers, playing six years and helping the team win the Grey Cup twice.

But it was hockey that was his true calling. Hatskin's first experience in owning a team came in the days of the Western Canadian Hockey League, where he owned the original Winnipeg Jets along with other franchises. (Incidentally, once the Jets became WHA–bound, Hatskin retained his junior team.)

But there's no question that Hatskin's greatest involvement in hockey came with the WHA when he not only stepped up as Jets owner, but pulled off one of the greatest signings in sports history—Bobby Hull. Bob Irving, legendary voice with CJOB, talked about the key role Hatskin played in giving the WHA the credibility it had by signing Hull.

"Ben Hatskin deserves full credit for being a key individual in the creation of the World Hockey Association in 1972. Without his drive, and certainly without him signing Bobby Hull, the WHA probably would never have gotten off the ground," Irving said. "He convinced the other potential owners in the league to pitch in and pay Hull's salary, and once they signed Hull, the league had instant credibility. Ben was a guy who got things done, and when he began his pursuit of Hull, he wasn't about to take no for an answer."

Hatskin's, shall we say, stubbornness in refusing to give up his pursuit of Hull was part of his personality; and that may have factored into the WHA's founders knocking on the door to the Winnipeg Arena. As *Winnipeg Free Press* reporter Maurice Smith documented way back on October 6, 1971, Hatskin was a major cog in the future plans of the Rebel League as it sought to put teams in western Canadian cities (Edmonton and Calgary also being on its radar). The article came out soon after a visit by Dennis Murphy and Gary Davidson to Winnipeg and a meeting with Hatskin.

"As of now, Hatskin won't commit himself for the public prints," Smith wrote, "but in conversations we've had with him, he's been more than enthusiastic concerning the prospects of the new league."

Hatskin, of course, came on board—along with a consortium behind him—and the rest as they say was history; well, except for that whole signing Hull thing. It all started with a bold declaration.

"How would you like to see Bobby Hull playing in Winnipeg?" Hatskin told Smith in an article printed in the *Free Press* on November 3, 1971, shortly after he spilled the beans on player inquiries coming in. "I'm prepared to give Bobby Hull $1 million if he'll sign a five-year contract with the Jets."

And it is Hatskin's personality that, unquestionably, played into his brash attitude.

"He was a sometimes gruff individual, but he also had a unique charm that worked well for him in many ways," Irving said.

But all that Hatskin did, he did out of love for his city and the possibility of what pro hockey could bring, even though it ended up costing him dearly in the pocketbook.

"He loved Winnipeg, and he knew he could make a splash. You went big or you didn't go at all. He always went big," Michelle Rahman told the *Winnipeg Free Press'* business reporter Geoff Kirbyson in the summer of 2014.

For all that Hatskin did for the Jets and the WHA, he became one of the most recognized names associated with the club and league. The Jets would later name their Most Exciting Player Award in his honour, and the league titled its best goalie award the Ben Hatskin Trophy. He's also a member of the Manitoba Sports Hall of Fame, the WHA Hall of Fame, and the Winnipeg Citizens Hall of Fame; and if his family has its way, there will soon be a street named after Hatskin in Winnipeg.

15 Mark Scheifele Wore an NHL Jersey on Draft Day

When the new Winnipeg NHL club stepped up to the podium in Minnesota to announce its first draft selection, it did so with little in place.

Kevin Chevaldayoff was only weeks before hired as the team's new general manager. The services of his incumbent, Rick Dudley (who played for the original Jets), were not retained amid a maelstrom of controversy. Head coach Claude Noel was not an Atlanta Thrashers import either—his arrival in Winnipeg had come a couple years prior with the TNSE–owned Manitoba Moose.

Other personnel, such as Craig Heisinger, were retained and became part of the draft process, where Mark Scheifele was taken with the seventh overall selection.

Scheifele was not an unfamiliar name among draft experts. As a member of the Barrie Colts and, perhaps fittingly, coached by Dale Hawerchuk, Scheifele had a ton of talent that was only starting to come to light.

In parts of two seasons—2011–12 and the lockout-shortened 2012–13 season—Scheifele showed signs of being the future of the Jets' frontline, and by 2013–14, still officially an NHL rookie, Scheifele was a comfortable fit on the team's roster.

But it all began in one of the most unique fashions in NHL history.

You see, the day Mark Scheifele was drafted was not only his entry into the NHL—it was also the official start of the Winnipeg Jets. Though the team was born on May 31, 2011, with the official announcement, the team was not yet named. Speculation was that the Winnipeg Jets' moniker was going to be renewed, but there were other names that were bandied about—the Polar Bears, the Ice, and the Falcons among them.

There was some natural trepidation on the part of Mark Chipman. Ties to the past can either work for you or against you, and when your team is attempting to forge a new identity, doing so with an old name can be a step in the wrong direction.

And yet, there was Chipman, at the Xcel Energy Center; a proud Winnipegger, but far from the only one in attendance. With a six-to-eight-hour drive behind them (depending how many speed limits they obliterated along the way), a contingent of Winnipeg NHL fans made the trip to the Twin Cities to see their first draft of a new era. It's perhaps fitting that the draft played host to the unveiling of the new Winnipeg team—just over a decade prior, the Minnesota Wild skated for the first time, returning the NHL to another frozen city after the beloved North Stars were ripped away and moved to Dallas.

With the eyes of the hockey world on him, Chipman made an announcement that has left an indelible mark in Winnipeg history:

Mark Scheifele performs during the annual skills competition.

"It's now my pleasure to introduce our executive vice president and general manager, Mr. Kevin Chevaldayoff, who will make our first pick, on behalf of the Winnipeg Jets."

And with the announcement, Mark Scheifele became the first, by name, member of the Winnipeg Jets.

But what about a jersey for Scheifele to wear? While the name was ready, the logo and sweaters were not. The new look of the Jets would not be unveiled until later that summer, first with an online reveal of the new insignias that was quickly followed by a mad rush on the Jets Gear store at the MTS Centre for the first souvenir ball caps and T-shirts.

Next came the jerseys, which debuted when four members of the squad, including Nik Antropov, Eric Fehr, Andrew Ladd, and Mark Stuart, stepped out of the back of a carrier plane at the 17 Wing base.

So instead of donning his team's colours, Scheifele—along with other Jets draft picks that day—instead pulled a generic (though admittedly sharply designed) NHL jersey over his head. It was the first time that a player had donned the sweater of the league rather than his club, and it's one that in all likelihood will not be repeated; well, at least until Quebec City gets its NHL franchise back.

Scheifele had a brief start in the NHL, getting into seven games straight out of the draft and registering his first big league goal before returning to the Barrie Colts. His second season followed the same pattern, and finally in 2013–14 he found a permanent roster spot as he shouldered the role of being one of the future cornerstones of the young franchise.

16 The 1990 Playoffs

If there was any team that was close to slaying the invincible dragon that was the Edmonton Oilers (well, other than the tandem of Steve Smith and Grant Fuhr's pad), it was the 1990 edition of the Jets.

The team was arguably at its biggest peak since the 1984–85 season. Finishing third in the Smythe behind the Oilers and defending Stanley Cup champion Calgary Flames, the Jets were transitioning from the old guard to a new group of players led by super rookie Bob Essensa, sniper Pay Elynuik, and developing defensive pairing Fredrik Olausson and Teppo Numminen, while the likes of Dale Hawerchuk, Dave Ellett, and Doug Smail were still along for the ride.

And the teams were about as even as they had ever been.

By 1990, the Oilers had been stripped of some of their uber-stars. Wayne Gretzky, of course, had been dealt to the Los Angeles Kings, while Paul Coffey found a new home in Pittsburgh, and Andy Moog had been shipped off to the Boston Bruins. Grant Fuhr, meanwhile, had sustained an injury and was inactive. Yes, they still had Mark Messier, Glenn Anderson, and Jari Kurri, but the team was showing signs of vulnerability.

"I think we expected it to be a very tough series," said Bill Ranford in an interview with the *Edmonton Sun* at the time of the Jets' return. "Winnipeg had a very strong team. They were pretty well-rounded. The question going in, was who was going to get the better goaltending?"

A good question indeed, and after the first two games it appeared that young Essensa was going to be the victor.

The first sign of hope came in Game 1, when, for just the second time in their playoff history, the Jets defeated the Oilers in a

7–5 shootout for the ages. Ranford, a native of Brandon, Manitoba, was the victim of the shellacking. The second game showed a little more even play, as overtime was needed to decide the contest. It was Mark Lamb, a relative unknown, who brought home victory for Edmonton, sending the series tied to Winnipeg.

And that's where the Jets grabbed a hold on Edmonton's neck.

First, the Jets beat the Oilers 2–1 with Dale Hawerchuk scoring the game winner in his last true celebratory moment in a Winnipeg Jets jersey.

Then came Game 4, one of the longest—and most memorable—games in Jets history.

Just over a minute into the second overtime, Thomas Steen broke out from a pack of players and made a beeline for the Oilers' net; and, had it not been for Reijo Ruotsalainen, he may have been the hero of the contest. In Ruotsalainen's panic, however, he was called with a hooking penalty, and without a clear break, Steen was denied a penalty shot.

Cue the dramatics.

The teams lined up to the left of Ranford with Steen, the captain of the Jets, taking the faceoff. Steen won the draw, pulled the puck back to Ellett. The veteran defenseman was already in shooting stance when he received the puck, quickly wound up, and fired a slapshot along the ice toward Ranford.

Goal.

The sea of white in the stands erupted as Olausson and Steen grabbed the instant hero in a moment of pure celebration. "It's the biggest goal of my pro career," Ellett later told the *Winnipeg Free Press*. "It's something we always try to do. I just had a clear alley. There was no way I was going to pass up the shot."

But as brightly as the fates seemed to be shining on Winnipeg, the Oilers weren't going to relent, especially with Game 5 returning to Northlands Coliseum. "We didn't panic when we came back home, I think we started to feel stronger and stronger about our game," Ranford said in the same *Sun* interview. "We felt as though the tide was starting to turn. Our mission statement was 'One game at a time.' I remember [head coach] Teddy Green being a Winnipeg boy, talking about getting that next win back at home, then getting back to Winnipeg."

Though the Oilers took the series, coming back from a 3–1 deficit to win the series 4–3 (and later the Stanley Cup), it was Ellett's goal that is the most memorable of the series and is still remembered by Jets fans today as being among the most, if not *the most* important in the history of Winnipeg hockey.

17 Victory Over the Soviets

For many players in the WHA days of the Winnipeg Jets, there are numerous memories to go around, especially for stars like Anders Hedberg.

Multiple Avco Cups, individual statistics that rivalled the NHL's best...those are the kinds of highlights some players may refer to as their fondest memories.

Not for Hedberg.

When asked, there was one solitary game that stands out as his favorite memory of playing in Winnipeg.

"It was when we beat the Russians," Hedberg said in a 2004 interview. "It was the first time a club had beaten them. They were touring around and beating up all the NHL teams, and they came here and we beat them up. That's the game that sticks out in my mind because it was more than a game—it was politics, it was free will, democracy vs. the dictatorship. It was the WHA vs. the NHL. It was the smaller city vs. Toronto and Montreal."

Need further proof of just how important game was? It also ranks high in the memory of one of Winnipeg's greatest broadcasters—CJOB's Bob Irving.

"I will never forget the game against Russia," the man known as "Knuckles" said. "The Winnipeg Arena held just under 10,000 people at that time, and it was packed to the rafters that night to see the Jets play a powerhouse Soviet team that included all of their great players, Kharlamov, Yakushev, Tretiak etc., and I swear the roof nearly came off the place when Hull, Hedberg, and Nilsson put on a show in leading the Jets to a 5–3 victory."

Indeed, it was the Winnipeg Jets who did the unthinkable when they upended the Soviet National Team, something no other club team to that point had been able to do.

The game itself came in the aftermath of the famed 1972 Summit Series. For years after that series, the Soviets—both as the national squad and as individual clubs such as the Red Army—toured across the two major North American leagues, taking on clubs as part of tours across Canada and the U.S. Among these games were the more well-known contests against the Philadelphia Flyers and the Montreal Canadiens. Additionally, the Soviets banded together for the 1974 WHA Summit Series, where the Rebel League put forth its top Canadians against the Russian squad as the NHL had done two years prior. The Soviets won this exchange with four victories, a single loss, and three ties.

No one likely would have predicted that the Jets would come out on top in the contest held on January 5, 1978, but then again, no other team—WHA or NHL—had the mix of international superstars that Winnipeg had; and make no mistake about it, this factored big time into the Jets coming out on top. Perhaps if the WHA had opened the '74 Summit roster to the international stars that it had (something the NHL didn't have when it essentially fielded its All-Star team as the Canadian squad), it wouldn't have come up so much on the short end of the stick.

Perhaps the most interesting part of the contest was how quickly the Jets showed they weren't going to have any fear. Within the first 10 minutes of play, Winnipeg was up 2–0 on the strength of two Bobby Hull goals on setups from Kent Nilsson and Lynn Powis (Lars-Erik Sjoberg and Hedberg also drew assists on the first and second goals, respectively). Ulf Nilsson then counted the third and fourth goals before the proverbial Russian bear was awoken and responded with three tallies. But soon after, the Soviets simply ran out of gas; a third goal from Hull in the dying seconds of the game sealed victory for Winnipeg, 5–3.

Unfortunately, reliving the heroics of the game isn't possible. Without a broadcast tape being available, the contest becomes an afterthought, unfortunately, in the greater hockey community. "I have always felt it's a shame that the Jets-Soviet game wasn't on TV," Irving commented. "It was only seen by the 10,000 or so who were actually in the Winnipeg Arena, and I don't feel the Jets ever got enough credit outside of Winnipeg for beating that Soviet juggernaut."

The 1978 game wasn't the only one that the Jets played against international squads. Russian clubs continued to pay visit to the Winnipeg Arena, including games both as part of the WHA series and the Super Series games of the 1980s. The Jets also took part in contests overseas, playing the likes of not only the Soviets (who they battled in Japan for a three game set) but also international tournaments like the Izvestia Cup and Volkswagen Cup. The Jets also faced national squads like that from Czechoslovakia (who the Jets also beat).

But it's the Soviet team that remains the most important international opponent in Jets history, and the game that Winnipeg historians will always point to as being one of the biggest moments in local hockey lore.

18 The Manitoba Moose Story

Once the Winnipeg Jets left at the end of their playoff run in 1996, there was a large void to fill in the hockey landscape. Though Hockey Canada did an admirable job by hosting the World Junior Championships in 1999 and Women's World Hockey Championships in 2007, along with exhibition and pre-tournament contests, the biggest occupant of Winnipeg Arena and later MTS Centre ice was the Manitoba Moose.

Originally based out of Minnesota, the Moose were primarily an unaffiliated International Hockey League team (though they had a loose agreement with the Jets) when Mark Chipman and an assembled ownership group picked up the club from south of the border. There was an air of familiarity for the team though, as one-time Jets Russ Romaniuk, Scott Arniel, and Randy Gilhen (who moved to the club straight from the Jets roster) were part of the inaugural team. Randy Carlyle, who already had some coaching experience from the Jets, was also part of the staff and, after Jean Perron failed as the new coach, was named as the lead bench boss.

While the familiarity was there, however, there could have been some understandable reservation for a city to go from NHL hockey to the IHL game, a step or two down the ladder. But as Chipman explained years later, the momentum of crowds attending hockey games needed to be maintained. "We thought there might be some reservation, but our view was you need something to keep hockey alive rather than stop and restart," Chipman said.

In picking up the Moose franchise, Mark Chipman and his partners were essentially working a swap, as he would later explain. Originally, the Jets were Minnesota bound and were to take up occupancy in St. Paul, while the Moose would come north. Of course, that didn't end up being the case.

Unfortunately, the Moose didn't perform well—at first—in the stands. As Mike Beauregard reported during *24 Hours Late Night*'s during the September 28, 1998, broadcast, the team was not the financial success that ownership was hoping for. In Year 2, as Beauregard reported, the Moose drew an average 6,300 fans through turnstiles, more than a thousand tickets off pace for what they needed to break even.

But the fortunes of Manitoba soon turned. That season, the Moose did get the bigger crowds they sought, finishing with an average of 7,300 and change. Even with a sag in the final year of the IHL (6,800), the team was still a viable entity and was one of six teams to move to the American Hockey League (the others were the Chicago Wolves, Grand Rapids Griffins, Houston Aeros, Utah Grizzlies, and Milwaukee Admirals).

The AHL brought about a lot of change for the Moose. Now, they were forced into affiliation and found a partner in Vancouver. Immediately, the impact was felt as Stan Smyl was brought in as head coach. Others later on, such as Randy Carlyle, Alain Vigneault, and Scott Arniel, were also Canucks hires, while the players were signees or draft picks by Vancouver. In early years this meant that also-rans like Steve Kariya and Brandon Reid populated the Moose lineup, but as the Canucks drafting improved, so too did the Moose.

The affiliation didn't just help on ice, though, it also marked a better financial state for the franchise.

"When we moved to the American League, we had a lower cost for player personnel because we got the majority of our players from Vancouver, so it became a viable business for all of us involved," Chipman explained.

Also improved was attendance. By the time the Moose moved to the AHL, attendance had risen to around the 7,000 mark and

The Manitoba Moose celebrate a victory during the 2005–06 AHL season.

reached a peak of 8,626 (sellout of the first two bowls of the MTS Centre) in 2004–05. This, of course, was the lockout season where the league was playing host to NHL'ers who had retreated back to the A while the big league was on hold for an entire year. Not only did names like Marc-Andre Fleury and Jason Spezza play on MTS Centre ice that season, but so did expected NHL rookies like Jeff Carter.

Of course, the Moose players themselves were no slouches. Ryan Kesler, Alex Burrows, and Kevin Bieksa, all future headliners in Vancouver, were centrepieces of a team that by season's end raised the Northern Division banner to the rafters of the MTS

Centre and just a few years later produced what is inarguably the team's best campaign—2008–09. That year, the Moose reached the Calder Cup finals. Led by a young Corey Schneider, the Moose were able to make a charge unseen in Winnipeg hockey since the golden years of the Jets.

"I remember this building, in that final series, was as loud as it is now," Schneider said in 2014 after playing against the Jets. "It was a really incredible experience as a minor leaguer."

Though they fell short of championship glory, falling to the Hershey Bears in six games, the Moose proved that not only were they contenders, but the parent club had a bright future. Perhaps fittingly, the Moose's last season was the same campaign where the Canucks made it back to the NHL finals.

Being a member of the Manitoba Moose though meant much more than just being a candidate to one day make it to the NHL. Talk to alumni and they'll say that they were well respected both by management and the city in which they performed.

"Even though the Moose were in the AHL, we were always treated like an NHL franchise," said Jannik Hansen, former Moose player and now Vancouver Canuck. "They made sure we had the best facilities to train in, and it was such a great hockey market. The fans there were really passionate about their team and were so good to us. It was a place that players truly wanted to come and play because of the way we were treated both on and off the ice."

"The people in Winnipeg are passionate about hockey," Canuck Alex Burrows said. "[There were] great fans that really supported the Moose. The other people were Craig Heisinger and Mark Chipman. Those guys were so passionate about the team, wanted to please the community so much and wanted to have a good product—a winning team—that made the fans proud."

As fate had it, the Moose ceased as a Manitoba team on Monday, May 9, 2011, playing their final game—a triple-overtime loss in the Calder Cup playoffs to longtime rivals the Hamilton

Bulldogs in Winnipeg. Just a few weeks later, the team, who was still to be owned by TNSE, relocated to St. John's and became the Ice Caps—the new affiliate of the Winnipeg Jets.

Fifteen seasons of playing in any one location in minor league hockey is incredible. Some teams last all of one season in a home; but no team in AHL hockey can ever, or will ever say, that it was the reason that the NHL returned home.

19 The Last Game

"It made the goodbye even tougher because we knew there was no going back."

—Scott Oake, CBC Reporter

Like tens of thousands of other onlookers, Oake watched the Jets play their final season—1995–96—after getting a reprieve when the original deal that would have sent the team to Minnesota fell apart. With another year, dubbed the "Season to Remember," Winnipeg had one last campaign of NHL hockey to enjoy; but the reality was the team wasn't going to stay beyond that day. But in a unique twist of fate, TNSE chose to end their affiliation in St. John's in 2015, electing to resurrect the Moose back in Winnipeg.

With the NHL schedule set, the countdown to extinction was on. The stay of execution wasn't going to last, and the Jets were down to their final games in Winnipeg. No matter what way you sliced it, the Jets were going to be on the move—all that could happen was a playoff run to keep the team going a bit longer.

Just as they did in 1994–95, the Jets' final home game was held against the Los Angeles Kings, and for fans in attendance it was a nervous day—the Jets had one last possible stay of execution ahead of them. Beat the team that sent them to the grave just one year prior and they were in the playoffs. Lose and they were going to try to claim said spot on the road (yes, the NHL put the last regular season and possibly final ever game away from the Winnipeg Arena) against the Anaheim Mighty Ducks, a team that now included Teemu Selanne.

As a commemoration, the team handed out metal key chains with replications of the ticket stubs of the first and last games for the franchise along with commemorative posters. But the focus of the game wasn't on free stuff—it was the action on the ice. Thankfully, the Jets did come through with the victory, with Shane Doan—the future of the franchise—getting the game-winning goal, followed by Keith Tkachuk potting an empty netter to earn his 50th goal of the season.

After losing to Anaheim in a lame duck game, the Jets readied themselves for the playoffs. If one thought that the new playoff format introduced just a couple seasons prior, where the top eight teams in a conference were ranked and met, was going to help the Jets, they thought wrong. Sure, the new format meant the club was able to escape the pressurized scenario of facing the Edmonton Oilers or Calgary Flames, but they now faced the Detroit Red Wings, who one season prior had been Stanley Cup finalists.

Uh oh.

The Jets, to their credit, battled valiantly, and had it not been for the heroic, 51-save effort of Nikolai Khabibulin in Game 5—where the Red Wings were already up three games to one—the Jets' story would have ended on the road at the Joe Louis Arena. But the clock struck midnight in Winnipeg, and the Red Wings easily put the Jets down with a final score of 4–1.

Fans remained in their seats as long as they could, while the players gave a final encore, waiving to the Jets' faithful and showing their appreciation. The last player to leave the rink was Teppo Numminen, one of the heart-and-soul players of the '90s Jets.

There's perhaps no better encapsulation of the game than the reflections of Brent Hawryluk, one of the Jets fans in attendance. "A few friends and I sat in one of the top rows (36) behind the net—all dressed in white including white pants and face paint. Norm Maciver scored the last ever Jets goal in our end of the rink, however, by that time the feeling throughout the building was that the Jets just couldn't complete at Detroit's level," Hawryluk recalled. "I remember watching the scoreboard clock many times throughout the game, with the realization that this could be the final time I ever see the team that I grew up with, watching and cheering for the Jets who provided us the opportunity to see the world's best hockey players in person, however it never sunk in. Even upon leaving the building, it still hadn't hit the four of us until we made it back to the car and my friend Max started crying, then the emotion truly set in for us all—our Jets were gone forever."

20 The Foundations

"We did a lot of things in the community, and I think that was the right thing."

—Kris King on the last season of Jets hockey

One of the hallmarks of the Winnipeg Jets and True North hockey franchises was their dedication to the Winnipeg community.

The first organized effort came with the Jets Goals for Kids Foundation, a program that, as former owner Barry Shenkarow explains, came from his wife, Rena.

"The team was doing a lot of stuff individually. It was my wife's idea to form the Foundation and to organize it and be able to raise more money for the community, and doing things like the 50/50 where the minor hockey team came in and sold tickets, and they got half [of the proceeds]," Barry explained. "It was her brainchild and her hard work that made it happen. In hockey, I believe it was the first in the NHL."

The beneficiaries varied but always focused on the youngest fans of Winnipeg hockey, including the local children's hospital, and one particular cause that sticks out in Shenkarow's mind. "At the time, they gave money to televise up north back to the hospital in Winnipeg when kids needed surgeries. They supported food banks for kids and all sorts of different things."

One of the ways that donations were raised back in that time was the Jets Wives Carnival. Another brainchild of Rena Shenkarow, the idea was borrowed from the city of Minneapolis that would hold a fundraising fair that included the Minnesota Vikings, Twins, and North Stars.

Darren Ford vividly recalls the goings-on at the Jets Wives Carnival, which he attended as a youngster. "You could buy mystery boxes wrapped up in Jets wrapping paper for I believe $20. You didn't know what was inside so it was fun to tear them open and see," he said. "You could also take a real shot on Pokey Reddick or Bob Essensa or take pictures with any player. I have many photos from those carnivals. They were great events for the kids, and the wives really took it on as their own event. And of course come junior high, we all wanted to see Mark Osborne's wife [laughs], Madolyn Smith."

When the Jets left Winnipeg, the Jets Goals for Kids Foundation lived on. In fact, public money from Operation Grassroots, as well as the sale of the "Memories to Cheer" cassette, benefited the charity; but Mark Chipman and True North Sports and Entertainment stepped up, founding the Moose Yearling Foundation. Established in October 1996, the Foundation took up the cause of Goals for Kids with proceeds benefiting youth activities and focused charities. It was during the Moose years that the annual gala, as well as the Flatlanders Spirits Festival were born.

When the Jets returned to Winnipeg, Chipman converted the charity to the Winnipeg True North Foundation. Once again, events were central to fundraising efforts, such as the Mike Keane Celebrity Hockey Classic. The Jets also teamed with Manitoba Public Insurance to create a license plate with partial proceeds benefiting the Foundation.

This 1990s patch served as a constant reminder of the Goals for Kids Foundation the team supported.

Following the Jets' first season, the Foundation announced it had donated over $1 million to 44 agencies.

"To reach over the million-dollar mark in monies donated to charities is a great accomplishment for the Winnipeg Jets True North Foundation," foundation Executive Director Dwayne Green said in a release. "This would not be possible without the generosity of those who support our fundraising activities, our event sponsors, our passionate fans, and all our volunteers and our internal staff and management who get behind all of our events. They are the reason we are able to help so many children in need around the province."

21 The MTS Centre Is Built

"Hockey in Manitoba has changed a little bit for now, but I can see them coming back to the National Hockey League one day. The new building will do that for you."

—John Ferguson Sr.

Give Fergy all the credit in the world—he knew the business of hockey. He was in Winnipeg along with a host of former Jets alumni and personalities for the closing of the Winnipeg Arena before the opening of the MTS Centre, then the new home of the Manitoba Moose.

There were many factors that contributed to the NHL returning to Winnipeg in 2011—willing ownership and an improved economy among them—but the presence of the MTS Centre may very well have been what tipped the scale in favor of True North Sports and Entertainment.

Opened in 2004, the MTS Centre stands in the heart of Winnipeg's downtown. With capacity for just over 15,000 fans, the building is the smallest in the NHL yet has nary seen a night that hasn't been a sell-out. The close confines make it, like its predecessor on Maroons Road, one of the loudest buildings across the landscape of the NHL. Additionally, it played host to numerous NHL exhibition games, acted as the practice and exhibition rink for the 2004–05 World Junior gold medal–winning Canadian team that sported the likes of Sidney Crosby, and was the primary rink for the 2007 Women's World Hockey Championship to go along with concerts that include the biggest names across the entertainment landscape.

Officially, the MTS Centre opened its doors on November 16, 2004, mere days following the last game of hockey played at the Winnipeg Arena. The night was celebratory for fans who jam-packed the new building whose main entrance stood at the corner of Portage and Donald, and it's a memory that still resonates with those who played on that first night, including Alex Burrows, who counts the opening game against the St. John's Maple Leafs among his best memories of playing for the Manitoba Moose. He said the sold-out arena was quite the site to see, "especially for the minors. To have 15,000 people watch your game, it's pretty special."

The creation of the MTS Centre, however, did not happen overnight, nor was it the only proposed facility to take over from the Winnipeg Arena, whose best days were behind it by 2002. Over the course of the original Winnipeg Jets' remaining years in the River City, a few different proposals were bandied about, none of which were taken more seriously than one by Manitoba Entertainment Complex Inc. As described in a proposal entitled "The Playbook," MEC was "committed to the construction of a new entertainment facility in Winnipeg," which was to be "utilized as a multipurpose entertainment and sports complex, with the major tenant being the Winnipeg Jets Hockey Club." MEC's plan called for luxury suites with a payment plan that went into 1997, but the conglomerate's plan to purchase the team from Barry Shenkarow fell through.

True North had elements of this proposal on its side. Much like MEC, the plan TNSE proposed also had a hockey franchise being the main tenant of a new arena, that being their own Manitoba Moose. In reflecting on the agreement for the MTS Centre, Chipman revealed that there were multiple factors that worked in favor of his group.

"I guess it's probably a combination of a few things—one part timing. We kind of had to let the wounds heal from our inability to get it done in '96," Chipman explained. "I think a big part was the viable business model that underpinned it. You can show the premier and mayor that this is a partnership that works. This isn't going to fail. We have a strong ownership group and we're going to take on the vast majority of the costs and we're going to take on all the risks.

"So really it was a $140 million project. We needed a little less than a third from these guys [government]. They were smart people, they did the numbers and in the case of the Feds [federal government], they'd get their money back almost instantly with GST on all the construction."

Additionally, the numbers showed for the province that its investment would be paid off by the time building was completed.

So with the plan in place for a new arena, the big question mark that stood was the location. A few areas were bandied about in the media and between hockey fans. Chipman had his own vision for the location. "The site that we were really considering was attaching to the Convention Centre."

But the site for the MTS Centre didn't end up being there, of course. Intended areas were otherwise spoken for, including by the Workers Compensation Board.

Enter David Thomson.

Thomson was the head of the Thomson Corporation at the time, a family-run business that included several subsidiary companies and later purchased news outlet Reuters. Through Osmington Inc., Thomson owned the building area once known as Eaton's. He was more than willing to join up with Chipman's True North Group.

"When it became known that we were attempting to build an arena that was going to be behind the Convention Centre and we were struggling to get that land assembled, the guys from Osmington, who owned this building [the building which are now TNSE's offices], Cityplace Mall, and the Eaton's parkade, said, 'Hey, if you want to build an arena, we'd like to be your partner.'"

With land ready, the conversion of Eaton's was set to begin (albeit once hurdles were cleared by those wanting to preserve the building). Elements of the former Canadian retail giant were retained, including its red brick exterior and the statue of Timothy Eaton (more on this later). On April 16, 2003, ground was broken on construction of the new arena, and roughly a year and a half later, the MTS Centre officially opened its doors.

The new facility was slightly smaller than the Winnipeg Arena and below capacity compared to other NHL venues; but Chipman did his due diligence during planning stages to confirm any dimensions that were needed to suit the league's needs.

"As we were developing our thinking on the building, I had the occasion to meet with the commissioner of the NHL for a couple reasons, whether it was AHL/IHL discussions or whatever. It might've been Mondetta being at Salt Lake City for the Olympics," Chipman said. "I had a conversation with him about the size of the building. There was a period of time where there was a minimum number of seats that was required. So I asked if that was really true, and he said, 'No, not really. You're building to fit your market.'"

Ever since that monumental opening day, the MTS Centre has been one of the darlings of North American sport and entertainment. It continually ranks as one of the busiest venues in Canada or the U.S., and with its primary tenant—the Winnipeg Jets—has assumed the position of being one of the best facilities in which to see hockey across the globe.

22 Experience the Anthem

There's no question that the Canadian national anthem is among the most beloved across the globe. Simply named "O Canada," the ballad is a source of pride, despite the humorous mockeries by those to the south of the Great White North.

Through the decades, it's been sung loudly and proudly in hockey arenas from Victoria to St. John's, but there may be no more passionate singing of "O Canada" than at the MTS Centre.

Throughout Winnipeg's hockey history, the city has played host to national games that bring patriotic, sell-out crowds to venues. From the third game of the 1972 Summit Series through the 1999 World Junior Hockey Championships and beyond, Winnipeg and Hockey Canada have enjoyed a relationship that most other cities only wish they had; but it wasn't until the return of the Winnipeg Jets that "O Canada" was sung with as much fervor as it is today.

Much like in any other city in Canada, the moments start fairly subdued and respectfully as anthem lead Stacey Nattrass begins to recite the lyrics.

But it's at a single phrase that gets people going—"True North!"

The show of appreciation by the Jets faithful to the group that brought NHL hockey back to Winnipeg is incredible to listen to as it can rock the foundation of the MTS Centre on some nights, and as Nattrass reflected, it was something that was born before the very first puck drop of the new era. "It kind of started softer for the first preseason game or two and then grew louder by the home opener," she said. "I do find that I have to concentrate on keeping a steady tempo though as it is tempting to slow down through that moment. It also always makes me smile, which can throw off the sound of my voice!"

Since those first nights, the chant has taken on a life of its own. Not only is "True North!" emphasized at hockey games, but also at other events at the MTS Centre, and as Nattrass attested, outside events are also picking up the newfound tradition. "I sing at a few annual dinners throughout the year," she said, "and there are definitely a few die hard brave souls that shout it out at those sorts of functions!"

Though the "True North" call has been with the Jets since the first game, a second tradition has come about since. Toward the end of the anthem, a cameraman will make his way over to one corner of the rink and focus in on one gentleman who stands, finishes the anthem with a salute, and gives the MTS Centre the "thumbs up" as fans clap, showing appreciation for the efforts of a past generation.

The gentleman is Len Kropioski, a veteran of World War II—and resident of Kenora—who has sat front row at every Winnipeg Jets game since the return of the team. So beloved is "Kroppy" that the Winnipeg Jets created a special pin during the 2003–04 season of the 90-plus-year-old veteran as part of their annual collection.

Of course, Kropioski doesn't do this for attention or for adulation, he does it simply to show his love of Canada. "I love my country, and anytime 'O Canada' is played or sung I stand up and I salute, doesn't matter where I am," Kropioski told the *Kenora Daily Miner and News* in January 2014. "It is just a wonderful country; I wouldn't trade it for nothing. Anything I did for my country I would do it again, I just love it."

It's a special moment that Nattrass is more than thrilled to do as a moment of sharing the spotlight. "I think it is amazing that we have this veteran, who travels from Kenora for each and every Jets game [he did the same for the Manitoba Moose by the way]. He stands in the front row saluting during the anthem, truly 'on guard for thee.'"

23 The Flight Helmet

"When Stewie brought it up to us, it was a great idea. What's a better thing than a flight helmet? A lot of guys have fun with it after a hockey game."

—Jim Slater, forward, Winnipeg Jets

If ever you get the chance to tour the Winnipeg Jets' locker room, it's highly recommended you take advantage of that opportunity.

Laying behind two steel doors in the underground parkade for the club sits this den for Winnipeg's professional hockey stars. Within are the stalls, bedecked in the deep blue uniforms of the team. The centre of the room holds the Jets' logo, which, as is tradition, cannot be stepped on. After games and practices, a carpet-covered plank is placed over the insignia to protect it.

But the sight that has the most appeal for the players but may otherwise be ignored is a different sort of helmet than one would expect to see in a locker room—a fighter pilot helmet.

The helmet was the conception of Mark Stuart. One of the leaders of the Jets, Stuart came to Winnipeg with Blake Wheeler as one of the last moves ever made by the Atlanta Thrashers organization, acquired from Boston for Rich Peverley and Boris Valabik.

In acquiring Stuart, the Thrashers were getting a leader. Already, Stuart had worn the assistant captains' "A" on his jersey with Team USA and helped the squad win the World Senior Men's Hockey Championship in 2008, matching an accomplishment he was part of at the Junior level in 2004 and at the U18's in 2002. Once Stuart arrived in Atlanta, he was given the "A" once again, an incredible show of faith in a fresh face to a locker room.

Almost three years to the date that he was acquired, Stuart approached ownership with the idea of bringing a player-driven recognition piece to the club. Mark Chipman took it from there.

"Chipper ended up finding a helmet for us," Stuart told Cassie Campbell-Pascall of *Hockey Night in Canada* in February 2014. "Andrew Ladd mentioned this was something we wanted to do and he [Chipman] went out and got us one. It's something a lot of teams do—something like this."

Andrew Ladd, the team captain, found great value in Stuart's recommendation. "I think it's great for recognizing guys that do some unsung things or things that go unnoticed by everyone out there but we know that are important to this room," he said. "So I think sometimes you see a lot of times guys that people out there wouldn't expect to see get it, but are playing big roles and keep this team on track."

Stuart was the second recipient of the helmet after Devin Setoguchi claimed it first on February 2, 2014. As part of the ritual, it is the winning player who bestows the honour on the next individual.

Jets head coach Paul Maurice, who just a few short weeks earlier came into his position, was thrilled with what his players had done.

"That's the players—I had nothing to do with that. I like all the things that are player traditions—all of them," Coach Maurice told Tim Campbell of the *Winnipeg Free Press*. "When I got here, I kind of asked what it is they did, not just in that way, but everything.

What is it that you guys do that makes this different? And the list was a little short. I had nothing to do with this. It was all them. But those are the little pieces that bind guys together, so I think it's awesome.

"And it's cool-looking, and it's not a great big goofy fedora thing."

24 Participate in the White Out

When Winnipeg made it to the playoffs in the 1980s and '90s, the atmosphere inside the Winnipeg Arena was unparalleled. Loud, boisterous, jam-packed-to-the-roof crowds filled the old barn on Maroons Road, cheering on their beloved Jets with dreams of playoff success.

And for the players, the uniform of choice by these fans was a sight that holds firm in their memories.

"The one thing that sticks out is the White Out," said Pat Elynuik, who played with the Jets in the late 1980s and early 1990s. "When we were playing Vancouver in the playoffs, all the fans got together and created the first White Out night. You see it around a lot of *SportCenter*s these days, and you see them doing similar things. It was pretty special that Winnipeg thought of that to cheer on its hockey team and that it's now spread throughout North America."

"I'll never forget the playoffs," Teemu Selanne added. "I think it really helped the players. There was so much intensity and energy in the building. It really helps you as a player."

The White Out was truly unique. Whether you were a reserved fan who would simply don a white T-shirt or Jets home jersey, or got more hardcore by painting up your face (or more), the display was nothing short of incredible as thousands of seat dwellers at the Winnipeg Arena would join together, young and old alike. At times the Jets distributed white pom poms to go along with the gear, creating an even more riled-up look and even more energy filling the old barn on Maroons Road.

The origins of the White Out came in April 1985. Rod Palson, an advertising consultant for the Jets, suggested that a simple promotion be struck—that everyone wear white to the pending playoff games that were coming to Winnipeg amid one of the team's most successful seasons. The notion caught fire, and soon, the Winnipeg Arena was a veritable sea of white.

For fans like Darren Ford, who ran jetsowner.com during the 15 year NHL absence from Winnipeg, being part of the White Out had its ups and downs, something natural when you consider the futility that unfortunately accompanied the Jets' playoff runs.

"My memories are fond and not-so fond depending on how you view them. They didn't last long as the Jets were an early

Wait in Line Two Hours to Meet a Jet

Back in the days of the Winnipeg Arena, meeting a Winnipeg Jet meant waiting outside the locker room after a game. To get this experience today, you're going to instead head to a public appearance. And though you'll wait a lengthy amount of time, it's worth it.

Whether for charitable causes or private contracts, it's not uncommon for Jets players to situate themselves across the city. And when fans come out to these events, they very often do so in droves, so much so that lineups snake through stores or go on for a block outside the hosting location.

With memories of years past in their minds, these events now become generational opportunities for fans. "With remembering how exciting it was to meet my Jets v1.0 heroes at autograph signings for store grand openings, I enjoy the excitement [son] Scotty exudes when he meets each of his Jets v2.0 heroes," Brent Hawryluk said.

exit to almost every best-of-seven first-round playoff series they ever played," he explained. "But beyond being short lived, they were the most exhilarating experiences imaginable. People would arrive so early for the game. The old arena would be jam packed for warm-ups. Complete pandemonium. Drums banging, chants, and general chaos, and the puck hadn't even dropped yet. Once the game was actually underway it was deafening. And a goal? My word…insane. Gives me goose bumps just thinking about it."

The difference in Ford's mind was that the pick-up was organic, with little artificial encouragement from Jets brass. "It was so real. So genuine," he said. "There were no white shirts on every seat that people were given as a promo. That's easy. Any team can give 15,000 white T-shirts away to create a White Out. But this was real. 15,000 people literally found their own white something, and wore it to the rink. It was a blizzard of white mixed with oddly yellow painted aisles [laughs]."

The White Out became so popular that it even spawned a song, "Jets Fight/Wear White" on the *Hockey Rock Winnipeg Style* recording that was produced during the 1995–96 season, and was the last image that the hockey world saw when the Jets took their final bow out of the NHL in 1996.

With the return of the NHL to Winnipeg, the question quickly became whether the White Out would be resurrected. There were people on both sides of the debate, but the message became loud and clear as the 2014–15 season concluded. The night the Jets qualified for the playoffs, True North began a new campaign, spelling it out in large, white letters: Our Team, Our Tradition.

25 Wear a Jets Jersey in Phoenix

Winnipeggers may be a lot of things—brave souls for weathering -40 Celsius just to have an outdoor celebration in February for example—but one thing they definitely are is a breed of people who doesn't forget.

Ever.

That's why one of the most common sights for an angry, nay, *vengeful* Jets fan between the years 1996 and 2011 was to see a Winnipeg Jets jersey in the stands at Arizona Coyotes game.

Yes, even though the Jets are a memory, they are very much alive in the hearts—the cold, bitter hearts of Winnipeg fans who still want their original team back; and in the opinion of at least one former Jet, the sentiment is mirrored.

Shane Doan, as discussed elsewhere in this book, is still with the Jets/Coyotes franchise and is the last standing member of the team. Touring across the Western Conference means that he will still see the sweater he wore in his rookie season at venues across the NHL landscape, including at his home rink. "It brings back some great memories for me," Doan said. "I was very proud to be an original Winnipeg Jet, and it's nice to see some fans still wearing the old jerseys. Winnipeg has some of the best and most passionate hockey fans in the world."

But what would the reception be for a Coyotes fan to see the former tog? You might be surprised. Jordan Farber of Winnipeg wore the old team's jersey in the new team's building five years before Winnipeg inherited the Atlanta Thrashers. The reaction he got might surprise you. "People loved it. [They were] high fiving me!" he said.

Farber, of course, is far from alone. Phoenix has become a preferred destination for Winnipeg snowbirds, and whether it's the baby boomers, golden eras, or their children that come down for a visit in the coldest of months in Winnipeg, going down to see a hockey game is pretty much a must do. Seeing NHL action unfold while you sit back in a T-shirt and shorts is an experience most in Winnipeg would only dream about.

But here's the kicker—the experience of wearing a Jets jersey in Winnipeg could have ended following the 2010–11 season. It was close. Very close. As in so close you could smell the tears of the Picasso-inspired desert dog.

As Mark Chipman told the Winnipeg Chamber of Commerce at a luncheon in June 2011, True North was as close as anyone to bringing the original boys home.

"We literally came within 10 minutes of acquiring [the Coyotes] in May 2010 when the City of Glendale met a 5:00 PM Eastern Standard Time deadline to wire the funds necessary to pay for the league's losses for the (2010–11) season," Chipman said. "We left somewhat disappointed but uplifted by the fact that the league had taken us so seriously and, as a consequence, had indicated it would just be a matter of time before we would actually acquire a team."

How ironic it would have been, not only because the team would go back from whence it came, but the Coyotes' extinction would have come at the hands of the same Detroit Red Wings that sent the Jets into the hangar for the last time.

Last minute funding from the city of Glendale, however, saved the Coyotes from moving back north, though some still question why. In 2013–14, the Coyotes sat last in the NHL in attendance with an average of 13,775, just 80.4 percent capacity (also a league low).

Could the Coyotes still be on the move? Only time will tell. Until then, don't expect to see Jets jerseys disappear from the stands in Arizona.

26 The Hot Line

When the Jets entered the WHA, there was a concerted effort to live up to the worldly aspect of the league's name.

Like the rest of the WHA, the team was bent on showing the hometown crowd the best players from across the globe. Though their first two seasons saw more of the trend carried over from the NHL of employing North American players, the gateway to Western Europe opened up in the third season.

There were Finns such as Veli-Pekka Ketola and Swedes like Lars-Erik Sjoberg who joined the Jets that year, individuals who helped shape the Jets not just into Avco Cup contenders but champions. Of the imports, there were none more important to the team's offence than a Swedish tandem: Ulf Nilsson and Anders Hedberg.

Nilsson and Hedberg had all the tools to be successful when they entered the WHA. Hedberg was a former Swedish Rookie of the Year while Nilsson was a standout in the World Championships among other accolades each had in their trophy cases when they entered North American hockey as pioneers of European hockey.

"We were part of what they called the globalization. It was needed," Hedberg said in 2004. "It would have happened eventually because players and talent come from everywhere. The borders are personality, not nationality. I think we were part of the Jets and Winnipeg saying, 'We're not only going to invite you in, but we're going to embrace you, because we think this is fun and this is good, and you can win with this.' So in this way, we were part of changing and opening up their minds so that the game could be played more than the traditional NHL style at that time."

Instantly, Hedberg and Nilsson were placed on a line with Bobby Hull, and the line gelled right away. By this time, Hull had already established himself as one of the big guns in the WHA and quickly took Hedberg and Nilsson under his wing. In the process, the trio became the most intimidating line in all of the WHA with all three scoring above a point-per-game pace. Of the 12 season totals among them, only one—a shortened season by Bobby Hull in 1976–77—had a point total less than 100. Now *that* is domination.

The time of the Hot Line had its share of celebrations, but not every moment was pleasant for the trio, in particular Hull who by this time was, shall we say, filially challenged, which made him an easy target for players on the other side of the ice. Despite being an NHL legend and arguably the biggest star in the WHA, Hull didn't get any special treatment, as Anders Hedberg recalled.

"One of the Hansons in Birmingham pulled Bobby's wig off his head, and he came out the next period wearing a helmet," the Swedish superstar recalled with a laugh.

Together, the Hot Line won two Avco Cups, were perennial All-Stars, and took home postseason hardware such as MVP and Rookie of the Year titles. With all the firepower and accolades they possessed, one can only imagine what would have happened if the Hot Line would have stayed together when the Jets entered the NHL; but like all other good things, the Hot Line met its end. This came in 1978 when, as ironic as it is, John Ferguson signed Hedberg and Nilsson to contracts that brought the duo to the NHL's New York Rangers. Although they performed well in the NHL (Hedberg had four 30-goal seasons in his seven years with the Rangers, Nilsson was a point-per-game player over five seasons), they couldn't bring a Cup to Broadway. The magic of the Swedish stars resonated but didn't shine brightly enough on the big stage.

Fortune being what it is, the last Hot Line games for the duo were not the last time they played on Winnipeg Arena ice. With the absorption of the WHA by the NHL, the Jets faced off against their former heroes. If fans were divided in loyalty during those games it's highly understandable. Hedberg himself had trouble wearing enemy colours on Winnipeg ice.

"I was so damn nervous, I could barely play here," he said. "It was very different."

Hull, meanwhile, played out the final season for the Jets in the WHA before retiring, but not before bringing Winnipeg its third Avco Cup. Hull returned to Winnipeg for its first NHL season, unretiring and playing 18 games with the club before being dealt to the Hartford Whalers. There, he retired for good, playing alongside onetime rivals and fellow hockey immortals Gordie Howe and Dave Keon.

Today, Hull, Hedberg, and Nilsson remain at the top of all-time player lists for the Jets. Their combined efforts ensured that the team stayed on top in the WHA, and they were recognized for their collective greatness, as the trio was inducted into the Rebel League's Hall of Fame in 2010.

27 Three Retired Numbers

There are two honours that a hockey player can receive at career's end that stand head-and-shoulders above all others.

One is to be inducted into the Hockey Hall of Fame, which tends to only recognize the stat marvels more than the players who made more rounded contributions to one or more clubs throughout their career. The other honour is one that tends to be a bit more open-ended and may actually be more meaningful to players—when a team you played for chooses to retire your jersey number.

Now one honour tends to be more plentiful than the other, but in the case of the Winnipeg Jets the numbers are essentially the same—the Jets have officially retired two numbers while a third was honoured by the Phoenix Coyotes. Similarly, three Jets alumni are in the Hockey Hall of Fame as of this writing.

Amidst these two honours are two parallel players whose jersey retirements came with controversy.

The first number retired by the Jets, likely not surprisingly, was that of Bobby Hull. The "Golden Jet," of course, was the heart and soul of the WHA era and gave Winnipeg instant credibility.

Hull's jersey retirement came on February 19, 1989, amid a transition era for the NHL's Jets. Hull's No. 9 had been worn by Doug Smail at the time (he transitioned to No. 12). The ceremony was memorable and stood the test of time as the lone Jets retirement for much of their NHL tenure.

Where controversy erupted, however, was what occurred in 2005–06. At this time, Bobby's son, Brett, was set to return to the NHL along with the rest of the league after the 2004–05 lockout year, and he signed on with the Phoenix Coyotes, who were the transformed Winnipeg Jets.

At the time, father Bobby decided to bestow son Brett his jersey number.

"I am very proud to have Brett wear the same No. 9 for the Phoenix Coyotes that I wore for the Winnipeg Jets," Bobby told the Coyotes' website. "My years in Winnipeg were some of the fondest and most memorable of my career. We had great teams and we won championships. Brett has had an incredible career, and I look forward to seeing him attempt to bring championships to the Coyotes while wearing my number.

"I want Brett to have as much fun wearing No. 9 as I did," said Hull. "It's a very special thing, and I think he feels the same way."

The article revealed, however, it wasn't just Bobby who made the decision—the recommendation came from GM Mike Barnett, who Winnipeg fans may remember as being the agent for two of the team's most hated rivals—Wayne Gretzky and Lanny McDonald. The thought, as writer Russell Brooks penned, came when Brett signed with the Desert Dogs in 2004.

"It is no less of an honour to confirm that Bobby Hull has happily agreed to temporarily un-retire his famous No. 9 in order for his son, Brett, to further enhance the image of the Hull name, wearing No. 9., scoring highlight goals in arenas throughout the NHL," Barnett said. "All hockey fans, and particularly our fans in Phoenix, will surely enjoy watching Brett Hull perform while paying tribute each night to his legendary father."

The visage never fully came to fruition. Brett played all of five games in the Coyotes' uniform before permanently retiring, returning his jersey to the rafters.

Incidentally, out of respect to Hull and Winnipeg hockey heritage, Evander Kane contacted the Golden Jet to gain his approval before wearing No. 9 for the new era Jets. Hull approved.

The second—and last—Jets number to ascend to the heights of the Winnipeg Arena ceiling was that of Thomas Steen, No. 25.

Steen, of course, was a career Jet after being originally drafted in the fifth round of the 1979 Entry Draft. His tenure began in the 1981–82 season and lasted through the 1994–95 campaign and included 950 games and 817 points. When the Jets were originally set to depart the NHL, Steen's jersey was retired during the "funeral" for the organization.

Steen travelled a bit after his time in the NHL, playing in Germany for more than three seasons before becoming an NHL scout. It was during this period that he returned to Winnipeg and was often found in the press box at the Winnipeg Arena and MTS Centre. This came before Steen entered a different arena—the political one—first as an unsuccessful provincial candidate and later as a city councillor.

"It was the greatest honour I could ever imagine," Steen said of the retirement. "It's with me all the time. I've been so proud of it. I'm so thankful."

The third Winnipeg Jet number retired probably isn't surprising—Dale Hawerchuk. However, since Ducky was still playing when the Jets left Manitoba's capital, it wasn't those who actually saw his career who viewed the ceremony—the retirement was done by the Coyotes.

The Coyotes raised Hawerchuk's jersey on April 5, 2007, nearly a decade after his last NHL game. Hawerchuk, of course, was *the* name for Winnipeg in the 1980s and remains one of the most popular alumni of the squad. Some fans will scoff at the notion of the Coyotes doing this, and inevitably will do the same if they choose to retire other jerseys, namely that of Teemu Selanne.

Incidentally, Winnipeggers did get the chance to pay thanks to Hawerchuk. In the early 2000s, the AHL's Manitoba Moose had a commemorative evening for Ducky. The No. 10 was raised in the Winnipeg Arena, though the number is not recognized as retired by the current Jets team.

The only other number to be retired in Winnipeg professional hockey history was that of Mike Keane. Keane, a native Winnipegger, finished his remarkable career—which included three Stanley Cup rings and being captain of the Montreal Canadiens—with the Manitoba Moose. The ceremony took place on February 12, 2011, during the team's last season in Winnipeg before it evolved into the St. John's Ice Caps. Keane retired from hockey just one season earlier.

28 Heartbreaking Trades

The unfortunate reality of being a fan of any sport is that at one point or another, your heroes will be traded.

Time and time again teams will pull blockbuster trades where elite superstars depart for pastures that either are greener elsewhere or, if nothing else, add green to their own pocketbooks. Phil Esposito and Stephane Beauregard are legends who were sent away from the loyal fan bases that made them local legends.

The Winnipeg Jets were far from immune to this, as two of the biggest names that ever graced the famed Arena didn't make it to retirement in the colours of the Jets—Dale Hawerchuk and Teemu Selanne.

First, to Hawerchuk.

Throughout the 1980s, from the time that he debuted with the Jets, Hawerchuk was the centrepiece of a team that battled valiantly with the likes of the Edmonton Oilers and Calgary Flames; but by the 1989–90 season, the core of the team had shifted. While a new wave of leaders like Pat Elynuik were beginning to make waves, members of the 1984–85 squad began to depart, including general manager and linchpin John Ferguson in 1988. As new general manager Mike Smith made his mark, Hawerchuk seemed close to departure.

Amid the 1988–89 season, rumours flew that "Ducky" was ready to move. In February, he addressed the buzz in an interview with the *Chicago Tribune*. "I would accept a trade more easily now than I would have a year ago," Hawerchuk said. "I'm tired about reading bull in the papers. I'm tired of coming to the rink with a negative-type attitude here. Maybe it's best for the hockey club to get a few players for me. That's not saying I want to be traded."

The countdown, it seemed, was on. In 1989–90, Hawerchuk became one of three captains of the Jets (Thomas Steen and Randy Carlyle were the others) instead of being the sole leader. That season saw his lowest production in a Jets uniform (albeit still at higher than a point-per-game clip).

Then, during the 1990 NHL Entry Draft, the moment came. Hawerchuk was sent to Buffalo alongside the team's first pick (Brad May) for Phil Housley, Jeff Parker, Scott Arniel, and the Sabres' first pick (Keith Tkachuk). The return paid off, but as good as Housley was (and make no mistake about it, he was good—a Norris Trophy finalist one season, playing in the NHL All-Star Game every season he was in Winnipeg, and a postseason All-Star once), the impact on the Winnipeg hockey community was hard to swallow. It wasn't until Teemu Selanne surfaced in the 1992–93 season that the Jets faithful had a new lead star to hang their hats on.

And his fate wasn't much different than Hawerchuk's.

Midway through the 1995–96 season, Selanne was sent to the Anaheim Mighty Ducks along with prospect Marc Chouinard and the Jets' fourth-round pick in 1996 for Oleg Tverdovsky, Chad Kilger, and Anaheim's third-round pick in '96.

The trade blindsided Selanne, as he was told about the move during a practice. As the *Buffalo News* described in its report of the trade, Selanne was devastated by the news.

"The 25-year-old Selanne stormed out of practice and ripped off the nameplate from above his locker. He left Winnipeg Arena without talking to reporters," the paper stated.

Jets brass was somewhat hard pressed to bring logic to the unthinkable trade—this was, after all, mere weeks away from the team relocating to Phoenix.

"I've got to put a winning team on the ice. We're going to be a winning team right now. We did this trade for now," Jets GM John Paddock told *TSN Inside Sports* reporter Rod Smith.

The real reason for the trade was revealed years later when Paddock spoke with Tim Campbell of the *Winnipeg Free Press* amid the 2011–12 season.

"It was somewhat worded to me that we couldn't have three $3 million forwards on the team," Paddock said. "That's how times have and haven't changed. It was a financial decision; we had to change the money around, and it still happens today."

The angst and disappointment, however, resonated with fans, and upon Winnipeg's return to the NHL, Selanne was given a hero's welcome, each and every time he stepped on MTS Centre ice.

29 Backgammon for Gretzky

Oh what could have been for the Winnipeg Jets if their brass was more confident in their board game play.

In the years following Ben Hatskin's sale of the team to a local group, the Jets were at a strongpoint in their history, putting together two Avco Cup–winning squads in three years. But the Jets' finances once again were faulty, and by 1978, with talk of merger with the NHL at its hilt, the Jets were sold to Michael Gobuty and Barry Shenkarow.

Both proved to be shrewd businessmen by all stretches of explanation—they brought John Ferguson to Winnipeg as general manager and ensured the team was in good standing when the NHL absorbed four WHA teams in 1979.

The tandem ownership was impressive. Gobuty's empire had been built on his original business, Victoria Leather, while Shenkarow was a highly successful lawyer. When the two bought into the WHA, the league was at an extremely weak point with teams folding, not the least of which was the Indianapolis Racers squad owned by Nelson Skalbania.

The Racers weren't quite a success story. In their four full seasons of play, they made the playoffs twice and did have some notable players such as Dave Keon and Michel Dion, but they struggled for the most part and midway through the 1978–79 season—the last for the WHA—they folded.

Before the Racers exited permanently onto pit row, however, Skalbania had one trick up his sleeve—signing Wayne Gretzky to his first pro contract at the tender age of 17. Though the NHL was not allowing under-agers to be signed to pro contracts, let alone be drafted that young, the WHA had no such restrictions and Skalbania rolled the dice in acquiring the future phenom.

Gretzky played eight games for the Racers, tallying three goals and three assists during the stretch before Skalbania, strapped for cash, was forced to sell off his young prodigy. Skalbania had two destinations in mind: the Edmonton Oilers and the Winnipeg Jets.

Skalbania had begun negotiating with Oilers owner Peter Pocklington, an old friend. Pocklington offered $500,000 for Gretzky, but Skalbania wasn't one to take the first offer. With Shenkarow and Gobuty in Indianapolis, Skalbania offered Gretzky to the Jets ownership tandem at the same price, but being new owners, Gobuty and Shenkarow weren't willing to spend that amount of cash for one player, and they countered with an interest stake in the franchise. Skalbania retorted with an interesting wager.

"He said 'I'll tell you what I'll do,'" Shenkarow recalled. "'I'll play you one game of backgammon—Gretzky for your franchise.' and I said 'No.' I wasn't going to play one game of backgammon and gamble the franchise."

That's not to say that all interactions ended there. "We ended up playing 15 games, and as it turned out I won the first one, but I wasn't going to make that bet," Shenkarow said.

So Skalbania went to the next in line, one Peter Pocklington, who was more than happy to pay the full asking price. Gretzky immediately joined the Oilers and helped the team make the WHA Finals, only to bow out to the Jets.

But Pocklington's best move was not to sign Wayne to a standard contract. Had he done so, Gretzky or another Oiler would have been presented on a silver platter to NHL suitors during the WHA Dispersal Draft. Instead, the agreement was for personal services, meaning Gretzky worked directly for Pocklington outside of hockey confines.

And did he ever, not just by winning four Stanley Cups and shattering almost every NHL record he could get his mitts on, but also by making the Winnipeg Arena his playground in the many battles between the Oilers and Jets.

But that's not to say that Shenkarow was afraid of a high-stakes wager.

When merger talks started in 1978, there were a few NHL teams that voted against bringing in the WHA clubs, among them three Canadian teams—the Vancouver Canucks, Montreal Canadiens, and Toronto Maple Leafs—who were concerned about television rights. Shenkarow knew he needed to change minds so he made one heck of a challenge.

"We needed to get a couple more votes, so I flew to Vancouver and met with the owners," Shenkarow recalled. "I said to them, 'Here's what we can do: We can play one game, a three-game or a five-game series. If we win, we get your vote. If you win, you can get all of our players. They wouldn't play us.'"

30 The WHA Dispersal

As the WHA prepared to merge with the NHL, there was a huge dose of bad news handed down to the participant teams—they were about to be stripped of their rich talent.

First, let's talk about the state of hockey at the time. Prior to the 1979 merger, talks had begun for the cash-strapped WHA—more specifically, six of its member clubs—to join the NHL. The NHL owners voted this down, and the WHA continued play for two more seasons but were so weak financially that the league started to dwindle. Among the teams that folded were the once powerful, Howe family–led Houston Aeros that sought to jump to the NHL as an expansion team in 1978. They didn't and soon after folded.

By the time the 1978–79 regular season completed, the Jets were one of only six teams, total, left in the WHA, and finally, four teams—Winnipeg, New England (or to be renamed Hartford) Whalers, Edmonton Oilers, and Quebec Nordiques—were going to be absorbed into the NHL. As the entire saga unfolded, there were mixed feelings in locker rooms across the WHA, including inside the Winnipeg Arena.

"At first we wondered whether it was 'official' or was it like the announcement the year before, where Houston was supposedly part of NHL expansion. [My rookie year was in Houston, so I had gone through that.] After confirmation I'd say [there was] excitement for most, although I remember some guys saying they figured they were finished. We had a lot of players who knew they could play well in the NHL," Scott Campbell said.

But the concessions that the WHA made meant that its teams weren't going to be anything close to what they had once been.

In a tactic that can at best be described as shady and at worst as clear-cutting the competition, the squads were made to return their players to the team that originally had them signed to contracts.

Up to two skaters and up to two goalies could be retained by the clubs, and the Jets chose to hold onto Morris Lukowich, Scott Campbell, and Markus Mattsson.

Campbell described his emotions after told he was going to be kept as, "Shock, despite being told there was a really good chance it would happen.

"A lot of very good players had to be let go."

Those who were lost were major losses. For Winnipeg, this included one of its new marquee names, Terry Ruskowski. Just months beforehand, Ruskowski helped the Jets capture their third Avco Cup, but now he was headed back to the Chicago Blackhawks, the team that drafted him back in 1974. Fearing that he would be sent to the minor leagues, Ruskowski instead opted to go to the WHA with the Houston Aeros where he spent the majority of his WHA career.

Jets GM John Ferguson, sufficed to say, was none too pleased about losing Ruskowski, but his hand was forced. "I'm not only giving up probably the best player in our league, I'm giving up the heart of our hockey club," Ferguson said.

The Jets did have a plan, though. Fergy, who lost Bobby Hull back to the Chicago Black Hawks, picked up the Golden Jet from the list of players the team had left open, with the intent to trade him back to Chicago in exchange for Ruskowski. Black Hawks management, however, didn't bite.

Additional players that the Jets lost included Kent Nilsson, Glen Hicks, Barry Long, Peter Marsh, Kim Clackson, and Paul MacKinnon.

Those who remained with the Jets were joined by players made available in an expansion draft. Along with the aforementioned

Hull, the Jets were able to get Peter Marsh back, but the rest of their selections had little in terms of spectacular skills. Names included the likes of Pierre Hamel, Bill Riley, and Gord Smith.

Though some WHA familiar faces like Peter Sullivan and Lars-Erik Sjoberg were retained by Winnipeg, the team was a mere shell of its former self. What was the WHA championship squad in 1979 was now just a 20-win team, finishing a distant 18 points out of an NHL playoff spot.

31 50-50s and Records

In the history of hockey, there is no accomplishment more revered than being a 50-50 scorer.

To attain scoring 50 goals in 50 games is a level of output that only the most elite snipers in NHL history have achieved. Only Maurice Richard, Mike Bossy, Wayne Gretzky, Mario Lemieux, and Brett Hull have reached this remarkable feat.

Or that's what the NHL wants you to believe.

You see, in the days of the Rebel League—the WHA—there were two other hockey superstars who reached this rarified level; two men who put fear in the heart of each and every netminder that stepped into the crease of a WHA net. And it probably comes to the surprise of no one that those individuals were two Winnipeg Jets—Bobby Hull and Anders Hedberg.

Hull was the first to reach the feat in the 1974–75 season. During his NHL career, the Golden Jet came close to the feat when he tallied 50 goals in 52 games during the 1965–66 NHL campaign. Hull wouldn't be denied in the WHA, as during that season he hit the mark before finishing the season with 77 goals.

Already, Hull had once held the NHL record for most goals in a season; now, he had broken Danny Lawson's mark for the WHA, which he had set in the league's inaugural campaign with 61 tallies.

Hedberg was next. Just two seasons later, Hedberg became the true first player to break the 50 goals in under 50 games when he hit the milestone in 49 games (also getting his 51st in the process). The accomplishment made Hedberg the first and only non–North American player to hit the mark, and he finished with a remarkable 70 goals. Not surprisingly, the tally count was enough to give Hedberg the goal-scoring crown. It was the second time a Jet led the WHA in goal scoring, and it was the only time in WHA history that a player scored at a goal-per-game rate higher than 1.0 (he only played in 68 games).

By the time the WHA closed up shop, Hull's goal record was still intact. His next closest competitor was Real Cloutier with a 75-goal season in 1978–79. It is one of a few major records that Jets competitors hold in the WHA.

That same 1974–75 season Hull and Andre Lacroix battled to establish a new points standard. They both topped Lacroix's 1972–73 124-point mark, but it was Lacroix who came out on top with 147 points compared to Hull's 142.

On another stream, Ulf Nilsson holds the WHA record for most assists per game played (1.147). Part of his remarkable accomplishment comes as a result of that same 1974–75 goal record season for Hull when the Swedish sensation tallied 90 assists. Had it not been for Lacroix, who put together 106 assists that same year, Nilsson would have owned that season's record.

Though Hull doesn't own the regular season record for goals (that honour belongs to Marc Tardif), the Golden Jet does own the career playoff scoring record with 43 tallies, two more than Mark Howe. Howe is also second to Ulf Nilsson on the career playoff assist record (53 vs. 51).

With these records in the spotlight of the WHA, one can't help but wonder what NHL records are owned by Jets. Teemu Selanne's rookie marks are well known, and elsewhere I discuss the speed records of the Jets, but there's one record few know about, belonging to Dale Hawerchuk. During the 1983–84 season, Ducky tallied a remarkable five assists in one period of play. Two goals were scored by Morris Lukowich, two by Paul MacLean, and one by Wade Campbell. And yes, Hawerchuk solely owns this record; pretty much the only assist mark Wayne Gretzky doesn't call his.

32 Operation Grassroots

"We believed the effort to save the Jets would work but only to stay for a few more years. Deep down I knew it was a waste of time, but at the time it was a valiant effort never seen in the NHL before."

—Dale Sawchuk, Jets fan, Operation Grassroots contributor

In 1995, the Jets' fate was sealed. As the lockout-shortened NHL season drew to a close, so too did the future of the hockey team. Economics of rising salaries, a weak Canadian dollar, and an arena with unused seats were taking their toll, never mind that a new venue was quickly becoming a pipe dream.

The group largely responsible for the bid to keep the Jets in Winnipeg was the Manitoba Entertainment Complex, but they knew they couldn't fund the team alone, especially with operating costs mounted in the red.

Public support was needed. The dollars needed to come from all levels of government. As recollected by writer Jennifer Beever in her article "Boosterism: 1, Journalism: 0" that appeared in the

Ryerson Review of Journalism's summer 1996 issue, $37 million was asked for at all three levels of government. When that money failed to come in from the federal government and additional dollars were being demanded by the NHL, Operation Grassroots began.

The motivator to start up was innocent enough, as Vic Grant, then host of CJOB's *Prime Time Sports* told Beever. "I had people phoning me up, saying, 'I'll give you $1,000. I'll give you $5,000. I'll give you a $10,000 cheque right now.'" Quickly, Grant had collected $50,000.

The radio station quickly took up the cause and began Operation Grassroots on May 15, 1995. Soon, kids were emptying piggybanks, and adults were writing cheques. Schools set up campaign tables while businesses pooled finances. It was a sight to be seen, all happening weeks after the infamous funeral when only a glimmer of hope was what fans had left that their beloved Jets would somehow, someway stay in Winnipeg.

Unfortunately, Operation Grassroots wasn't the love-in that many would have hoped for and began to swirl with controversy. Jim Silver, a University of Winnipeg professor and member of the "Thin Ice" movement that opposed the use of public dollars to fund the team, documented the trials and tribulations he and other opposition to the campaign faced in his book, also titled *Thin Ice*.

"Nothing was more important to the future of the city than to Save Our Jets. The occasional critic was cut off immediately. Opponents of the huge public expenditure needed to keep the Jets in Winnipeg were attacked," Silver wrote. "Members of Thin Ice received calls from young men whipped into a frenzy by the station."

Thin Ice was also concerned with the lack of equal representation in media that their side was getting. "We found it difficult to get the media to cover what we were doing and saying," Silver told Beever. "When we were covered, we were buried in the story. The coverage [was]...100 to one for the proponent."

The Jets gave out this poster to fans who supported Operation Grassroots.

Still, the rally cry continued on. A public gathering on May 16 netted a ton of support and a promise of $62 million from the city's business community; but it was all for naught. The Canadian government announced it would give $20 million to the Jets and a new arena, not the $37 million MEC needed. Overall, the fund collecting fell $28 million short.

The moment of defeat was a bitter pill for fans to swallow, including a young Darren Ford, who snuck into the Westin Hotel with a friend before what he hoped to be the announcement that Operation Grassroots was a success.

"We overheard the devastating news that, on the contrary, everything had fallen apart. And I mean everything. The Jets weren't staying. They were being sold to the first buyer," Ford said. "I vividly recall Scott Taylor [*Free Press* at the time] whisking to a pay phone [the way reporters had to communicate back then] and whoever was on the other end heard something to this effect: 'That's it, it's over, this team is moving, likely to Minneapolis.'

"I was frozen. I remember walking outside past the legion of fans who still thought an exciting announcement was moments away. I was heading against the grain, going home. There would be no announcement. All I can remember was going home and crying on my bed for what seemed like an eternity. Winnipeg was dead to me just as I was about to graduate and head on to university."

Still, Operation Grassroots did a lot to unite the Winnipeg community and passion shone through. Though the combined effort fell short, it ignited a desire for NHL hockey that did not extinguish until 2011.

33 Military Ties

Stepping out of a carrier jet to show off your new team's gear is unique to say the least—but when you're the Winnipeg Jets, it was all too appropriate. This is what happened when the team unveiled its jerseys in the summer of 2011, which showed off the new logo that paid tribute to the city's ties to the Royal Canadian Air Force.

Designed by the Jets' organization and Reebok together, the logo closely replicated the RCAF insignia that, among other places, was found on the jerseys of the team that entered—and won—the 1948 Olympic gold medal for shinny.

"We felt it was important to authenticate the name Jets, and we believe the new logo does that through its connection to [Canada's] remarkable Air Force heritage, including the rich history and relationship that our city and province have enjoyed with the Canadian Forces," Mark Chipman said in a release.

Dorian Morphy, the Jets' senior director, managing, marketing and brand management, expanded on the design in the same statement from the team, talking specifically about the aircraft depicted on the logo—one of the chief differences between this crest and the RCAF emblem.

"The design cues for the plane were inspired by the military jets flown by the Air Force over the years. So not only were we able to establish a new identity for our brand, but we were able to maintain a traditional, time honoured look to the logo," Morphy said.

The Jets gave fans this special puck during their 2014 Military Appreciation Night.

Of course, no action could be complete without signoff from the men and women the Jets were recognizing, and that came fairly easily. On the heels of the logo's unveiling, Maj.-Gen. Alain Parent of 17 Wing, talked briefly about the connection with media.

"A hockey player has to be fast, agile, fit, and a team player," Parent told media, including the *Winnipeg Free Press*. "These are all characteristics of the men and women of the Canadian Air Force."

This, as longtime fans of Winnipeg hockey knew, wasn't the first time that True North had paid tribute to the rich history of the military in Winnipeg. Indeed, the history of pro hockey in Winnipeg had included this tie.

"We have always had a close relationship with 17 Wing throughout the years, dating back to our annual Manitoba Moose Military Night," Morphy said. "We are thrilled to be able to continue this relationship in a significant way.

Fittingly, perhaps, those tributes included that 1948 RCAF jersey. This jersey was worn in 2008 and was done up pretty much exactly like the Air Force sweaters. To add to the special tie, the Moose included the names of the 1948 gold medalists on a patch on the back of the jersey, as well as a yellow ribbon emblem that read "Support Our Troops" in English and French. Other jerseys included a camouflage design that incorporated a similar reverse crest as the 2007–08 season uniform, only this one had the names of those who had died in service inscribed. Another camo model was worn in 2010–11, while the prior year's version paid tribute to the centennial of the Canadian Navy and Marines and featured the Canadian Military Services logo on the chest crest.

The tradition of military commemoration was once again picked up by the Jets during the 2013–14 and 2014–15 seasons. On both occasions, the Jets wore camo jerseys for their pregame skate before games against the Ottawa Senators, and the jerseys were later auctioned off with proceeds going to Canadian Armed Forces charities. Additionally, in an unforgettable moment, armed forces veterans were invited to wear their gear for each night, and following the conclusion of the contest, had the opportunity to join the Jets players and personnel on the ice for a special photograph.

34 The Olympic Line

During the 1992–93 season, the Jets roster included three prospects that would change the fate of the team through the end of its time in the NHL—left winger Keith Tkachuk, centre man Alexei Zhamnov, and right wing juggernaut Teemu Selanne.

Coming into the NHL almost simultaneously (Tkachuk actually debuted late in the 1991–92 season), the trio formed one of the most dangerous prospect lines the league had ever seen. One can only wonder what might have been had the trio been able to stay together, rather than seeing Teemu traded to Anaheim during the 1995–96 season and Alexei Zhamnov sent to Chicago after season's close.

Individually, their track records are nothing short of phenomenal; but together, they were downright intimidating, even in their first season.

"As a line, they were scary and I'm sure a nightmare for the opposing players. Great energy and atmosphere," former teammate Luciano Borsato reflected. "Teemu's first year was unforgettable, as we all know. He was so exciting to watch, so enthusiastic when he scored and all the guys were excited for him. Alex had the most skill of anyone I had ever played with. Scary talent. Walt [KeithTkachuk] became such a force and great player, and nobody could move him in front of the net."

Keith Tkachuk, Teemu Selanne, and Alexei Zhamnov were the most popular Jets in the 1990s.

The first year that the trio came together was 1992–93, and at the time, the group of future NHL superstars had a fourth member of a stud stable—Evgeny Davydov. Davydov, like Tkachuk, debuted late in the 1991–92 season and took Winnipeg by storm when he tallied seven points in just 12 games after coming across the pond from CSKA Moscow.

So you can imagine the excitement when another seemingly hot Russian prospect, Zhamnov, was signed after a brief holdout. Fans at first weren't sure if the forward—who took the No. 10 once belonging to Dale Hawerchuk—was worthy; but it didn't take long for Zhamnov to gain legions of fans, and by season's end he had 72 points to his name. That same season, of course, was Selanne's 76-goal, 132-point campaign. Tkachuk counted 28 goals and 51 points while Davydov hit 28 goals and 49 points. It marked the first—and thus far only time—that an NHL team had four rookies tally more than 20 goals. To put it in perspective, there are several teams now that have trouble getting four players of any kind to hit that plateau.

Before 1993–94, Davydov was traded to Florida, leaving the trio on a solid line—Tkachuk on left wing, Zhamnov at centre, and

Selanne at right wing. A couple different names were attempted for the line, including the UN Line, but ultimately it was the Olympic Line that stuck, with the U.S., Russia, and Finland represented. Local clothier Mondetta, known for being global in its approach to marketing, created several Jets themed apparel pieces, along with souvenirs such as a poster that trumpeted, "A Spirit of Unification," and at the forefront of the campaign was the Olympic Line, alongside Sweden's Thomas Steen and Canada's Bob Essensa.

It's almost impossible to not look back at the Olympic Line and think about what could have been. In 1993–94, Selanne's season was cut short by an Achilles' tendon injury during a game with the Anaheim Mighty Ducks, putting the line's rise on hold. One season later Zhamnov broke out and cracked the top 3 NHL scorers, but the season was cut short due to an early player lockout. Tkachuk's breakout came in 1995–96 as he hit the 50 goal and 98 point marks, but by the time the season was complete, Selanne had been traded and the Jets' fate had been sold to Phoenix. Zhamnov never made it to the desert—he was traded before the 1996–97 campaign began for Jeremy Roenick.

There's no question in the minds of Winnipeg hockey fans that the Olympic Line ranks among the greatest in 1990s hockey; the only question is how great they could have been had all the pieces been able to stay together.

35 Selanne Tribute and the '90s Return

It's a moment that no one thought possible.

Throughout the Jets 2.0's run in the NHL, the running theme had been that the team wanted to keep a strong distinction between the eras of Winnipeg NHL hockey. One story that unfolded came courtesy of proud Winnipegger and wrestler Chris Jericho, who refused to remove a Dale Hawerchuk jersey when he was to be interviewed during a Jets game and was asked by 2.0 staff to remove said sweater. Urban legend also stated that the sale of vintage Jets jerseys and other gear was going to cease as the new team moved in.

But all those were memories dashed on January 11, 2015, in Anaheim, California. The Jets, playing the Ducks on the eve of Teemu Selanne's No. 8 being raised to the rafters of "The Pond," emerged from their locker room for their pregame shoot around wearing 1990s jerseys sporting the No. 13 and even wearing the commemorative patch of the Stanley Cup Centennial.

It was a sight to behold and stirred up memories for fans young and old. The fact that everyone on Winnipeg wore No. 13 (while Anaheim players suited up in old school Mighty Ducks jerseys that had the No. 8 on it) didn't actually seem out of place, given how quickly Teemu would move through the Winnipeg Arena—at times it seemed like there were multiple Teemus on the ice.

"We could think of no better ways honour Teemu," was the simple message that the Jets put out on Facebook that night, and not surprisingly, loyal Jets fans responded with a resounding thumb's up (or more appropriately, "Like").

"Awesome to see those jerseys on the ice again #thirdjersey," one fan wrote, while another said, "classy move, by a classy organization! Go Jets Go!!!"

Indeed, it seemed that all had been forgiven, and it's not surprising that it's Selanne that brought about the renewal of the old jersey. More than any player in Jets 1.0 history, it is the "Finnish Flash" who was the most revered of them all, active or retired. The times that Selanne came back to Winnipeg as a member of the Anaheim Ducks were among the loudest games in the history of the building.

Understandably perhaps, Selanne didn't quite know what to expect on his first return visit to the city during the 2011–12 season. "Two years ago when I first came here, I didn't know what to expect, and it was very overwhelming," he said in 2013.

Because of how the NHL schedule and makeup was laid out, Selanne only played twice in Winnipeg during the 2.0 era, thanks in part to the Jets being positioned in the Eastern Conference rather than the West. The 2011–12 season saw the Jets host Anaheim, while the 2012–13 lockout meant inter-conference play was wiped. With a new schedule format awaiting the Jets when they arrived in the Western Conference in 2013–14, only one game was to be played on home ice against the Ducks. Thus, October 6, 2013, was earmarked as the game to get tickets for—the last time Teemu Selanne would skate as an NHL'er in Winnipeg.

Though Selanne was held off the score sheet in the 3–2 Ducks victory, he was named the game's first star. Humbly, Selanne reflected to a massive press scrum after the contest that he didn't feel he deserved to be named a star, but Winnipeg wouldn't have it any other way.

And as Winnipeg poured its admiration out for Selanne that night, just as those who made the trip down to Anaheim did for the jersey retirement night, Selanne fed it right back.

"In some ways, it made me feel like I was on the home team," Selanne said of the 2013 game. "This is a very special building. The people really made me feel like I was home. I have so much respect for them. I am so thankful that I was able to play here in front of these fans and start my career here. I'm very lucky."

36 The King and Tie

For all the trades that had fans slapping their foreheads in frustration, the Jets did pull off some amazing deals in their day; and there might not have been any that was greeted with more adulation by armchair general managers than the one that brought Kris King and Tie Domi to Winnipeg.

During the 1992–93 season, the Jets were starting a new era that featured speedsters like Alexei Zhamnov and Teemu Selanne; but what they lacked, especially after the departure of Bryan Marchment and Shawn Cronin, was muscle to protect their young prospects. They needed the types of protection that Wayne Gretzky, in his day, received from Dave Semenko, but looking up and down their roster, there was little to be found.

Thus, on December 28, 1992, the Jets sent Ed Olczyk to the New York Rangers for Kris King and Tie Domi.

Already known as two of the toughest players to ever grace a sheet of ice in the NHL, King and Domi arrived to much fanfare. King, a more strategic player, was a leader in wait who wasn't afraid to hit hard and drop the gloves when needed, while Domi, celebrated for his heavyweight, bare-knuckle tilt with the likes of Bob Probert and Marty McSorley, was the perfect grappler.

As King recalled, he was somewhat banged up as the Rangers were squaring off with the Boston Bruins, a team notorious for their bruising style of shinny. That night, both King and Domi were held off the rink as healthy scratches, something that aroused King's suspicions.

"Sitting in the press box, we [Tie and I] looked at each other and said, 'Something isn't right. We should be out there.' We were getting run around a little bit and started to think something was up," King recalled. "The next day at practice, for the first time in the four years that I had been there, [head coach] Roger Neilson didn't run the video session—Wade Campbell did. Shortly thereafter, Roger called me up to his office. He told me he had some news for me—bad news and really bad news.

"I said, 'What would be the bad news,' and he said, 'You're being traded to Winnipeg.' I asked, 'If that's the bad news, what's the really bad news?' and he said, 'Tie's going with you.'"

And so, after a brief lunch farewell from their Rangers teammates, King and Domi were bound for LaGuardia Airport. They touched down in Winnipeg at 12:30 in the morning, not a good time to be doing anything during the doldrums of winter in Winnipeg, as King soon found out.

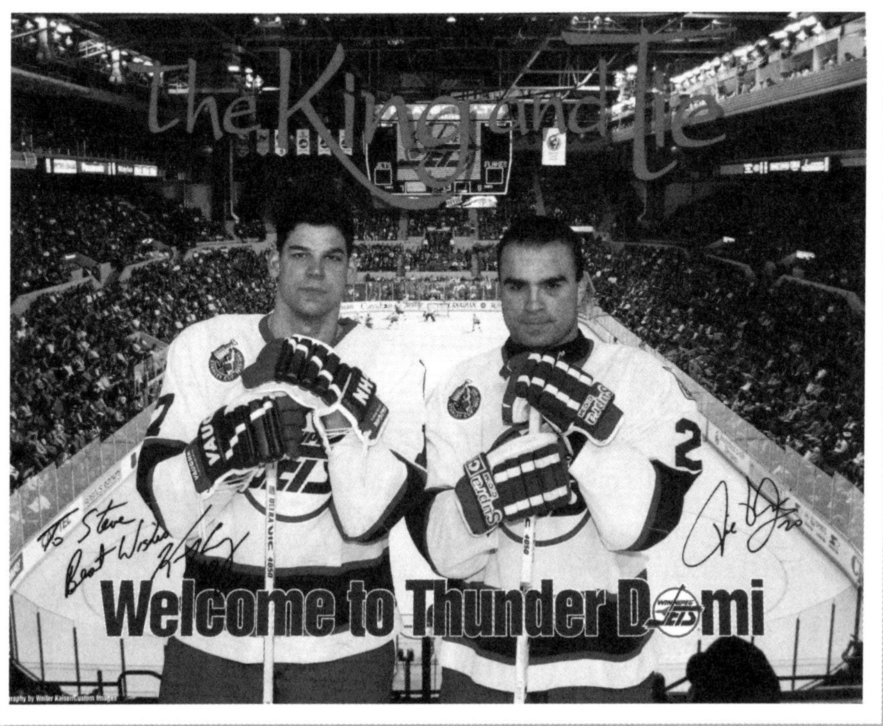

The Jets welcome Kris King and Tie Domi to Winnipeg with this commemorative poster. (Steve Feldman)

"We were met by John Paddock. He had a winter parka on—you could barely see his face," King explained. "It was -35 degrees. They had a couple rental cars for us. Paddock gave me mine and mine wouldn't start. It was one of those 'What the heck just happened?' moments."

With that, King found the place he would ply his trade for the next four seasons, right up until the time the Jets moved to Phoenix. Though Domi played through the midway point of the 1994–95 season, when he was sent to Toronto for Mike Eastwood and a draft pick that became Brad Isbister, King found a true home.

"It didn't take long after getting to Winnipeg that we realized this was going to be a very positive change for me and my family," King said. "It was the greatest move of my 15-year career."

That first partial season saw Domi collect 249 PIMs (to go along with three goals and 13 points) while King counted 136 PIMs (in addition to eight goals and 16 points). The impact was even larger than that—with protection, the young, speedy prospects had room to move around the ice and develop their skills. The duo continued to dominate the rink and later reunited in Toronto, continuing their reputation as the best tag team in the history of the NHL.

37 Shane Doan: The Last Jet

One of the first things that happened once the Winnipeg Jets left for Phoenix was the countdown to the last member of the team being active in the NHL.

It didn't take long for the numbers to dwindle, especially when the retirements from the big league start near day one—Randy

Gilhen elected to stay in Winnipeg and play for the new Manitoba Moose rather than make the trip to Phoenix.

Slowly but surely, the team was deconstructed. While some players like Alexei Zhamnov found new life with other teams, the announcements of skates being hung up started to pour in, to the point where that by the time the NHL returned to Winnipeg, only three players were left—Teemu Selanne, Nikolai Khabibulin, and the only member still with the franchise, Shane Doan.

Doan was one of the last draft picks of the original squad. He was selected seventh overall in the 1995 draft after a junior career that saw the Halkirk, Alberta, native win two consecutive Calder Cups with the Kamloops Blazers, the latter of which also saw Doan named playoff MVP.

"It was a great honour to be drafted by the Winnipeg Jets. Growing up in Alberta, I was hoping I would be drafted by a Western Canadian team and when the Jets drafted me I was thrilled," Doan said of his selection.

Doan was given little time to rest on his laurels, though. The prospect made the Jets Opening Night squad for the 1995–96 season and had a fairly good showing during the Dead Puck Era with Winnipeg, tallying 17 points in 74 games. The most important marker among his seven goals, inarguably, was the game-winner for the Jets in their final home contest in the regular season—a victory over the Los Angeles Kings.

That last year featured one of the most impressive locker rooms in the Jets NHL tenure. At season start, those occupying stalls included scoring threats like Olympic Line and roughians like Kris King. Looking back today, Doan believes that the assembled group could have gone far with more years together. "We had a great team with some amazing players. Guys like Tkachuk, Selanne, Zhamnov, Numminen, Khabibulin, Olczyk, Drake, Janney, Manson…" he recalled. "If we stayed together, I think we could have been a very good team for a long time."

Doan found a welcome home in Arizona and quickly established himself as one of the franchises faces. Though it took him a bit to get his scoring stride in place, Doan went on to become a star, putting together a string of nine consecutive seasons of 20-or-more goals, led the Coyotes to their first playoff series victory, as well as the first advance past the second round in the teams' combined history.

On top of all that, Doan became a national standout. In 2003, Doan won his first international gold as part of the World Senior Men's Canadian squad and one year later was part of the World Cup of Hockey champions. Just a few years later, he was captain of that same Senior Men's squad when it won the gold.

With Selanne's retirement following the 2013–14 season and Khabibulin's inability to land with an NHL team after playing only four games with the Blackhawks, Doan was (unofficially) the last Jet skating. Through the 2014–15 NHL season, Doan was still with the team, now geographically named the "Arizona Coyotes," as captain. The accomplishment of spending all his time with the franchise is special to Doan, and he still holds dear that first season with the Jets.

"I only got to play one season in Winnipeg, but I have some great memories of my time there. The fans were amazing, and the White Out I played in was incredible. I'm so glad that Winnipeg got an NHL team back. The city and the fans deserve it."

38 Wayne Gretzky and the "Last Puck"

If there was any player who terrorized the Winnipeg Jets more than any other, it was "The Great One," Wayne Gretzky.

Gretz was unapologetic of the way he victimized Winnipeg, too.

His records against the Jets included most short-handed goals in one playoff game (two) and most assists in one period (three, though he did accomplish the same feat four other times, twice against the L.A. Kings), but most importantly he had a huge hand in ensuring that Winnipeg never advanced past the division finals.

Gretzky also hit one of the biggest milestones of his NHL career against the Jets—his 2,000th NHL point. The moment came on October 26, 1990, as (not surprisingly) an assist on a Tomas Sandstrom goal. That no player has been able to hit that benchmark is nothing short of remarkable and speaks to just how good Wayne was, even though he wasn't the most liked person to ever step foot inside the Winnipeg perimeter.

But for all the evils of Wayne Gretzky in relation to the Jets, there may have been no greater dastardly deed than what he did on the night of May 2, 1995.

This, of course, was the final game (v. 1.0) of the Winnipeg Jets' NHL history. One game after being eliminated from NHL playoff contention and seemingly on their way to Minnesota, the Jets faced off against the Los Angeles Kings for what looked to be their final contest in the NHL.

Give the Jets credit though, despite being the epitome of a lame duck game, they put up one hell of a fight, levying 43 shots against Kelly Hrudey. Only one got past him—off the stick of Randy Gilhen—but it wasn't enough as the Kings scored two against Tim

Chevaldae. (The less said about the number of shots L.A. put on net the better)

As time wore down, the Jets' faithful stood in disbelief as their team was gone. Only one man seemed to really be active between players and fans—Wayne Gretzky.

In plain sight of the arena, Gretzky skated over to one of the officials and grabbed the last puck that was used in the game.

Yep, you read that right. The "Great One" pulled off the "Great Heist" as he snuck the puck away. He was later spotted by television cameras and mouthed that he indeed had taken the last puck.

The word that shot around media circles in the coming days was that Wayne was going to return the puck to Winnipeg, but no one's certain if it ever was given back to Winnipeg brass. After all, with the 1995–96 season now in place, the Jets' "last puck" was as meaningless as Mark McGwire's 70th home run baseball (with all apologies to one-time Oilers co-owner Todd McFarlane). Still, the puck should rightfully have come back to Winnipeg.

The following season, Gretzky played his final game against the Jets, but actually ended up missing the final game for his team—the St. Louis Blues—against Winnipeg on April 8, 1996 (a 2–2 draw). The trade, which came as a shock to the hockey world (albeit not as strongly as the first swap that saw Wayne go to Los Angeles in the first place) came one day after Gretzky's Kings lost to the Jets, 4–3.

But Gretzky's kicks at the Jets carcass didn't end with the last game puck, not by a long shot.

In May 2000, not even a season after he had left the ice, Wayne bought a 10 percent stake in the Phoenix Coyotes, and when the NHL emerged from the lockout season of 2004–05, he assumed head coaching duties for the one-time Jets.

The position, interestingly, brought Wayne to Winnipeg on a couple occasions, as the Coyotes played exhibition season contests at the MTS Centre, one of which came against none other than the team that scooped up Gretzky in the WHA—the Edmonton Oilers.

Truly, Wayne robbed Winnipeg of so much in his tenure in the NHL between milestone pucks and playoff series victories that you'd expect him to be public enemy No. 1; yet still, in the basements of red-blooded hockey fans across the city, there sits memorabilia of the Great One, speaking to just how universally loved he truly was.

39 The Rivalry with the Oilers

"Our problem, if you will, was always getting past Edmonton. We could play with and beat Calgary, but in a seven-game series, we had trouble getting by the Oilers. There were a few times we had them in a very tough position and we couldn't finish them off. It was probably the most disheartening thing."

—Laurie Boschman, forward, Winnipeg Jets

The use of the term "rivalry" usually refers to a series between two foes where they battled back and forth, splitting victories over the course of their history. This is what makes the Jets' history with the Edmonton Oilers so (sadly) unique—the battles were decidedly lopsided. During eight seasons, the Jets met the Oilers in the playoffs six times. Each and every time, the Oilers came out on top, often in a series sweep.

The lack of success in the NHL playoffs with Edmonton was a stark contrast to what had taken place just a decade earlier, when both teams were in the WHA. Over the course of the seven year run of the Rebel League, the Jets and Oilers met twice in the playoffs. The first encounter in 1975–76 saw Winnipeg sweep Edmonton in the opening round of the postseason 4–0, while the second matchup—the last series in the history of the WHA—was a lopsided 4–2 victory, assuring the Jets immortality as the final champions of the league.

Once the teams entered the NHL, and more specifically as a lanky centre named Wayne Gretzky developed, the rivalry became very uneven. There was a very pronounced sense that this Oilers team, borne from the ashes of a WHA crew that itself was successful, was going to break out. In short order, the Oilers amassed a team of prospects that many pegged as being the class of hockey for years to come.

Among those who knew it was Boschman. In 1982, Boschman was a member of those Oilers who were on the upswing and gelling as a crew when he was traded to Winnipeg in exchange for Willy Lindstrom. Though Boschman was excited for the opportunity to come to Winnipeg, there was that sense of what he would be missing out on. "I was looking forward to the move," he said, "but Edmonton was at the infancy of their five Stanley Cup run so that was a little disappointing just because you knew with Gretzky, Coffey, Fuhr, Moog, and all those players, you knew they were on the verge of something special."

As we all know now, that promise came to fruition. The Oilers were *the* team of the 1980s, winning four Stanley Cups in a five-year stretch after losing to the New York Islanders in the 1983 Finals. In those years, the Jets managed but one win against Edmonton. The playoff series in 1990 proved to be the most heartbreaking, as the Mark Messier–led Edmonton squad came back from a 3–1 deficit to take the series, 4–3.

So what was it about the Jets teams that made the Oilers so dominant? Obviously a lot of credit goes to that opposing squad, but as then-owner Barry Shenkarow denotes, internal issues also hampered development of the Jets into a squad that could come together and beat Edmonton.

"The problem is that because we never got around them, we kept changing the team, trying to get better so we could beat them," Shenkarow said. "In hindsight, that was a mistake because we had great teams. The fact that they had Gretzky, that extra advantage, they were just too good. The year we had six 20-goal scorers [1984–85], we didn't beat them, so we made moves, and quite honestly we shouldn't have."

The fall of the Oilers' dynasty, unfortunately, coincided with the Jets' own trouble making the playoffs. In their remaining years in the NHL, Winnipeg didn't meet Edmonton in the playoffs. Though Edmonton remained Smythe Division champs for the 1991 and 1992 postseasons, they avoided the Jets, either because Winnipeg didn't qualify for the playoffs ('91) or bowed out to the new rival Vancouver Canucks ('92). Edmonton then went on a four-year stretch of not making the playoffs whilst the Jets bandied about in qualifying and losing either to the Canucks or Detroit Red Wings.

When the new Jets team entered the NHL in 2011–12, there was high anticipation for a renewal of the rivalry, but to date that has not happened, with both teams struggling to crack the crowded Western Conference playoff picture. But with a sense of history behind them, there is still an atmosphere of the rivalry that the players recognize.

"Obviously, playing in an atmosphere like this was as close to a playoff game as you can get in the regular season," said Oilers' left winger David Perron following an overtime loss to Winnipeg early in the 2014–15 season. "It was really fun."

40 First 2.0 Win

"Visiting the MTS Centre tonight is the shorthanded Pittsburgh Penguins. The Pens make the trip to Winnipeg without superstars Sidney Crosby and Evgeni Malkin (no confirmation if Mario Lemieux will make the trip, but why start now). While the Penguins proved last season that they can still play solid hockey minus their big two, hopefully the Jets can take advantage of the missing stars and record their first win of the season in front of their hometown fans."

This was the pregame analysis of Davide Capone of Winnipegwhiteout.com as the Jets went into action on October 17, 2011. The game was seemingly Winnipeg's for the taking, as Capone alluded to, with the two biggest names on the Penguins roster MIA. Still, the team faced an uphill battle with the likes of Jordan Staal, Marc-Andre Fleury, and Kris Letang active.

By this time, the Jets were also 0–3 on the season. Their first game was a loss to the Montreal Canadiens at the MTS Centre, but the next two games were road battles with Chicago and Phoenix. The Blackhawks game was a write-off going in—no one would have given them a chance against the 2010 Stanley Cup champs, though they were game in the 4–3 loss. Phoenix stung a little bit more—a 4–1 defeat in what would have been appropriate for a first victory in the NHL, slaying the demon dog that haunted Winnipeg hockey fans for 15 years.

The game against the Penguins—who had beaten Jets 1.0 in their first-ever NHL contest—held the potential for history to be made back at the cozy confines of the MTS Centre. A sold-out noisy crowd ensured that Marc-Andre Fleury, who in the past had his troubles in Winnipeg as he developed in the AHL, would be thrown off his game.

The Jets struck first blood just eight seconds into the game as Kyle Wellwood tallied on assists from Alex Burmistrov and Nik Antropov. "Welly," as he had been affectionately become known by fans, was already becoming a cult hero in Winnipeg. Often regarded as a player with limitless potential, Wellwood was now a veteran in the NHL and had already bounced around through three cities (Toronto, Vancouver, and San Jose).

The second goal followed later in the period. This time it was Tanner Glass getting the marker. The backline forward was also well travelled, including stints in Florida and Vancouver when he was picked up by the Jets as a free agent. Glass, a Regina native, played just that single season with the Jets before ironically departing for Pittsburgh but found a cult following as a 16-point bruising forward as part of the GST Line.

So with two goals up on the board, the Jets were sitting strong as the first period ended; but no lead in the NHL this early in a game is safe (well, at least no two-goal lead), and Pittsburgh showed just how fragile that lead can be when a distance shot from Zbynek Michalek beat goalie Ondrej Pavelec during the second period.

But it was after that goal that Pav really bunkered down and secured the Jets' victory. Pavelec was a 2005 second-round draft pick by the Atlanta Thrashers. After finishing his CHL career with the Cape Breton Screaming Eagles, Pav spent some time in the minors with the Chicago Wolves before backing up Kari Lehtonen. Once Lehtonen was off to Dallas, Pav took over in net and since has been or shared the starting goalie duties for the franchise.

Following the contest, Pavelec reflected that he had to do more to aid the skaters in front of him. "I didn't play well in those first games, so I was trying to help the team to get the win and keep them in the game," he told the *Globe and Mail.*

When the final horn blew, the Jets had their first victory, igniting a huge party in the MTS Centre and in the locker room, as well. Even curmudgeonly coach Claude Noel couldn't help but be happy.

"We just played better," Noel said in an interview with the *Globe and Mail* following the game. "We played with more urgency and more pizzazz. I think [the players] were fed up."

The Jets added 36 additional wins to finish above .500 for the season, but fell short of the ultimate goal—the playoffs. Still, the first game gave the Jets the confidence they needed to compete in the tough Eastern Conference.

41 Jimmy Mann and First Jets Draft Picks

The "first" of so many things tends not to always be the most successful; in fact the "first ever" notation tends to be about as much fame as said piece will get.

For example, consider smartphones. Long before iPhone and Android waged war, IBM issued the first ever combined computing/telephony device.

So it's not surprising then that first draft picks often get a pass from longtime team followers. Pat Falloon, for example, was the first pick of the San Jose Sharks, and while the Foxwarren, Manitoba–born skater did well out of the gate, his career fizzled pretty quickly.

A similar fate befell the Winnipeg Jets' first ever NHL pick—Jimmy Mann. Though he was never projected to be a scoring ace, Mann had an air of being the next great heavyweight in the tradition of Dave "The Hammer" Schultz or Tiger Williams. Mann showed this potential in his rookie season of 1979–80 when he led the league in penalty minutes with 287. Nevermind that he didn't even reach the 10-point mark in an era chock full of 100-point getters—Mann was a beast.

The only problem was, he tanked. Quickly.

The following season, Mann split time between the Jets and Tulsa Oilers. His hard-hitting style began to become a liability, unfortunately, and came to an unfortunate summit during the 1981–82 season in a case that reached such a high profile that it was covered by the *New York Times*. On January 13, 1982, Mann attacked Pittsburgh Penguins forward Paul Gardner, after a cross check to Doug Smail's face. Mann threw two punches, breaking Gardner's jaw. The result was not only a 10 game unpaid suspension handed down by the NHL, but also a court case that resulted in a $500 fine to Mann, the first ever for an on-ice incident in Manitoba.

Mann's time with the Jets lasted two more seasons, including some time in Sherbrooke with the then AHL affiliate squad, before making his way to Quebec during the 1983–84 season. He finished his career in 1988–89 with the Indianapolis Ice of the IHL, ending a career that started with such promise as a bruiser, and unquestionably having Mann as the protector for Dale Hawerchuk and Co. *a la* Dave Semenko would have proved valuable for the club.

Now the Jets' selection of Mann was not the only blip in the first selections the Jets made through the years. Any time you make a selection in an NHL Entry Draft you are taking somewhat of a crapshoot, and there is none that is more deeply analyzed than the first player taken by each team. Overall though, the Jets didn't do too bad, but like their play on the ice at times, they were very streaky when it came to those primary picks.

For the next three seasons following Mann, the Jets did well with their first selections, taking Dave Babych, Hawerchuk, and Jim Kyte. Andrew McBain in 1983 turned out decently for Winnipeg as well, chipping in back-to-back seasons of 30-goal hockey before being sent to Pittsburgh prior to the 1989–90 season.

But the next season Winnipeg's sweet selection streak fell with Peter Douris, who played less than 25 games with the team, spending more time in the AHL. He eventually found a semi-permanent home in Boston before rounding out his career in Germany.

As bad as Douris was, he was an All-Star compared to 1985's top pick, Ryan Stewart. Taken 18th overall, Stewart had better than a point-per-game clip in the WHL. Unfortunately, he never got the true sniff test in the NHL, only playing three games in Winnipeg. He did, however, get a goal in those games. Stewart's career ended in the British Hockey League of all places.

The next few seasons were decent for the Jets at the draft podium. In 1986 came the selection of Pat Elynuik, followed by Bryan Marchment (albeit he had much more success with other teams), Selanne, Stu Barnes, and Keith Tkachuk. It can be argued that the 1991 pick of Aaron Ward was also a smart pick. Ward didn't play a single game with Winnipeg but went on to win three Stanley Cups in Detroit and Carolina after being sent to the Red Wings for Paul Ysebaert (who, by the way, didn't even play a full season with the Jets).

Another two-year-itch started in 1992. First was the drafting of Sergei Bautin, which is covered elsewhere in the book. The following year the Jets picked Mats Lindgren who, while being traded for Dave Manson, never had any high value in the NHL, tallying only 128 points in 387 career games (ironically though, Lindgren ended up with the Manitoba Moose in 2002–03). The Jets then redeemed themselves, first by picking Deron Quint, who had a few decent seasons with Phoenix, and Shane Doan.

With the new incarnation of the Jets, Mark Scheifele and Jacob Trouba have proven themselves to be worthy of their high selections, while Josh Morrissey and Nikolaj Ehlers have yet to suit up in Winnipeg. Don't worry though; they have plenty of time to show whether they'll join the list of great or not-so-great first picks in Winnipeg Jets draft history.

42 Trophy Winners in the NHL

While the Jets dominated individual player honours in the WHA, the NHL haul was a bit more sparse.

Across the 16 seasons in the NHL, only five players went home in June with hardware in hand—and each only did so once.

Not surprisingly, two of those players were Dale Hawerchuk and Teemu Selanne. Both Ducky and the Finnish Flash took home the Calder Memorial Trophy as Rookie of the Year after 100-point-plus freshman campaigns. Both were also dominant in their years—Hawerchuk tallied 258 votes in his year, easily outpacing runners up Barry Pederson (93) and Grant Fuhr (87), while Selanne (250) more than tripled his nearest competition—Joe Juneau (75) and Felix Potvin (63).

But those weren't the only trophy winners.

The same year that Hawerchuk took home the Calder, Tom Watt won the Jack Adams Trophy.

Watt was a rather unique case in hockey. Rather than, say, retire from the game and move into the CHL and rise through the ranks to get up to the NHL level, Watt instead came to the NHL via the CIAU. In 1965, Watt, who studied and played at the University of Toronto, became the team's head coach. Over the course of 15 seasons at the helm of the Varsity Blues, Watt led the team to nine league and 11 conference championships. One season before coming to Winnipeg, the Vancouver Canucks gave Watt his break as an assistant coach.

Watt was brought to Winnipeg in 1981 after Mike Smith had a disastrous year at the helm. Watt brought about a huge change to Winnipeg, producing a 48-point turnaround and giving the Jets a playoff berth. For his efforts, Watt was named as the Jack Adams recipient.

Watt, however, wasn't the only Jack Adams winner in Jets history. Nearly 10 years later, Bob Murdoch, a former grinder in the NHL, found himself at the helm of the Jets. The season was 1989–90, and the Jets were coming off a 64-point season in which they finished last in the Smythe Division and just two points ahead of the Toronto Maple Leafs in the "battle" for basement dwellers in the Campbell Conference. Murdoch led the Jets to a 37-win, 85-point season, good enough for fourth in the conference.

The final trophy in Jets history came at the conclusion of their last season. Perhaps due to this being the swan song for the team, Jets captain Kris King was recognized with the King Clancy Memorial Trophy. As documented by the Hockey Hall of Fame in its 2008 program "Legends," King was named the winner of the trophy both for his participation in the Jets' Goals for Kids Foundation and for his individual work with the Manitoba Muscular Dystrophy Association and Ronald McDonald House. It was a rare time that a member of a relocating franchise was given an individual honour.

Though these five awards represent slim pickings for individual recognition, The Jets did, however, have other postseason honours during their stay in the NHL, as several players were named to the postseason NHL All-Star Teams. These included Dale Hawerchuk (2nd team, 1985), Phil Housley (2nd team, 1992), Teemu Selanne (1st team, 1993), Keith Tkachuk (2nd team, 1995), and Alexei Zhamnov (2nd team, 1995). Additionally, four Jets freshmen were named to the postseason All-Rookie Team, including Iain Duncan (1988), Bob Essensa (1990), Selanne (1993), and Boris Mironov (1994).

43 Mikhail Smith and the Russian Invasion

After John Ferguson's departure from the Winnipeg Jets' front office in September 1988, the Jets looked to their assistant general manager, Mike Smith, to lead the team on an interim basis. Made sense—this was just a couple weeks before the NHL season began.

For whatever reason, the Jets found him to be a suitable enough interim replacement that just three months later, he was made permanent GM, starting one of the most tumultuous periods the Jets ever had. In the five-year period that Smith was at the helm, he traded away Dale Hawerchuk and just about every member of the '80s powerhouse team. In fact, virtually every player who came to the Jets during the 1990s was a direct result of Smith's penchant for making trades, good or bad.

Now to be fair, Smith's trading was fairly decent. He did, after all, manage to secure the likes of Tie Domi, Kris King, Ed Olczyk, and Nelson Emerson, players who contributed to the (limited) success the team had in the NHL. Yes, there were bad trades (Kris Draper anyone?), but what GM hasn't had their share of duds? After all, Markus Naslund ended up in Vancouver in exchange for Alex Stojanov.

But free-wheel trading was not the main calling card of Smith—that "Trader Mike" title belongs to Mr. Milbury, ex of the New York Islanders front office.

Instead, Smith's moniker is "Mikhail," and with good reason—he loved drafting Russian players. Truly, Smith was on a mission to bring players from the former Soviet Union to the confines of Winnipeg. Maybe he figured they'd be most likely to play here, given the reasonably similar weather conditions.

At Smith's first draft, he brought two Russians under the Jets' fold—Evgeny Davydov and Sergei Kharin. Davydov wasn't that bad a pick. In his lone full season with the Jets—1992–93—the speedy forward was part of the quad of rookies who scored at least 20 goals. He was traded after this inaugural campaign.

In 1990 Smith again hit the Russian waters and again came away with a successful nab—Alexei Zhamnov. He also picked Sergei Selyanin, who never left Russia (save for one IHL game with the Russian Penguins).

Then the floodgates opened.

In 1991, four Russian prospects were picked up. Only one spent a significant amount of time with the Jets, hulking defenseman Igor Ulanov, who went on to play more than 700 games in the NHL. The others—Yan Kaminksy, Dimitri Filimonov, and Sergei Sorokin—played a combined one game in the Jets' uniform.

But if you think that's bad, look at 1992.

This was the height of "Mikhail's" love affair with Mother Russia. To his credit, Smith made a shrewd decision in selecting Nikolai Khabibulin. Khabby's time in Winnipeg was exciting, and he went on to have an amazing NHL career that included a Stanley Cup with the Tampa Bay Lightning. Smith also selected Boris Mironov in the second round of the draft, and he ended up playing through to the 2004–05 NHL lockout.

That's where the adulation ends, though. Smith's first selection—17th overall—was Sergei Bautin, a lumbering D-man who spent parts of two seasons in Winnipeg. The other Kremlin imports played a grand total of zero games in Winnipeg: Alexander Alexeyev, Artur Oktyabrev, Andrei Raisky, Yevgeny Garanin, Andrei (not Alexander) Karpovtsev, and Ivan Vologzhaninov. In case you lost count (and I don't blame you if you did), that's nine players from the former Soviet Union. Today's NHL Entry Draft doesn't even have that many rounds.

The following season, Smith started to taper off, drafting "only" six Russians. Notable names? Does Ravil Gusmanov or Harijs Vitolinsh (12 games, 0 points between the two with the Jets) count? I didn't think so.

That 1993 Entry Draft was Smith's last with the Jets as he was released from his duties in January 1994, just prior to the start of the lockout-shortened NHL season. Smith would go on to find other jobs in hockey with the Chicago Blackhawks and Toronto Maple Leafs.

Ironically, a couple years after Smith's departure, the Jets seemed to pay tribute to the onetime GM, as during a short run of games in the 1994–95 season, the team donned red helmets on the road instead of the traditional blue lids.

44 The Winnipeg Arena Story

St. James is one of Winnipeg's most contrasting neighbourhoods. Its citizens are quiet and reserved. Its streets give you the feel of suburbia at its finest—lots of green grass and trees, schools and parks for children, and community centres for all. The neighbourhood is also home to one of, if not Winnipeg's best mall—Polo Park. For decades, it's been a hub of retail activity, with clothing stores, kiosks, and a movie theater attached.

And yet, for so many Winnipeggers, St. James was better known for being the epicentre of the sports world. In summer, it was the open-air Winnipeg Stadium that drew crowds, but the rest of the year it was the Winnipeg Arena.

Standing from 1955 to 2004, the Winnipeg Arena was *the* home of hockey for the River City. It was born out of need, the

The Manitoba Moose and Winnipeg Jets alumni close out the Winnipeg Arena.

latest and biggest of its kind in the Manitoba capital, taking over for Shea's Amphitheatre, itself a 5,000 seat facility. At initial construct, the Arena had a seating capacity almost double that of Shea's—9,500. That number grew and shrank through the years as demand came and went.

Initially, the Arena was the home of the Winnipeg Warriors who were part of the minor pro circuit known as the Western Hockey League. The team, during its years of activity, featured the likes of Billy Mosienko, Ted Green, and Eddie Johnston on its roster, and the club was a success, winning the Edinburgh Trophy in 1956. Owner J.D. Perrin, Sr. also ran two junior hockey clubs in the building—the Winnipeg Braves and St. Boniface Canadiens.

After the demise of the Warriors, Perrin retained ownership of his teams, renaming the Canadiens the Winnipeg Warriors. Ultimately, the teams became property of Benny Hatskin and his ownership group. Originally, Hatskin kept junior hockey as the main tenant of the Winnipeg Arena before he and his group founded the WHA's Winnipeg Jets. Incidentally, one of the junior teams, now known as the Winnipeg Monarchs, continued to play in the Arena until 1977.

Over the course of the near 24-year history of the Jets in the WHA and NHL, the Arena underwent various expansions, eventually having a capacity north of 15,000 seats. The Arena saw several magical moments in its time, including Avco Cups, Teemu Selanne's records, Dave Ellett's famed goal against the Edmonton Oilers, the 1972 Summit Series contest, and the 1999 World Junior Hockey Championship.

But it wasn't the moments that told the story of the Winnipeg Arena—it was the fans. At times, Winnipeg Arena rivalled, if not superseded, Chicago Stadium as the loudest hockey venue in North America. Close confines meant that already passionate crowds were that much more boisterous. On playoff nights, the White Out seemingly broke any semblance of sound measurement.

The noise in the Arena made it an intimidating venue to visit for any opponent, much like the MTS Centre is today, and it helped create a true spirit for the players.

"Certainly, when it was full to the rafters with over 10,000 people, there was an awful lot of excitement," Joe Daley said. "There were a lot of great memories in that building for me. I enjoyed playing in it. It was a great hockey atmosphere; the fans were great all through the years. It was something special, especially when we got to close out championships in the building. It was a lot of fun."

In 2004, with the MTS Centre completed, the Arena shut its doors. Early in the 2004–05 AHL season, after a brief stay of execution, the Winnipeg Arena hosted its final hockey game. The occasion was momentous. Legends from Winnipeg's hockey past—from Teemu Selanne to Ulf Nilsson to John Ferguson—were brought back for a final curtain call in the Winnipeg Arena. Though the Moose lost to the Utah Grizzlies (poetically an affiliate of the Phoenix Coyotes), the night could not be spoiled as fans cheered their heroes, past and present, and stayed in the Arena as late as they could that night.

The magnitude of the night wasn't lost on the Moose players, either. "Hearing the guys talk, it's actually a great honour to have been part of it," said Moose forward Jesse Schultz moments after the final whistle blew.

For the record, it was the Moose's Lee Goren who was the last hometown hero to play a game on the Winnipeg Arena ice. "It's an honour," Goren said following the contest. "There's a lot of guys that have come through here who have been awesome players and did great things. To be out there on the last night was great."

Within months, the Winnipeg Arena was torn down. Years later, while creating a memorable opening sequence for the Jets' first game back to Winnipeg, *Hockey Night in Canada* dedicated part of its opening to the now-empty lot on Maroons Road, with fans walking in the spot where their heroes once skated.

Truly, the Winnipeg Arena will never be forgotten.

45 Andrew Ladd and the '05 Juniors

When the Winnipeg Jets arrived from Atlanta, there were a few question marks that existed personnel wise; perhaps none bigger than the future of Andrew Ladd.

One year prior, Ladd came to the Atlanta Thrashers after winning his second Stanley Cup with the Chicago Blackhawks. Already marked as a leader, Ladd, who entered the NHL with the Carolina Hurricanes, was handed the "C" almost immediately upon arrival to his new squad.

Flash forward to the summer of 2011, and Ladd was without a contract when he arrived in Winnipeg. It didn't take long, however, for the man who would become known as the heart and soul of the new Jets to sign a pact with the club's new ownership.

This wasn't Ladd's first experience playing in the MTS Centre. That came several years beforehand.

Back in 2004, Ladd was a member of the Calgary Hitmen in the midst of his second year with the club when he was invited to be part of the group of prospects who would hope to survive the cut and represent Canada at the World Junior Hockey Championships, just across the border in Grand Forks, North Dakota.

And that roster, before it drove through customs at Emerson, was assembled in Winnipeg.

Future Jets captain Andrew Ladd warms up at the MTS Centre in an exhibition game prior to the 2005 World Junior Hockey Championship.

The MTS Centre played host to the final selection camp, trimming down invitees to a final roster that looked to win back the gold medal for all of Canada, and among those left standing was Ladd, who stood proud on the forward line at the end of camp.

Before the tournament started, Canada played two exhibition games, both of which were landslide victories—a 6–0 thumping of Finland and 5–0 thrashing of the Swiss.

Those two contests remain memorable for Ladd. "One of the memories I have is just how crazy the MTS Centre was when we were playing our exhibition games. We had a lot of fun there," Ladd said.

Once the tournament started in Grand Forks, no one could match Canada's fire power. The team went undefeated, capping off its amazing run with a 6–1 lopsided victory over the Alex Ovechkin– and Evgeni Malkin–led Russian squad.

That roster may have not only the greatest to ever play hockey in Winnipeg, but indeed the most dominant in the history of Canadian hockey. "That was a cool experience," Ladd reflected. "With the lockout, we had so many great players going into camp. If you look down the line of that team, there are a lot of superstars in the NHL right now."

Just as a reminder, that roster of superstars that Ladd teamed with included Sidney Crosby, Jeff Carter, Patrice Bergeron, Michael Richards, Corey Perry, Ryan Getzlaf, Dion Phaneuf, Shea Weber, and Brent Seabrook.

While some members of the team would call the '05 Juniors their greatest moment in hockey, Ladd's was still to come. In 2005–06, as a rookie, Ladd won the Stanley Cup with the Hurricanes. Just a few years later, he was part of the team that brought Lord Stanley's mug back to Chicago for the first time since the era of Bobby Hull.

Ladd's first three years in Winnipeg involved leading by example as he tallied at least 20 goals three times and in the lockout-shortened 2012–13 season had a near point-per-game pace. In 2014–15, he was named a finalist for the Mark Messier Leadership Award, while also being one of the most active Jets off the ice for community events.

Incidentally, that same '05 World Junior Championship that saw streams of Winnipeggers make the journey to Grand Forks, also featured other future Winnipeg Jets, including Michael Frolik (Czech Republic) and Al Montoya (USA).

46 The Memory of Rick Rypien

On opening night for the Winnipeg Jets, there was excitement that filled the MTS Centre. From players and coaches to staff and fans, each and every individual in the building knew they were part of history.

As joyous as the night was, there was still a thought of sorrow and mourning for a fallen hero who didn't get the chance to play for the new NHL team—Rick Rypien.

By all accounts, Rypien was a special player. Tough, ornery, and full of passion, Rypien played his heart out at every opportunity. Sure, he was often relegated to fourth line duties, but he was the type of skater who would not only draw a crowd on the ice, but also the adulation of fans.

Rypien's road to the NHL began in the Alberta Junior Hockey League and quickly transitioned to the Regina Pats of the WHL. It was here that Rypien drew the attention of scouts after being named the team's MVP and most popular player as voted by fans. That season was 2004–05, a campaign where Rypien, an overager for the junior ranks, was introduced to Craig Heisinger.

Michael Hutchinson's mask features a sticker to honour No. 11 Rick Rypien.

"I had watched him play junior, and he was a good hardnosed player, I watched the Wheat Kings pound him into submission one night, and went to watch practice the next day because Curtis Hunt was a friend of mine and Rick was blocking shots in practice," Heisinger told reporters, including Michael Remis of *Illegal Curve*, shortly after Rypien's passing. "I remember going down to the dressing room and saying, 'Tell me more about this guy,' and it went from there. He was a true character guy, the coach Curtis Hunt really went to bat for him; we offered him an amateur tryout. There wasn't a long line, his agent couldn't say yes fast enough."

Following the conclusion of the Pats' season, Rypien joined the Moose and contributed two points in the eight-game tryout while also being a strong role-player in the playoffs. Soon after, Rypien was signed to a full AHL contract by Heisinger and later to a two-way pact by the parent club Vancouver Canucks. Rypien made the most of that first full pro season, scoring his first NHL goal during his first shift of play.

Over the next couple years, Rypien travelled back and forth between Vancouver and Manitoba before finally earning a full-time roster spot during the 2008–09 NHL season. Unfortunately for Rypien, it was also where clinical depression took hold. Attempting to handle his illness along with a battery of injuries, Rypien began taking leaves of absence. His most active season of NHL hockey came in 2009–10, where he played 69 games for the Canucks after signing a two-year contract that off-season. The following season was again split between the Canucks and the Moose.

Early in the 2011 off-season, Rypien was reunited with Heisinger, as he signed on with the Winnipeg Jets. Just weeks later, however, the courageous player lost his battle with depression. He was just 27 when he passed away, but the impact he made on his family, friends, teammates, and community was immeasurable.

For that first Winnipeg Jets game and ever since, players have worn a sticker on their helmets of No. 11—the number Rypien was to wear for the club—while staff wear a similar pin or one with "RR" in memory of the fallen brother.

47 Play Against the Jets

Let me be clear—I recognize that this is one that isn't easily accomplished—it takes years of dedication and self-sacrifice to get to the point where you play against the Jets. The people who get to do this in any given season only number in the hundreds.

Yet it makes the list because it is such a unique experience—being the visiting team that comes into the MTS Centre to square off against a hometown boys in blue. Players, coaches, and other personnel across the NHL will tell you repeatedly about the unique atmosphere in the building and in its predecessor, the Winnipeg Arena—a lot having to do with the ever-looming presence of the Jets faithful, who will ferociously taunt and boo opponents.

The atmosphere creates a very unwelcome feeling for anyone who comes to play wearing another jersey, even if they're a talent who grew up in the 'Peg.

"It's a different feeling than other buildings," St. Louis Blues forward Alexander Steen remarked. "It feels like the fans are right on top of you. It's definitely a different atmosphere than in other buildings."

Steen, of course, is far from the only NHL'er from Manitoba. Even with the Jets gone, the province has bred a multitude of big league players.

Among those players is Ryan Reaves. A native of Winnipeg, Reaves entered the NHL with the St. Louis Blues after playing in the juniors with the Brandon Wheat Kings. As one could imagine, playing in Winnipeg where he grew up remains special, even though he's years into his career.

"When I played for Brandon, we came here and played the one or two games while the Winter Fair was there," Reeves said

"It's a big deal when you're playing in junior, but this is the NHL. Coming back here and getting a goal in front of them is special."

The same sentiment is felt by another Winnipegger—Travis Zajac. Zajac is certainly familiar with playing in a hockey-mad city as a member of the multiple Stanley Cup–winning New Jersey Devils; but as he commented, there's a whole other air to playing in the city where he grew up. "It's always an exciting game for me. As soon as you get off the plane, this city just breathes hockey. You like to be in that type of atmosphere," Zajac said.

For those who haven't grown up in Winnipeg, they're more likely to get the vitriolic treatment, but there's a bit of a combat to this that some players have—experience playing in front of the MTS Centre crowds from the days of the Manitoba Moose. Skaters like Montreal superstar defenseman P.K. Subban are able to use this history to their advantage (unfortunately).

"It's a great building to play in. Most of us here played in Hamilton, played playoff series here. We know the energy in this building," Subban said after his Habs beat the Jets in a 2012–13 game.

The energy is also felt by those who once suited up in Winnipeg, even after they come back as members of a longtime nemesis squad.

"I love coming back here. The people love the game, they get excited about it," said former Jets and Moose forward Dallas Eakins while he was head coach of the Edmonton Oilers. "They're highly encouraging people. I walked from the hotel to the rink twice today, and both times, I had no less than five people rolling down their windows, wishing me good luck tonight. Just great people and great Canadians."

As the NHL continues on, more players will get that opportunity to square off with the Winnipeg Jets and in doing so will understand the rare, and fortunate chance it is to play against one of the most beloved franchises in all the league.

48 A Relocation Destination

"The lockout changed everything."

—Mark Chipman, chairman,
True North Sports and Entertainment

The 2004–05 season had a gigantic effect on the National Hockey League. It was the first time in major North American sports history that a league lost a full season of play for any reason, let alone a labor dispute between its players and management.

The season lost meant a lot of things to a lot of businesses—jobs were temporarily on hold if not all-out eliminated in markets as businesses related to the game weathered an incredible storm. A number of players who otherwise may have held on for one more season retired while others who may have debuted in 2004–05 spent another year in juniors or with the AHL.

Coming out of the disposed season, the NHL had a new financial reality. A salary cap meant that small markets like Edmonton were now better positioned to be competitive with the Toronto's of the world. The setting also meant that there was now a glimmer of hope for a city like Winnipeg to once again house an NHL franchise.

Recognizing the opportunity, Chipman, along with other parties at True North, began to get their ducks in a row as they marched toward what hoped to result in a return to the NHL.

Give Chipman all the credit in the world—he did his due diligence. Though well familiar with the structure of the NHL, being the owner of the Manitoba Moose, he sought out and took advantage of networking opportunities. This included furthering relationships with Canadian clubs similar in structure as to what would be the case for Winnipeg.

"Post-lockout, we spent time in Edmonton and Ottawa and worked on relationships that we had developed in years prior, and really began to understand the modern economics of the team," Chipman said. "With each meeting, it became more, 'Maybe this will work.'"

The next step came in 2007, when the NHL opened its doors to five cities to make presentations, justifying themselves as potential homes for hockey. True North's brass was among those presenting with an eye toward the cities being spots for expansion or relocation, the latter of which is a situation the NHL only takes on in extreme cases.

"The National Hockey League never stops thinking. It's an unbelievable machine. The depth and breadth of what they're doing is incredible," Chipman said. "They were being proactive. With a couple years of the new economic system under their belts, they were looking at potential new markets, starting the process of identifying where they might go to next."

Chipman's eagerness to participate paid off, as queries started to come to his office that centred around relocation. Even before the Phoenix Coyotes talk really started to heat up, there were exploratory movements made surrounding other teams possibly moving to Winnipeg.

"Right after that, we started getting introduced to concepts and possibilities," Chipman said. "Nashville, a very brief conversation with Pittsburgh before they turned around and got their building committed. It was a bit laughable at the time but those were the kinds of things that grew out of that presentation in '07. They became serious about us and it just kept moving."

The process, however, wasn't easy. As stated before, the NHL has steadfastly maintained a position that relocation of a franchise is a last resort, and True North—and Winnipeg as a whole—remained hopeful that there would be a future for the NHL in the River City. The most important part was that the higher ups in the NHL saw that there was indeed a viable market for its brand of hockey in Manitoba.

"After the Jets left, Winnipeg's NHL connection remained strong through such distinguished players as Mike Ridley, Grant Ledyard, Mike Keane, and James Patrick, and today's NHL includes more Winnipeg standouts such as Jonathan Toews, Patrick Sharp, Duncan Keith, and Travis Zajac," the NHL Commissioner said in a 2011 interview. "In addition, the Manitoba Moose always developed quality players for its NHL parent club. So there were always hometown heroes for the fans of Winnipeg to support and there was always hope that the Jets would return. The passion of the community never seemed to wane."

49 Dance with Dancing Gabe Between Puck Drops

When the action on the ice at the MTS Centre takes a short break, there are some things you can count on—a rush to refill on beer, a human exhibition of whacky games in pursuit of gift cards, and lots of crowd shots of smiling, excited fans.

And the most excited fan you'll see is Gabe Langlois, better known as Dancing Gabe.

Since the early 1990s, Gabe has been strutting his stuff in Winnipeg. Go to any sporting event—the Bombers and Goldeyes included—and you'll see the smiling face of Dancing Gabe as he makes his way from aisle to aisle, revving up the Winnipeg faithful.

It all started innocently enough—a fan described by *Winnipeg Free Press* columnist Gordon Sinclair Jr. as being "Rain Man" like in his ability to recall and output statistics about his beloved Jets getting up and rallying his team on with a semi-choreographed series of moves that gets fans around him jazzed, much like the famed episode of *The Simpsons* that introduced the world to Dancing Homer.

"I guess one day he couldn't help himself—he got so excited he started dancing. After every game the media would say, 'Well, there goes our Dancing Gabe,'" Angelina Langlois, Gabe's mother, said in the documentary *The Return of the Winnipeg Jets.* "He counted himself as part of the team. It was like his job to be at every game."

Momentum built slowly, and it didn't take long before Gabe became an unofficial feature attraction at Winnipeg hockey events. Through the Jets' final season and Manitoba Moose days, there was Gabe, eternally adorned in the jersey of his home team, dancing his way into the collective heart of Winnipeg.

Gabe has been front and centre at some of the most exciting days in Winnipeg history. He was in the first row of the crowd at The Forks when the announcement came that the Jets were coming back to Winnipeg, he was shown North America–wide when just weeks later Mark Chipman proclaimed that the Jets would be retaining their former name, and he travelled to Toronto in 2007 for the Bombers Grey Cup Championship Game against hated rivals the Saskatchewan Roughriders.

There may be no fans that get more excited by Dancing Gabe than children, who will jump out of their seats when Gabe approaches their section and starts juking and jiving. Whether he's rocking on an air guitar or performing his own spin-o-rama, he gives off a natural charisma that gives such emotion that it connects, inarguably, even with the most glued-to-their-seat beer zone bum.

But more than just a rally figure in Winnipeg, Gabe is a kind soul. His visage carries a permanent smile, and he's seemingly always finding a way to bring that infectious grin to others, both at the rink and in every-day situations. One such testimonial came through the blog Winnipegbusstories.com. A reader, identifying herself only as Mandy, shared the following tale in 2014.

"I got on the number 14 back in February with my arms laden with parcels and shopping bags," she wrote. "I rode the bus for about 10 minutes to my destination. As I stood up to get off the bus, a man touched my arm to get my attention and handed me my wallet, which I had unknowingly dropped. I looked up into the man's face to thank him. My good Samaritan was none other than the legendary Dancing Gabe! If he ever comes across this, I just want to let him know that he made my day."

So revered is he, that MyToba.ca president and CEO Kevin Klein declared that Gabe should be bound for the Manitoba Sports Hall of Fame.

"Anyone who has ever met Dancing Gabe knows he is a very polite and positive man," Klein posted on May 21, 2014. "I watch him at every stoppage of play as he takes to the stairs to generate excitement from his fellow fans. It's amazing to see how the thousands of fans Gabe entertains treat him like a rock star! As time has passed I have been fortunate to catch some Goldeyes, Bisons, and Bombers games and at each one there is Dancing Gabe leading the home-team charge."

And you won't get any argument from the population of Winnipeg.

50 The Versatility of Dustin Byfuglien

Back many moons ago, hockey looked like a much different sport.

Goalies didn't have pads, skaters didn't have helmets, and there was this odd position between the forwards and defensemen called a "rover."

The rover was a seventh man on the ice, who quite literally roamed the entire rink, acting as a fourth man on offence and a third man on defense depending on which role was needed in a particular game situation. Among the more popular rovers of the era—this being the early 1900s—was future Hockey Hall of Famer Fred "Cyclone" Taylor. Though the NHL and predecessor NHA did not have a rover, other leagues like chief professional rival Pacific Coast Hockey Association did; but by the time the NHL was the only major league standing, the rover was gone for good.

Which is a shame for today's NHL, when you consider that the prototypical rover occupied a spot on the Winnipeg Jets' lineup—Dustin Byfuglien.

"Big Buff" was one of the marquee names who came to Winnipeg in 2011–12 and had such amazing versatility that he was able to play either forward or defence. If he really wanted to, Byfuglien likely could have been a netminder, too.

"I think Dustin Byfuglien can do whatever he sets his mind to, I really do," Paul Maurice said of Big Buff during the 2013–14 season. "He has a really good stick, he's strong. He scores the big goal but creates some other things from the blue line."

Byfuglien was born in Minnesota to parents who never married. He split his time growing up between the metropolis of Minneapolis and rural Rouseau. Later, his mother married into hockey, tying the knot with WHA and NHL'er Dale Smedsmo. Byfuglien fell in love with the sport right away and as fate would have it, moved to Canada for major junior play with the Brandon Wheat Kings. After just a few games over parts of two seasons, Byfuglien was moved to the Prince George Cougars.

In 2003, the Chicago Blackhawks drafted Byfuglien as a defenseman—the spot that he occupied in his junior development. After spending much of his first two seasons of pro hockey with the AHL's Norfolk Admirals, Byfuglien found a more permanent spot on the team for the 2007–08 season. Soon after the call-up became

Dustin Byfuglien follows through on a slap shot from the blue line during the 2014–15 season.

permanent, Buff moved up to forward and found a new home. That first season he finished fifth in team scoring and earned his first NHL hat trick.

"At first I didn't like the move because I didn't have experience playing forward. I had no choice but to adapt, so I did," Byfuglien told USAhockeymagazine.com in 2009. "Playing with good players like we have, I adapted quickly, and now I'm pretty much there to stay."

The move paid off in spades for the Hawks. In 2010, Byfuglien was an instrumental part of the team bringing the Stanley Cup back to Chicago for the first time since the early 1960s. Buff tallied 16 points in 22 postseason games including 11 goals.

One year later, however, Byfuglien was on the move, the casualty of a Chicago system that was pressed up against the salary cap. He found a new home in Atlanta with the Thrashers before they relocated to Winnipeg. By the time that first NHL game was played on MTS Centre ice, Buff was back at his former position on D and remained there for most of the Claude Noel era of Jets hockey. Along the way he was named to the 2010–11 NHL All-Star Game as the lone Jets rep, but he did not end up playing due to injury.

Once Paul Maurice became head coach, however, Buff was moved back to forward as a right winger. Early in his tenure, Maurice told Scott Edmonds of the Canadian Press that he saw Buff as being more than happy in his new position.

"I really like the way he's into the game on the bench, he's finishing checks, he's engaged in what he's doing," Coach Maurice said. "He doesn't at all look like a player who's waiting for this experiment not to work and 'I'm going to go back to where I want to.'"

That doesn't mean that Buff doesn't go back to D when called upon. During the 2014–15 season, the Jets were down three of their starting defensemen and Buff was brought back to the blue line. In his first game back on D, Buff scored on a rocket from the blue line while going +2 for the night.

"He makes it seem seamless, but that's not an easy thing to do," Jets captain Andrew Ladd said after the game. "I think for the first period it was different to see guys coming at him rather than the other way, but he's a pretty special player to go from being one of your top forwards to being one of your top defensemen the next night."

51 A Season to Remember

The 1995–96 campaign for the Winnipeg Jets was one of the most unique in sports.

Most often when a team packs up its bags and moves to a different city, it does so at the end of a season, or at the very least with a move imminent as the last few games tick off the calendar; but to know at the start of a season that it will be your last in your current home base? That's a rarity.

Dubbed the "Season to Remember," the 1995–96 year for the Jets was, one way or another, going to be the last in Winnipeg. Originally, the team was Minnesota-bound, but as the crew found out later on, it was Phoenix that was going to be the new destination for this brand of hockey.

One can only imagine the strife and emotional turmoil that players went through as they battled to stay focused on the ice while facing a constant barrage of questions about their future. Kris King, captain of that final team, talked openly and candidly about the experience.

On preparation for the season:

"Really early in training camp, we got together as a team and said we're going to get a lot of questions. Every time we leave this town we're going to be asked the same question: 'What's it like to be a lame duck team, and how are you guys going to approach this year?' We just said, 'We're professionals and we owe it to our fans in Winnipeg to play as hard as we can whenever we're there.' We had our ups and downs as expected and no matter what happened, we wanted to give our fans, for the lack of a better term, a good show. We approached it that way."

On keeping focus:

"When things got tough, we got a little bit tougher. We had to reel the guys in and say, 'We've got to do this the right way and refocus ourselves,' and every time you'd go to another city they'd say 'You're leaving, and you're just playing it out. You're going to do this and you're going to do that.' And if enough people keep telling you that, you tend to start to believe it a little bit. It was our job as leaders in that room to bring everyone back to reality and remind them what we all agreed upon at the start of the year, that we were going to play hard and play every night, and we were going to leave Winnipeg, for the lack of a better term, with a bang and for the most part I think we did a real good job in tough circumstances to do that."

On saying goodbye to Winnipeg:

"It was hard. I was there for a short amount of time, there were guys there for longer than I was, but Winnipeg grows on you and you didn't want to disappoint the people because our fans were so good to us and it was such an honour to play there. Unless you had been there, you didn't realize just how lucky you were to play in a great hockey city like that. You talk about the weather and the cold, but what you don't know about is how passionate their fans are and how well they treat you and just how great a memory it is, and now when you look back, I've played 15 years, played in Toronto

This pocket schedule commemorates the final season of the original Jets.

and New York; people ask me, 'Where was the greatest place you've played?' It doesn't take long to say, 'Winnipeg, by far.' They look at you a little bit crazy. But you can't explain it to people, and to this day it's one of those things I'm proud to say I was part of that group."

On being the last captain:

"Being the last captain was an honour. A lot of it had to do with the fact that I was able to stand in front of cameras and microphones in the other cities and say the right things. I think the players needed someone who could do that for them. I had no problem with that, and for the most part was able to get the guys' minds back in line and throughout other things. It was important for us and for the people in Winnipeg. You can't hide when you go for dinner or a movie or with your kids to Chuck E. Cheese's. It was important for us to leave on the right note, and for the most part I was proud of how our guys handled it and how they approached it. It wasn't easy, but it was memorable for everybody."

52 Zinger

When the Jets left Winnipeg bound for Phoenix in 1996, there were very few pieces that remained in Winnipeg to hang back for the new adventures with the Manitoba Moose. Of the players, only Randy Gilhen stayed, and there were a couple behind-the-scenes personalities; and among these individuals there was no one who meant more to the team's future than Craig Heisinger.

Born in Winnipeg, Heisinger was the epitome of the "rise through the ranks" style of success story that fans love. Focused on a career surrounding a hockey team, "Zinger," as he is known to co-workers, mediates, and fans, started as an equipment manager in the Manitoba Junior Hockey League, slowly making his rise to the WHL, first to the Winnipeg Warriors and then to the Brandon Wheat Kings.

After four years in Brandon, Zinger got the call that so many people dream of, but only a few get—the opportunity to be with the Jets. As a member of the equipment management staff, Heisinger became a recognized name among the boys in the locker room, earning a reputation as a dedicated worker. Unfortunately, with the move of the Jets to Phoenix, Heisinger was faced with the decision that would change his life—move with the team and retain a position with the Coyotes or remain in Winnipeg. Zinger's choice was family-focused as he stayed in Winnipeg.

Fortunately, there was already someone scouting Zinger locally—Mark Chipman. "When we bought the [Moose] in 1996, I don't know how many people told me this, but they said the first guy you've got to hire is Craig Heisinger," Chipman told the *Globe and Mail* in 2011. "It came from former NHL players and members of their front office. I just so vividly remember everybody telling me the guy to hire to be the caretaker of your team is Craig. And where a lot of people left, Zinger never ever thought about leaving."

Midway through the Moose's run as the chief hockey team in Winnipeg, Zinger got the unique promotion to assistant general manager of the team. It was there that TSN Radio 1290 host Andrew "Hustler" Paterson met Heisinger and saw the passion that he had, and saw just how many hats he wore up front and the dedication he had to the AHL club.

"Knowing from where he started, to being the assistant GM and working within hockey operations to what he does on the road is an absolute revelation," Paterson said. "The more I was in contact with Zinger, the more I respected him as a guy who worked his ass off to get into that organization and truly, above all, loved the city of Winnipeg. He could've been gone the day the Jets walked out the door. He chose to stay and had incredible pride in the Moose brand."

It didn't take long before Heisinger was named general manager of the Moose, and it was here that he carved out his spot in Winnipeg hockey lore. If there's anything that genuinely differentiated him from other AHL GM's, however, it was his steadfast method of running the team as if it was independent. Often, Zinger would go on scouting missions and became renowned for finding talent and fostering their growth in the Moose organization, even if they had not yet signed a contract with the parent Vancouver Canucks.

Probably the most famed of these players is current Canuck Alex Burrows, who was a direct signee of Heisinger's.

"I'd say he's the top guy that's made me a Canuck," Burrows said of Heisinger. "When I first started playing pro hockey I was playing down south in the U.S. and no one really looked at me. One day, he gave me the chance to come to Manitoba for a chance with the Moose and he kind of liked me. Even when Vancouver was calling and telling him to play their guys [the Vancouver draft picks], he said, 'I'm going to keep playing Alex because he's playing better and he's helping us win.' If he would have just folded and listened to Burkie [then Canucks GM Brian Burke], I probably never would have made it."

Thus, it's not surprising that when TNSE made the jump to the NHL, Heisinger's services were retained. With the new NHL organization, Heisinger was named the senior vice president and director of hockey operations and assistant GM, as well as taking on general manager duties with the St. John's Ice Caps affiliate team. It's Zinger's outlook, as he told the *Globe and Mail* in 2011, that helped propel him to a spot that he has today from such humble beginnings, "I've always been of the attitude I've had to work every day to earn people's respect, never try to demand it."

53 Fergy Brings Savard to Winnipeg

One of the common misconceptions about the Winnipeg Jets was that the team had trouble attracting big name hockey players to play in the River City.

Okay, so maybe in some cases that was true—it took a move to Phoenix, for example, to get Jeremy Roenick to don the franchise's jersey; but there were a few cases where big name players did travel to the land of the frozen chosen, namely Hall of Famer Serge Savard.

Savard, of course, is well remembered for his time with the Montreal Canadiens. The first defenseman to win the Conn Smythe Trophy as playoff MVP, Savard was an integral part of the Habs' dynasty in the 1970s who won multiple Stanley Cups. Though never a Norris Trophy winner, Savard was nonetheless one of the most feared rearguards in the league. Savard starred in the 1972 Summit Series and served as captain for two years.

It took cajoling by John Ferguson, once a teammate of Savard's in Montreal, to coax the retiring Savard to return to action.

"I didn't really want to come back," Savard said. "I was receiving calls from John [Ferguson]. I saw that the Jets weren't the same as the year before or else I wouldn't have come back, but the club was going for first place. I hadn't enjoyed the game the previous few years. Things were on a sour note with the Canadiens. There were a lot of young defensemen waiting in line. I made the right decision. But I felt wanted by Winnipeg, and the atmosphere was very different."

Additionally, Savard had his family's interest at heart. Though the Canadiens had not properly released Savard from his career in the NHL, there was still the obstacle of relocating his family, which he told the Hall would have kept him from returning to hockey.

"If Montreal had not forgotten to file my retirement papers, there's no way I'd have played in Winnipeg," Savard explained. "But I was very happy to be playing. If my family had been against the move, I would never have considered it. Their attitude surprised me. I think my family missed my involvement in hockey."

But shave the story down from Savard's biggest excuses and you see that it was his relationship with Fergy that probably had the most influence. The two were best friends, and as the stories tell the duo would hit the track together among other adventures.

Perhaps the most legendary story of the two came following the Summit Series, where Fergy was an assistant coach with the team and Savard a player. As the Montreal Canadiens re-told on their website, Ferguson had each member of his team sign a hockey stick. Fergy kept the stick tightly clutched the entire journey home. As the victorious Canadian team deplaned, they were greeted by a welcoming committee that included Canadian Prime Minister Pierre Elliott Trudeau. Savard, quick-witted as he was, exclaimed, "By the way, Mr. Prime Minister, John Ferguson brought you back an autographed souvenir from Moscow."

Despite this, Fergy found great value in bringing Savard to Winnipeg. Though he wasn't with the Jets long, the impact was felt fairly quickly for a squad that was starting to gel and was in need of veteran guidance.

"He always talks to you and gives you a little encouragement," a young Paul MacLean told Kathy Johnson in the January 22, 1982, edition of *Jet Stream*, just a short time into Savard's tenure in Winnipeg. "He will tell you if you should come down deeper or stay out farther. He just helps everyone with his presence. When he's on the ice you want to work hard because he's there.... He's really helped the whole team in the month he's been here, and it's going to get better."

Savard helped the Jets gain entry into the playoffs in his first year. The next season, in which he tallied 20 points in 76 games, was his last in the NHL. The retirement of "The Senator" ended up with him returning to Montreal, this time as general manager, where he won two additional Stanley Cups.

54 The Miracle of Redmond

Parents, skip this chapter in the book if you're reading this to your kids.

This isn't one for the faint of heart.

You see, this is one of the unfortunate tales of what can happen in hockey, a game of blades, wood (or composites) and galvanized rubber. The reality of hockey is that injuries happen, and while some are tame, others are admittedly gruesome and push that line between simple wound and injuries that put the game in perspective—that there are things more important than a simple game.

The Jets, over the course of their history, have thankfully had few moments of this level of panic; but the new era of the team brought about one such incident—the leg injury of Zach Redmond.

Redmond had all the potential in the world when he was selected by the Atlanta Thrashers 184th overall in the 2008 NHL Entry Draft. He opted to complete his time with Ferris State University before signing his first big-league pact with the team that drafted him mere weeks before its transfer to Winnipeg. Initially Redmond spent time in the AHL, first with the Chicago Wolves (the Thrashers' farm team) before coming to St. John's.

Amid the shortened 2012–13 season, Redmond was called up to Winnipeg and seemed destined to have a solid spot with the team. In an eight-game stint with the Jets, Redmond tallied four points, including potting his first NHL goal.

Everything seemed to be going his way, until a horrific incident occurred during a practice in Carolina. Jets head coach Claude Noel described the situation to Ed Tait of the *Winnipeg Free Press*:

"What took place is we were trying to get our extra players conditioned, and there was a one-on-one battle at the net where he tripped up and landed on his back. The player that was tied up with him happened to step on him. It's a fairly wide cut.

"He lost a fair bit of blood and he's in some pain. It looks like it's a vein. It cut him through the sock.... I don't know if it cut through the pant, but there was a fair amount of a loss of blood there quickly and we got it tied up and put pressure on it. He'll be fine."

The injury, however, could have been much more severe, had teammate Anthony Peluso and a group of trainers and coaches not worked quickly to stop the bleeding, applying pressure and fashioning a tourniquet quickly. Already, Jets head athletic therapist Rob Milette figured that Redmond had lost a litre of blood.

"He lost a lot of blood there and his heart was definitely struggling," Milette told Ed Tait. "We were monitoring his vitals, checking his pulse. His pulse was really weak and really slow. He was pale. He was starting to tell us he was getting thirsty and that told us he had lost a lot of blood."

But as remarkable as the day was, and the heroism that unfolded, the next step was even more incredible. Just six weeks later, Redmond was back on the ice. The speedy return was amazing in the eyes of Jets head physician Peter MacDonald.

"It's nothing short of a miracle considering what's he's been through," MacDonald told *Free Press* scribe Gary Lawless in early April 2013. "We're all aware of what happened. Considering the magnitude of the injury and the insult, not only to the leg but the whole body, it's quite miraculous."

Though Redmond didn't compete in the NHL again that season, he did play with the AHL affiliate St. John's Ice Caps. Roughly one year to the day that he started skating again with the Jets, he tallied a goal in one of his short stints back in the NHL. It was a special moment for the prospect.

"I'm still young in my career so scoring a goal at any point… after the injury you can say that's a little bit more special, sure. But a second goal in the NHL is going to be cool either way," Redmond told the *Winnipeg Free Press*' Ed Tait.

55 Dale Hawerchuk and the Molson Cup

Perhaps the most recognized player trophy name of any award given in the 1980s and 1990s was the Molson Cup, if only because it was mentioned at every single hockey game played in Canada (well, except for the Nordiques who had the O'Keefe Cup, but that's a discussion for another book).

Molson, of course, was and still is one of the biggest breweries across the nation, crafting ales for thirsty fans in attendance at arenas, bars, homes, and just about anywhere else someone can view our beloved sport, and to tie itself tightly to shinny, the company sponsored this trophy that was connected to the ritual three-star selection at the end of each contest. At season's end, the player who had the most selections was named winner of the Cup for their team.

It probably isn't shocking that Dale Hawerchuk won the most Molson Cups. Given his dominant spot within the ranks of the team, it's not surprising that "Ducky" won the Cup six times in seven years, including during his rookie campaign of 1981–82 where he topped the 100 point mark, a rarity among first-year stars. By the time his second season started, Hawerchuk was already showing the signs of leadership that Winnipeg sorely needed. Though nervous, Hawerchuk took on the role of captain just a couple short years later, and as he told the Hockey Hall of Fame, the honour helped shape the player he would become in subsequent years.

"It was a little intimidating," Hawerchuk said in an interview on the HHOF's Legends of Hockey website. "But there were guys around to help. Randy Carlyle was captain in Pittsburgh. [The Jets] probably thought the captaincy would help me, which it did. I accepted it and it made me a better player and better person."

Only once during these six years did Hawerchuk score fewer than 100 points, and he still scored at higher than a point-per-game pace. Additionally, those six seasons all saw Hawerchuk lead the Jets to the playoffs.

It was a fortunate find for the Jets, who took Hawerchuk with the first overall pick in 1981. Unlike today where the first selection has routinely become a superstar quickly, those surrounding Hawerchuk didn't often live up to the hype. Consider that Doug Wickenheiser, a fellow centre, didn't even reach a pace of a point every two games in his career and Gord Kluzak, felled by knee issues, didn't even reach 300 games. In fact, you have to look back to 1973 (Denis Potvin) and forward to 1984 (Mario Lemieux) to find the closest players to Hawerchuk's draft year to find Hockey Hall of Famers.

By the end of his run in Winnipeg, Hawerchuk had done more than anyone else in the team's NHL tenure to bring the club respect. Though they were cellar dwellers before, Hawerchuk raised them to not only be perennial playoff participants, but Cup contenders. So important was Hawerchuk to the River City that his wedding was given the same treatment as royals would get...well... if they lived in Winnipeg.

Beyond the Molson Cup lay so many more honours for Hawerchuk, including being called to suit up for his country on several occasions. None, however, are as well remembered than his being part of the 1987 Canada Cup team. In that tournament, Hawerchuk lined up with Wayne Gretzky and Mario Lemieux, forming one of the most dangerous trios in Canadian hockey history, and it was Ducky who won the faceoff in Canadian territory that sprung Lemieux and Gretzky for the historic goal that put Canada on top of the Soviets in dramatic fashion. "We won it because we gelled into a very good team," Hawerchuk said in the same interview. "Each man did whatever the coaches asked him to do, and every player on the roster was very important in the whole picture of the team."

Hawerchuk's tenure with the Jets ended after nine seasons. He went on to play five years in Buffalo, part of a season in St. Louis, and one full and one partial season in Philadelphia before hanging up his skates in 1997. Though he never won a Stanley Cup, Hawerchuk did eclipse the 500 goal and 1,400 point plateaus and left an indelible mark on the Winnipeg hockey landscape.

56 Eat a Jumbo Jet Dog

The intermissions at Winnipeg Jets games are ritualistic. Whether it was the Winnipeg Arena or the MTS Centre, the tradition carries on, as the arena bowls empty and fans do the "circuit."

The circuit involves shuffling across the concourse of the building in a circle. At times you'll stop to talk to friends, get a beer or check out the souvenir store; but for hundreds, if not thousands of Jets fans, it's an opportunity to get one thing and one thing only—the famed Jumbo Jet Dog.

Coming in at a foot long, this is no ordinary hot dog. Using Nathan's Famous Hot Dogs as the base, the hot dog then is topped with any number of delicious extras, from traditional fare like melted cheese to unique Winnipeg favourites like pierogi pieces.

The creation of the Jumbo Jet Dog has a bit of heritage to it, as Andrew Paterson explains. Though today he's best known for being one half of *Hustler and Lawless* on TSN1290, he was under the employ of the Manitoba Moose when the team moved into the MTS Centre. He remarked that the creation of the Jumbo Jet Dog in part was a carryover from a favourite back at the Winnipeg Arena.

"One of the things they were looking to do was step up with some great, new concession options, but also take a little bit of Winnipeg Arena history with them," Paterson said. "Those of us who were in the organization at the time, Kyle Balharry in particular, always talked about the toasted hot dogs you would get in the north end of the Arena back in the Jet days. [The Moose] did a version of it when they were back in the Arena, but when they went to the MTS Centre, they released what at the time was the Toasted Moose Dog, which was a hot dog on a grill; but then they took it to the next level and added a bunch of cool things on it."

Here's where the MTS Centre has gone the extra mile. Whereas in the Winnipeg Arena the famed dog was only available at one spot on the concourse, the Centre has it at multiple locations on both levels, allowing fans to chow down on the monstrous offering. Ultimately, as Paterson explained, it was demand that not only brought about this expanded offering, but retained it on the menu.

"At the end of the day it's dollars and cents. People absolutely loved it. They expanded to a couple other locations. Then when the team went to the NHL, the upstairs was going, it really exploded

"They've done a ton of work in the 300 level, really changing the experience for fans and have moved a couple of those locations; but talk to the people who run the concessions, I'm sure it's consistently one of the top selling items, very popular, and for my money, the top hot dog in the NHL."

It isn't just Paterson who's given the Jumbo Jet Dog top marks. Witness the review of Jordan Falconer of StadiumJourney.com:

"If you are really hungry, try the Jumbo Jet Dog—a MTS Centre feature and fan favourite," Falconer wrote. "The Jumbo Jet Dog is a very large hot dog that will run you $9.25 but will fill you up. It is also available in a combo for $13. In addition to the regular toppings, additional toppings available are what make this a monster. Bacon bits, pierogie pieces, chili or nacho cheese are available for an extra $1.50 each. Try the pierogie pieces and if you are not worried about spilling on your jersey, go for the nacho cheese and chili!"

57 Two Members of the Miracle on Ice Team

The first season for the Jets in the NHL was pretty much nothing to write home about. Save for the important firsts, the Jets were abysmal on the ice, finishing tied for the last spot in the Smythe Division with the Colorado Rockies (only ahead on the technicality of more wins) with a 20–49–11 record and sitting 18 points out of a playoff spot.

If there was anything to make the inaugural season in the league noteworthy, it was the achievement of one player—Dave Christian.

Christian spent less than a quarter of the season with the Jets, in which he played at better than a point-per-game pace (18 points in

15 games), but his absentia can be excused—he was pretty occupied winning a gold medal at the Olympics as part of the famed Miracle on Ice squad.

Christian's path to international glory was somewhat of a birthright—the Warroad, Minnesota, native was the son of Bill Christian and nephew of Roger Christian who, just 20 years prior, were part of the 1960 Olympic Gold Medal–winning U.S. squad while uncle Gordon Christian won a silver on the biggest international stage of them all in 1956. Additionally, Bill and Roger owned Christian Brothers Hockey Company, perhaps best known as being a premier hockey stick manufacturer.

As one might expect, the lineage meant that Dave and his brother, Eddie, grew up playing hockey.

"I don't ever remember ever learning how to skate," Christian told the *Star Tribune* in an interview for their Boys' Hockey Hub website. "I just can't remember. It just seems like that's what I did."

Christian's progression in hockey, which included his father's tutelage as coach in many instances, led him first to play college hockey at the University of North Dakota, a program that most notably produced Jonathan Toews but was also home to Jets alumni Doug Smail, Bobby Joyce, Russ Romaniuk, and Phil Sykes. It was from UND that Christian was plucked for the Miracle on Ice team by Herb Brooks (who was the coach of the rival Minnesota Golden Gophers).

By this time, Christian had already been picked up by the Winnipeg Jets—40th overall in the 1979 Entry Draft. With his NHL career ready to start following the Olympics, forward Christian was placed on D by Coach Brooks, a move that proved to be brilliant as the speedster counted nine assists in the seven-game tournament.

Christian's flash of brilliance on the ice in that remarkable 1979–80 season was followed by a stellar NHL career. As a member of the Jets, Christian quickly evolved into a leader, earning the captaincy of the team for the 1981–82 season, the first year Winnipeg gained entry into the NHL playoffs. During his additional three full seasons of Winnipeg hockey, Christian amassed 71 goals while playing near point-per-game shinny while he helped shape the young hockey team.

Christian's stay with the Jets was all too brief as he was traded to the Washington Capitals before the 1983–84 season and later spent time with the Boston Bruins, St. Louis Blues, and Chicago Blackhawks while also wearing thc red, white, and blue for Team USA in a number of tournaments including three Canada Cups before finishing his career in his home state with the IHL's Minnesota Moose.

After hanging up his skates, Christian was inducted into the U.S. Hockey Hall of Fame alongside his father and uncle. Phil Housley, Ed Olczyk, and Keith Tkachuk are the other Jets alumni who have received this honour.

But Christian wasn't the only Jets alumnus to play in the Miracle on Ice tournament. The other also entered the NHL immediately after the Olympics—Dave Silk. "Silky" was a standout leading up to the Winter Games, tallying 48 points in 56 national team games. At the tournament itself, Silk counted five points in seven games.

Selected 59th overall by the New York Rangers in the 1978 NHL Entry Draft, Silk went to the Rangers' organization after the Miracle on Ice for two games (not earning any points) before heading to the AHL and the New Haven Nighthawks. He spent a couple more seasons on Broadway and with the Nighthawks before spending time with the Boston Bruins' and Detroit Red Wings' organizations.

Finally, Silk came to Winnipeg for the 1985–86 season and found a spot on the big roster for 32 games, in which he counted six points (two goals, four assists). He also spent time with the affiliate Sherbrooke Canadiens.

Silk's playing career came to an end in Germany after playing in 249 NHL games.

58 Fergy's Enclosure at the Winnipeg Arena

When the Jets entered the NHL after the WHA absorption, the team was stripped almost bare of anything recognizable. Only two players were able to be retained from the WHA squad while some personalities behind the scenes shifted, as well.

John Ferguson was the constant retained from the last days of the WHA.

Ferguson was by far one of the toughest general managers in the NHL during the high production years of the 1980s, which probably comes as no surprise to anyone who watched him in his playing days. On their website, the Montreal Canadiens described Ferguson, who was a five-time Stanley Cup champion while he played his entire career with the team, as such: "'Fergy' had but one mission on the ice: to help carry the Canadiens to victory. A lot of men have claimed that they would go through a wall for their team. In John Ferguson's case, it was no exaggeration. Strong, skilled, canny, fearless, and mean, Ferguson neither expected nor gave any quarter."

With this hard-nosed attitude brought forward, Fergy transitioned from on-ice ruffian to off-ice general. This was evident in the Summit Series where, as assistant coach, he encouraged Bobby Clarke to slash Valeri Kharlamov and take him out of the game.

A few years later, Ferguson was the coach and general manager of the New York Rangers and, among other moves, brought Ulf Nilsson and Anders Hedberg to the NHL, just one year before becoming the Winnipeg Jets GM for their final year in the WHA.

Though some execs may fear having to assemble a team with limited resources available to them, Fergy enjoyed the challenge, as he reflected in an interview in 2004.

"Starting the NHL from scratch was really good," he said. "I hired everybody from the stick boy to the office staff to the training staff to the players and the coaches. It was pretty exciting."

Make no mistake about it—through shrewd drafting and a trade record that was pretty damn good, Fergy put together a squad that was good enough to be considered a Stanley Cup contender, and had it not been for the Edmonton Oilers being in the same division, may have escaped to the Campbell Conference finals.

Fergy's true toughness shone through and he is remembered by fans and ex-players as being nails tough. Although those close to him will say he was kind in his own way, it was his fiery temper that is probably what he's best remembered for, and it was that temper that led to one of the most unique constructs in NHL history—a plexiglass shield in front of Fergy's perch in the press box.

For those who haven't toured a media box, the areas are generally open air. Sure, this may be a hazard for fans seated below clumsy writers jostling their drinks, but to get a full feel for the game a media member must be able to get the sound of the action and reaction as easily as a paying ticketholder would. The same open concept applies for private booths such as those for team personnel, namely the general manager, and this was the case for many years at the Winnipeg Arena.

That is, until John Ferguson required an enclosure.

There are three beliefs as to why the protective plexiglass was installed for Fergy. Story number one comes from the GM himself.

"I can remember being up in my pigeon hole in the press box and one night I almost came out the window," Ferguson said in 2004. "My chair was on rollers and I was holding on with my fingertips. Then I decided I should put some glass in so I could see out and they couldn't see me coming in."

Story number two belongs to Winnipeg Jets veteran Scott Campbell.

"I used to get a laugh when a bucket of ice cubes would pour down from the press box where Fergy was sitting after a few blown calls by the referee," the former forward recalls. "I think they eventually put glass in his box."

And finally story number three, courtesy of longtime Winnipeg hockey journalist Scott Taylor.

"It's pretty simple—Fergy was pretty loud—he yelled and screamed and used words you wouldn't want around your children. He didn't like referees or bad plays very much," Taylor explained. "One Friday night game he really lost it, and in the old world of paper everywhere, in the second period it came out of his little booth in the press box. I sat in the next seat closest to his so I'd often look around the corner to see what his responses were on things, so all this paper came out. For the next game on Sunday, there was a Plexiglas tomb encasing Fergy. He just didn't want to be heard and seen anymore, and I don't think the people sitting below him wanted paper dropped on their heads, either. That was the story, and that's what happened."

59 Bryan Little's Hat Trick

From the time that the Jets returned to Winnipeg, there was a giant albatross that hung in the MTS Centre.

Yes, the playoff drought (which ended in 2014–15) was a major burden that players, personnel, and fans alike were carrying and did everything possible to break, but the reality was that the team was the Atlanta Thrashers, a franchise that since its inception in 1999–2000 had only made it to the postseason once (and didn't have a single playoff victory).

No, this monkey on the backs of players was different—since game one, no player had scored a hat trick. More than 70 two-goal games had been amassed by the likes of Evander Kane, Andrew Ladd, and Blake Wheeler, but no one had been able to pull off the trifecta.

All that changed though in 2014–15. The Jets were in the midst of one of the hottest starts to a season that they've had in a long time when they faced the Colorado Avalanche on December 5. One season earlier, the Jets were the new kids in the Western Conference, having finally transferred over from the East, and were greeted by an Avs team that was seemingly on the rise to being an elite team again out of the onetime Campbell Conference, with the emergence of a new group of superstars. The Jets, meanwhile, were seemingly treading water, and going into the new season seemed more destined for the Connor McDavid Draft Lottery than for the playoffs.

Whatever the cause, this was one of the nights that will forever be looked at as a breakout moment for Winnipeg, in large part thanks to one player in particular—Bryan Little.

To this point, Little had already been one of the most dependable players on the team. An original Atlanta Thrasher, Little was drafted 12th overall in the 2006 NHL Entry Draft after an impressive period with the Barrie Colts. After winning the gold medal with Canada at the 2007 World Juniors, Little saw playoff action with the Chicago Wolves of the AHL and then ascended to the Thrashers for the 2007–08 campaign, becoming the franchise's first player to score in his first game with the club.

Fast forward to the Jets and Little was occupying a spot on the top line with Wheeler and Ladd. The trio clicked incredibly well, and through the first three NHL campaigns for the Winnipeg era, Little had two 20 goal seasons under his belt.

Bryan Little is known for recording the first hat trick in the history of the new Jets franchise.

On this faithful night, it was Little who potted the three goals as an anxious Winnipeg crowd, that had started to become a bit quieter in the stands after struggling through non-playoff disappointments and continued frustrations with the on-ice product, erupted with one of the loudest displays in team history. When the hat trick goal came, ball caps poured onto the ice in a display of tribute and full-building celebration.

After the game, the jubilation carried through in the locker room. Little, not surprisingly, earned the Flight Helmet for the game. With reporters surrounding him, Little explained how he was only half aware of everything unfolding.

"Honestly, two and three goals I didn't celebrate because I didn't know they went in," he told the assembled scrum. "The first one, it looked like his glove was crossing the line but I wasn't sure, and the second one I thought it hit the crossbar, so I didn't know until after."

Of course, the humble Edmonton native soon turned talk toward his teammates and who would be the next to turn the trick. "We've had a ton of two-goal games. I didn't know it was going to take this long, but we've got guys that can do it."

And while Little was elated, it's possible there was one person who was happier than he—Jets captain Andrew Ladd, who spoke highly of his linemate.

"It was nice to see a hat trick finally. It was nice to see [Little] get it," Ladd told reporters. "He's a guy that goes quietly about his business and doesn't get the recognition he probably deserves, so it was great to hear the crowd chanting his name and a good night for the whole team."

Funny enough though, it didn't take long for the Jets to get hat trick number two. Just a few weeks later, Mathieu Perreault potted four goals—tying a franchise record—against the Florida Panthers. The game, which took place on January 13, 2015, is as much remembered for Perreault being unable to tally goal number five, which would have landed one lucky Manitoban a $1 million cheque from Safeway.

60 Luke and the 7-Up Commercial

"Typically, we feel really ignored here. In Winnipeg. It's just Winnipeg"
—Anonymous Jets fan, Budweiser "Fan Brew" commercial

The Winnipeg Jets were never truly short on talent, but gaining attention from outlets that would bring the boys into the spotlight was seldom seen. Probably the biggest exposure came, not surprisingly, in the form of Bobby Hull, who, among other endorsments, had a tabletop hockey game named for him.

But getting anyone to sit up and pay attention to the Jets was just what the interviewee in the aforementioned Budweiser commercial said—despite being in the centre of Canada and being one of the heaviest populated cities with national headquarters for several business, Winnipeg has often been overlooked when it comes to the spotlight.

"I always lamented that the Jets always got the short end of the stick by the national media and even locally at times," Curtis Walker said.

So rare it is that the Jets become part of a national campaign, that when any site of the blue, red, and white gives the team an opportunity for its heroes to be nationally showcased, especially with an endorsement deal, you know that fans are going to flock.

That's what made Morris Lukowich's deal with 7-Up such a tout point for the Jets back in the day. In the early days of the Jets, Luke was unquestionably the face of the team. For the first five seasons of NHL hockey, Lukowich was a 30-plus goal scorer four times.

The commercial showed Lukowich in mock NHL action then later with other "Jets" players (the quotes to emphasize that the others in the commercial were scrub actors in Jets unis) celebrating a presumed victory over their opponent. What made the spot more special was that it was a combined focus on three Canadian NHL'ers—one being Michel Larocque, goalie for the Canadiens, and a very young Wayne Gretzky.

Though the Jets weren't a big deal in Canada, some of the players did get some international ad time, namely Teemu Selanne. Scour YouTube hard enough and you can find a commercial that features Selanne sitting in a sports bar, watching Jets highlights with other patrons, drinking milk.

Other ads had more of a local flavor. Several fans will readily recall McDonald's using players such as Shawn Cronin and Evgeny Davydov to promote locally, while Tie Domi became the subject of a Pizza Hut campaign. For the modern Jets team, Evander Kane was a spokesperson for the *Winnipeg Free Press* during the inaugural season, while several players, from Jacob Trouba to Jim Slater, have promoted everything from home builders to car dealerships on local radio.

But when you're talking about advertisements that resonate, there is none that spoke to fans louder than a 2011 Budweiser commercial. Months before the Fan Brew video, or even before the purchase of the Thrashers, a seemingly innocuous shot of a sports bar that had the familiar logo of the 1990s Jets on a wood plaque got people in Winnipeg talking. After all—one would reason—why would the NHL allow the display of a former team's logo in a sponsor ad about Canadian hockey teams? It was the sort of image that got even the most firm non-believers buzzing that Winnipeg was going to soon be an NHL city again.

61 Igor Kuperman

Look up and down the landscape of video games and there is but one title that every hockey fan will tell you that is needed by a truly passionate player—NHL '94.

The second game produced for the Super Nintendo system and Sega Genesis was a landmark title that brought the digital game leaps and bounds ahead of any predecessor. So vaunted is it that its creator, EA Sports, recreated the game as a mini version of its 2014 title to mark its 20th anniversary.

Today, the game is still played on old systems and on simulators, and is done so with little notice to the contribution to the game made by a former Jets front office worker; but if you scroll through the game's credits, you'll come across a very important name in Winnipeg (and Soviet) hockey history—Igor Kuperman.

In the world of NHL '94, it was Kuperman who gave players their rankings in the game; but in the much larger world of international sport, Kuperman was a groundbreaker, equally as important to the movement of Russians migrating to North America as the athletes themselves, and on a Jets team that was embracing players who were once hidden behind the Iron Curtain, Kuperman was not just invaluable, as journalist Harvey Rosen described—he was an all out necessity.

"The arrival in Winnipeg of Evgeny Davydov, a rightwinger, is imminent, and next season, Alexei Zhamnov shouldn't be far behind. Other names of note to remember are those of Jan Kaminsky, Sergei Sorokin, and Sergei Selyanin," Rosen wrote in the February 19, 1992, edition of Winnipeg's *Jewish Post and News*. "It's no accident that he's [Kuperman] here in a hockey organization—farsighted GM Mike Smith was aware of the coming wave, and that he'd need some sort of liaison to ease matters when dealing with the Soviet Ice Hockey Federation."

Back in the U.S.S.R., Kuperman was a hockey journalist himself; but in choosing his career path he did so under iron-fisted rule. In 1991, shortly after his arrival to Winnipeg, Kuperman spoke to Steve Springer of the *Los Angeles Times* about the working conditions of a hockey reporter back home.

"[Leonid] Brezhnev liked hockey," Kuperman told Springer. "So when the [Soviet] teams lost, you could write no bad things about them. You could say it was bad refs," Kuperman said, "or bad ice, or that they [the Soviets] had no luck.

"When they played in North America, the first explanation was the smaller rinks. Then, you could say it was acclimatization or that [the North Americans] were using their refs."

Safe in Canada, Kuperman became valuable to the Jets as more than just as a communications guru with Russian players and agencies. Quickly, he became a consult for Mike Smith and was even brought to the NHL Entry Draft. Ed Willes, a former reporter for the *Winnipeg Sun*, talked with fellow journalist Lucas Aykroyd about an interaction between Kuperman and Smith at the draft table during, wait for it, Smith's peak time of drafting Russian players.

"Igor Kuperman...told me Smith was committed to taking Russians throughout that draft," Willes said, "and in the late going, he flipped his list over to Kuperman and asked if he recognized any of the names. Igor was surprised to see [Nikolai] Khabibulin was still available and told Smith to take him."

Though Kuperman stayed with the organization when the Jets moved to Phoenix, there were bigger things on the horizon. With the fall of communism, Kuperman became heavily involved in Russian hockey Olympic teams and was among the founding fathers of the Kontinental Hockey League. Today, Kuperman is most often associated with Pointstreak, an organization, as their website states, whose mission "is to provide innovative technologies to enhance the experience of the global sports community."

62 Take a Jet to Work

Imagine coming to work one day to see that your shift is going to be taken alongside Blake Wheeler, or walking into your lunch room only to find Michael Hutchinson at the water cooler.

To most hockey fans, that sounds preposterous—but if you're a Winnipeg Jets fan, that's a reality that could happen; and it's all because of Jim Slater.

Slater is best known to Jets fans as a grinding forward, generally found on the third or fourth line. An original draft pick of the Atlanta Thrashers, Slater had been with the franchise longer than any other player, through the 2014–15 season. He had grown a strong fanbase in part because of his play on the ice, but also because of his dedication to Winnipeg as a whole.

Through countless demonstrations, Slater has shown himself to be one of the most generous Jets with his time. He's been a "Mo Bro" for the local Movember movement, donated Jets game tickets to "Cvet's Pets" and made appearances on behalf of other charities. The reason for this generosity, as he explained, comes from his upbringing.

"I've always felt that the fans support us when we play hockey, and it's important to get out in the community and support them, too," Slater said. "I feel it's an obligation for us to help out in any way we can. The way my parents raised me, any time I can lend a helping hand, I'm willing to do that, and a lot of guys in here are, too."

Perhaps the most unique thing Slater has done is to introduce a community to Winnipeg—Take a Jet to Work. Quite literally, the program involves Slater and his teammates going out to Winnipeg organizations and getting in on their workday; and it's not just holding a shovel at a construction site or posing for pictures in an office—Slater and his teammates get down and dirty.

Witness, for example, the Jets using a blowtorch at a car restoration shop or going through a full training route with the police's tactical support team rather than just hitting the gun range. There's no special treatment here—the players are put to work as they're shown the ropes of different places of business in Winnipeg.

The origin of Take a Jet to Work, as Slater explained, dates back to Slater's days with the Thrashers, and it has exploded in his new city. "It started back in Atlanta with just a couple of things, but this has really taken off here in Winnipeg," Slater said. "People here really love their hockey, and any time you get the chance to be out there, be a part of it and meet them on a personal level, it's great. It's been a great thing for myself, the Jets organization, the fans, and this community. It's fun for me, and I know it's fun for them, too. I'm proud to be a part of it."

As one may expect from someone as humble as Slater, who does all this work with little wanted in return, he won't identify one job as being his favourite thus far. "They're all good in their own ways. There hasn't been a bad one," he said. "It's good because a lot of guys want to come to them. I try to take one, two, or three guys with me every time now."

63 #Helmetpardy

It was the incident that became a meme and almost gave birth to a new tradition in Winnipeg hockey lore.

And like so many sporting moments that involve fans and players, it started with alcohol over-indulgence.

The infamous incident took place on Wednesday, November 6, 2013. The game was a seemingly innocent contest between the Jets and powerhouse Chicago Blackhawks. The Hawks were en route to a 4–1 victory when, with 6:00 left in the contest, Chi-town forward Brandon Bollig ran Winnipeg's Adam Pardy so hard along the boards that one of the panes of plexiglass gave way.

As Pardy tried to recover and hold the pane back from striking fans (he is, of course, a Winnipeg player), a fan reached forward and dislodged his helmet. The same individual then put it over his own head.

At the same time, beer was poured on Pardy and his stick was taken, as well. "It got over the side of my face, down to my jersey," Pardy told a scrum following the game as reported by the *National Post*. "I don't know if you can still smell it in my clothes, but the bench was definitely smelling a little booze there for the last six minutes."

The incident quickly turned into an apology by the Blackhawks while the helmet grabber made a sizeable donation to True North's charitable foundation.

But the incident didn't just stop there. Nay, there began a movement by local DJ Dave Wheeler for there to be a "Helmet Pardy" the next time the Blackhawks visited the MTS Centre—November 21.

"Nov. 21 at MTS Centre vs. #Blackhawks is officially #HelmetNight. Show the Hawks fans that we don't need to steal helmets, we have our own!" Wheeler said in a Tweet as part of the declaration.

Soon, the campaign picked up steam on Twitter, aided no doubt by an exchange involving leading hockey personality James Duthie.

On November 20, Duthie posted the following:

"@ChrisLeeWpg: @tsnjamesduthie Inform the hockey world, Winnipeg is preparing for a #HelmetPardy I endorse this."

Other media started weighing in with their support, including local CBC radio and Troy Westwood of TSN 1290. All seemed to be set for a new tradition to be ignited in Winnipeg. To this point, fans had their rallies against other teams in the form of mid-game taunts rather than a pre-collaborative effort.

All the "planning" though was for naught, however, when a proclamation came from True Executive chairman Mark Chipman.

"Earlier this week, we learned of a media-promoted stunt to have Winnipeg Jets fans wear helmets to the game on Thursday, November 21 versus the Chicago Blackhawks," Chipman said in a November 20 statement on the Winnipeg Jets website. "I would like to let our fans know we in no way endorse this idea and in fact and wish to personally advise that we will not permit fans to wear such headgear at tomorrow's game.

"I sincerely believe we have the best fans in the entire National Hockey League. Their passion for the game is unequaled. However, this is about professionalism and respect for our great game and for the NHL. These are principles we attempt to follow in all aspects of how we play and present the game of hockey."

And with this announcement, #helmetpardy was put on the shelf, but not without its share of detraction from hockey media.

"It's a shame so many people are allergic to a good-natured joke nowadays," Matt Larkin of *The Hockey News* penned. "I suppose the Jets are worried fans will toss helmets onto the ice, but couldn't you say that about any hard object? Will they ban shoes and car keys next? Stay tuned."

The momentum of the helmet has passed, but that doesn't mean that the Jets and Blackhawks have simmered. The proximity of the two hardcore hockey centres and frequency of playing one another will factor into a rivalry that will emerge, something that was anticipated eagerly by one Winnipegger on the Blackhawks squad.

"It would be great to have a rivalry with the Jets," Jonathan Toews said in 2011, before the start of the first season for the new Jets team. "To keep coming back here and have a little competition with some of the guys here would be awesome."

64 Alexei Zhamnov

Hockey fans across North America and Europe are very familiar with "The Forsberg," a unique deke where a player will seemingly keep a puck tied to their stick on a string as they shift it back and forth, eventually putting it past a helpless goaltender with just one hand on their weapon. It's humiliating for the netminder and eye-popping for fans to witness.

But let's make one thing clear—the name of the move is not "The Forsberg." In reality, it has to be called "The Zhamnov," since it was the red-haired Russian who did it long before Foppa made his presence known in the NHL.

Zhamnov was among the last true superstars to emerge from the ranks of the Jets before the team moved to Phoenix, and was one of the players who didn't make the trip to the desert. He was traded to the Chicago Blackhawks during the summer of 1996 in exchange for Jeremy Roenick.

Through four seasons with the Jets, Zhamnov maintained better than a point-per-game pace that started with his rookie campaign. The same season that Teemu Selanne was breaking NHL records, Zhamnov was putting on a show of his own following contract arbitration squabbles. In 68 games that season, Zhamnov scored 25 goals and totalled 72 points. He followed up the performance with 26 goals and 71 points a year later despite only playing in 61 games.

But it was the lockout-shortened 1994–95 season that was Zhamnov's greatest. With just 48 games to play, Zhamnov still hit the net a career-high 30 times and counted 65 points, good enough for third in the NHL in scoring. The highlight of the season came toward the end of the short campaign. With the Jets on the road in

Los Angeles on April 1, 1995, Zhamnov put on an amazing performance, tallying five times on the tandem of standout Kelly Hrudey and future Hall of Famer Grant Fuhr.

And appropriately, the last goal unfolded with "The Zhamnov."

After blueliner Stephane Quintal caused a turnover, linemate and countryman Igor Korolev chipped the puck forward to a streaking Zhamnov, who broke in alone on Fuhr. Some fancy handywork later, the puck was in the back of the net and Zhamnov had tied a franchise record with his fifth marker of the game, sealing off one of the most impressive single efforts in Winnipeg hockey history. (As a sidenote, however, the Jets as a team weren't as impressive and ended up with a 7–7 tie).

For his efforts, Zhamnov was named to the NHL's postseason All-Star Team for the only time in his career. He was also named as a finalist for the Lady Byng Trophy, as he collected a mere 20 penalty minutes.

The following season, however, Zhamnov's stellar play was somewhat stilted. Thanks to injury, he only played in 58 games (though he managed 59 points). Unfortunately, the Detroit Red Wings were able to keep Zhamnov at bay through the playoffs as he registered just three points in six games.

By the time his career was done midway through the 2005–06 season, Zhamnov had four additional seasons of 60-point hockey under his belt. Though he didn't win the Stanley Cup, he did win three Olympic medals, including a gold in 1992, a silver in 1998, and a bronze in 2002.

Today, Zhamnov is dedicated to Russian hockey, acting as general manager of Vityaz Chekhov through the 2014–15 season, the same organization he played for during the 2004–05 NHL lockout; and in the storied history of a franchise that once practically bled the red of the Soviets, he is inarguably the greatest Russian import in Winnipeg hockey history.

65 Shop at Joe Daley's Sports and Framing

There are few Jets who have remained as loyal to the Winnipeg hockey scene as Joe Daley.

The subject of just about every interview about Jets hockey past, Daley was the netminder for all seven seasons in the WHA, garnering three Avco Cup rings and individual honours in the process. The Manitoba native came to the Jets after a run in the NHL that included stints with the Pittsburgh Penguins, Buffalo Sabres, and Detroit Red Wings.

The lure of being able to continue his professional career in front of friends and family was simply too much, and Joe rolled the dice coming to play in the WHA, becoming one of the most recognized faces of the team in short order (something accomplishable in part because he was one of the last netminders to stay maskless).

But as popular as Daley is with Winnipeg and hockey media, he's just as popular with fans, partly because of how accessible he's made himself to Winnipeg hockey faithful; and it's not just through his multiple charitable appearances—it's as simple as walking into his sports memorabilia shop.

For decades, Daley, along with son Travis, has been a fixture in the Winnipeg hobby world, and walking into his shop is a must for anyone who wants to pick up a souvenir or marvel at some of the memorabilia Daley has inside. From game-used jerseys to autographed photos, Daley has it all, along with a bevy of artefacts from his playing career.

The shop, as Daley explained, came about after he and his family moved back to Winnipeg. After his playing days were done, the family moved out to B.C., but after four years they returned to Winnipeg and immediately sought a business venture.

"Once we got here, my son, Travis, was sitting around with me on a weekend and said, 'Dad, why don't we find a little business we can grow with?' So we scoured the newspaper ads for things for sale and came upon a little shop that was up for sale," Daley recalled. "We bought it and thereafter moved to St. James Street and were there for 24 years."

The vast majority of that period had a lot of foot traffic from hockey or football fans before they ventured over to the Winnipeg Arena or Winnipeg Stadium for an evening of sports entertainment, but following the departure of professional sports to downtown Winnipeg (MTS Centre) and the University of Manitoba (Investors Group Field), the Daleys decided to move themselves, and relocated to the St. Vital area of Winnipeg.

Now here's the interesting dynamic of the shop—many athletes will go into business, putting their name on a shop or restaurant for the pure marketing purpose; very few, however, spend a significant amount of time in the venue. Sure, maybe they'll pop in once a week (as Michael Jordan was rumoured to do for his Chicago-based restaurant), but will they spend a significant amount of time there? Not so much.

That's not the case with Joe. It's rare to walk into the store and not see Joe behind the counter, ready to not only serve you with a smile, but also talk shinny.

"Having Joe in the store enriches the experience by having an in-person link to the pro hockey game itself. He can discuss the sport itself as honestly and candidly as the hobby store industry," collector Robert Brown said. "Joe's focus, of course, is on the current events and the day to day of Jets 2.0, but when you pose a question or relive a thought about Jets 1.0, he will without hesitation segue into those 'glory days,' and you will learn things only someone who was there can speak about."

It was that relationship that keeps customers like Brown coming back. While the pull of being able to talk with a former

NHL and WHA star would certainly bring a crowd in for initial look, it's Daley's ability to keep the conversations going that makes the experience a repeat endeavour for so many fans. It's that same personal relationship that, perhaps surprisingly, keeps collectors like Brown from hounding Daley for his signature (though he's more than willing to sign anything and everything for his fan).

"Joe and Travis are people I consider honest to goodness friends as well as someone I happen to do business with," Brown said. "One day I would like to get a picture of Joe and I and have him sign it 'To Robert,' and get it mounted with a bunch of Joe Daley cards and get the mounting done by Travis. I enjoy each minute I spend with the Daley as much as you would enjoy time spent with friends. I've never thought to ask for a friend's auto, so it never really crosses my mind to ask Joe."

66 Captains Roll Call

The colourful history of the Winnipeg Jets has a number of different captains in its midst, and often their runs as leader didn't last long.

In fact, very few captains wore the "C" for more than two years. Not surprisingly, it's Dale Hawerchuk who owns the record at five seasons as captain, six if you count the year he shared the honour with Thomas Steen and Randy Carlyle. It's a record that, by the time this book hits the shelves, could be equalled by Andrew Ladd. At press time, Ladd completed his fourth year as leader of the new team.

The leaders of the Jets are as follows:

Ab McDonald, 1972–74

One of the first hires of the Jets, Ab came home to Winnipeg after spending a long NHL career with Montreal, Chicago, Boston, Detroit, Pittsburgh, and St. Louis. Gaining the "C" in Pittsburgh as its first captain, Ab brought a ton of leadership to Winnipeg and instantly became the head of its club, knowing that his time in the WHA was going to be limited as he was in the twilight of his career. Under McDonald, the Jets made it all the way to the Avco Cup Finals in their inaugural season.

Dan Johnson, 1974–75

Johnson's leadership of the Jets came hot on the heels of McDonald's retirement. It was the third and final season Johnson played for the Jets. Originally a signee of the Toronto Maple Leafs, Johnson is better known in NHL circles as being an original member of the Vancouver Canucks. He also played in Detroit before moving to the WHA. The Winnipegosis native tallied 111 points in his 232 games played for the Jets.

Lars-Erik Sjoberg, 1975–78, 1979–80

Sjoberg inherited the "C" from Johnson after just one year with the Jets. A true superstar from Europe, Sjoberg was a past Player of the Year Award recipient in Sweden and represented the nation in the Olympics and other tournaments. An expert on the blueline, Sjoberg had all the qualifications to be a great leader from his rich experience with Leksands and Vastra Frolunda, Sjoberg led the Jets to three Avco Championships and was given perhaps the greatest honour of his pro hockey career, as he was named the Jets first captain in the NHL, becoming the first European player to wear the "C" in the league.

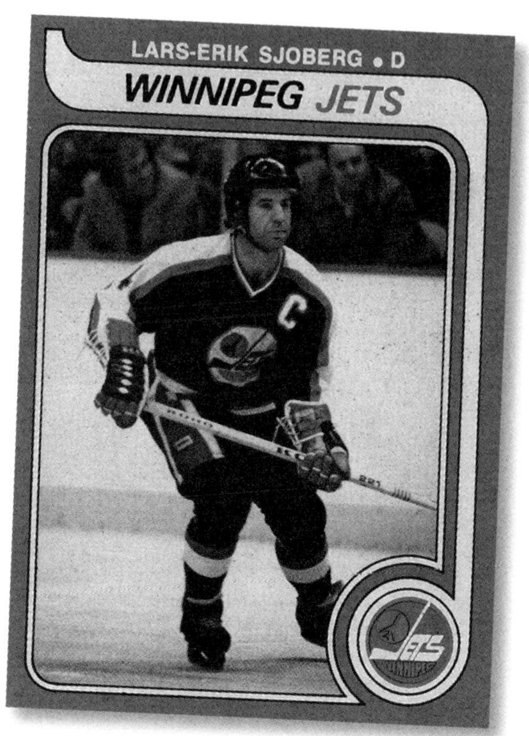

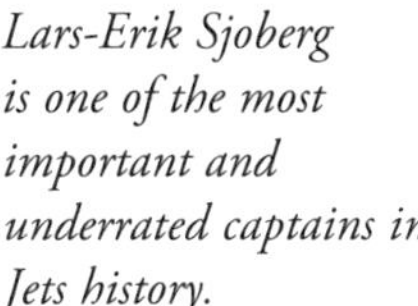
Lars-Erik Sjoberg is one of the most important and underrated captains in Jets history.

Barry Long, 1978–79

Due to injury, it wasn't Sjoberg who was the Jets' captain for the final year of the WHA. Instead, it was a future Jets coach who took the reins for that last campaign. A couple years prior, Long had been acquired from Edmonton after being named to the 1974 WHA Summit team and maintaining a near point-per-two-game pace with the Oilers. Once in Winnipeg, Long showed he was invaluable to the Jets and truly stepped up in that final season, putting up 41 points in 80 games on the blue line. Although Long was reacquired by Detroit at the WHA absorption time, he was later reacquired by Winnipeg and retired as a member of the Jets during the 1981–82 season.

Morris Lukowich, 1980–81

"Luke" was the Jets' first standout superstar when the club entered the NHL, and after Sjoberg's retirement became the club's captain for a tumultuous season, even though the year was fantastic for Lukowich individually, as he tallied 67 points in 80 games. Lukowich quickly became one of the faces of western Canadian hockey and for the second straight season represented Winnipeg in the NHL All-Star Game.

Dave Christian, 1981–82

As the Jets continued to rotate their captain, the next-in-line player was Dave Christian, who assumed the leadership role after being the Jets' leading scorer in 1980–81. Christian helped bring along Dale Hawerchuk with the club, and under his leadership the Jets made their first NHL postseason. Unfortunately, the 1981–82 campaign proved to be Christian's last full season in Winnipeg, as he missed time with a shoulder injury and was traded to Washington midway through the following campaign.

Lucien DeBlois, 1982–84

DeBlois was the latest Jet in rotation to take the captaincy and became the first player in the team's brief NHL history to be the anointed leader for more than one season. DeBlois was fairly well travelled when he came to Winnipeg, having already played for the Rangers and Rockies. DeBlois was hardly a "transitional" captain, though it's easy to perceive that with Hawerchuk coming hot on his tail. During his two seasons with the "C," the Jets made the playoffs twice while DeBlois put together 27- and 34-goal campaigns.

Dale Hawerchuk, 1984–90

Hawerchuk's individual accomplishments are talked about elsewhere in this book, but for this purpose the most important fact is that under his leadership, the Jets reached the height of their

Burton Cummings

For the 1991–92 NHL season, the 75th anniversary of the league, all member teams chose a celebrity captain. For the Jets, the choice was natural—Burton Cummings.

Best known for being part of The Guess Who, Cummings was a rock legend whose hits included "American Woman" and "These Eyes," but on top of being born in Winnipeg, Cummings has remained part of the community. Throughout his time living in the River City, Cummings would be called upon to sing the national anthems at Jets games.

Cummings remains part of Winnipeg, as a part-owner of local restaurant chain Salisbury House and continues to tour.

regular season and playoff success. The Jets never had a better leader-by-example, and Hawerchuk did all he could to keep his team motivated, even amid an ever-changing lineup.

Thomas Steen, 1989–1991

Steen, along with Randy Carlyle, had two seasons of shared captaincy, but there may have been no player who was more emblematic of being the heart and soul of Winnipeg. Playing his entire career with the Jets, Steen was one of the faces of the franchise as he became an unquestioned leader. His experience was especially valuable to the club as it transitioned from the Hawerchuk era to the new world. Steen's career included nine consecutive seasons with at least 50 points.

Randy Carlyle, 1989–91

While Steen led up front, the chief of the blueline was Carlyle. One of the last players to go helmetless in the NHL, Carlyle was a fixture on the Jets blueline after coming over from Pittsburgh, where he was also a captain. Carlyle's leadership and longevity led to him staying in Winnipeg until his retirement following the 1992–93 season. Carlyle's leadership was retained, as he became a coach with the Jets following retirement.

Troy Murray, 1991–93

Coming from Chicago, Murray was immediately handed the Jets' captaincy upon his arrival in Winnipeg. The former Selke Trophy winner was valuable to the Jets during a tumultuous year of change in 1991–92. Unfortunately, Murray himself became expendable in 1992–93 as a new generation of Jets leadership began to emerge, and he was sent back to Chicago, but not before leading the Jets to the 1992 postseason.

Dean Kennedy, 1993

Kennedy's tenure with the "C" was short lived. He only served for a portion of the 1992–93 season as a go-between after Murray was traded away. Kennedy himself had only come to the Jets in 1991 amid a second trade in as many years between Winnipeg and the Buffalo Sabres. Kennedy was part of the grooming process for future leader Keith Tkachuk but did an admirable job in helping the Jets maintain a record that led to them making the playoffs that year.

Keith Tkachuk, 1993–95

Love him or hate him, no one can deny that Tkachuk was the leader the Jets needed during seasons where their future was in doubt. He was calm, cool, and able to do amazing things on the ice as the role of the power forward gained more prominence during the early '90s. Tkachuk's play on the ice led to him being one of the Jets' superstars in the team's waning years, and, after putting together a 50-goal campaign in the team's final season in Winnipeg, he was named the first captain of the Phoenix Coyotes.

Kris King, 1995–96

With controversy surrounding Tkachuk after signing a pricey contract, the decision was made to pull the "C" off his jersey and hand it to Kris King. There was no one better for the Jets to have at the helm for their last season, as King was a natural-born leader both on and off the ice. More known for his hands being balled up in fists than being used for a scoring touch, King was a gritty forward who defended the team's superstars at every point needed. At the end of the season, King was recognized for his leadership in the team's community activities with the King Clancy Award.

67 The Kris Draper Trade

In 1989, the Winnipeg Jets were a team in transition. The old guard was starting to disappear while a new breed of future superstars was being drafted.

Already that day, the Jets had picked Stu Barnes fourth overall. Barnes went on to play in Winnipeg for parts of three seasons before becoming a passed-around proven leader, putting an exclamation point on his career as captain of the Buffalo Sabres.

The next two picks for the Jets—Dan Ratushny and Jason Cirone—proved to be busts. Second-round selection Ratushny played one game in the NHL for the Vancouver Canucks, instead gaining a measure of international glory as part of the 1992 Canadian Olympic squad. Cirone, taken early in the third round, did manage to play for the Jets—all of three games, tallying two penalty minutes.

The fourth pick became a boom for an NHL hockey club—a Selke Trophy winner and an integral part of four Stanley Cup championship teams. That player was Kris Draper.

At the time of selection, Draper was a member of the Canadian National team in the same era as Ratushny. His best days on Canada's squad were still to come as he'd claim two World Junior

Championship gold medals (1990 and 1991), a Senior Men's Championship, a World Cup of Hockey championship, and even be part of an Olympic team.

But in 1989, Draper was a fresh-faced player who Winnipeg was unsure of. In his first year at the pro level, Draper split time in Moncton and Winnipeg, tallying his first NHL goal in a three-game audition with the big club; but the majority of his time was spent with the Ottawa 67's of the OHL. Over the course of the next two years, Draper added two more goals to his Jets numbers and four penalty minutes. Unspectacular output to be certain, but surely the young prospect had a potential suitor?

In turns out he did.

When Draper asked Jets management to be traded, it didn't take long for the Detroit Red Wings to come calling. In exchange, the Jets got a term that many clubs use as a throwaway to this day—future considerations.

"A lot of these future considerations are nothing," longtime Detroit Red Wings executive Jimmy Devellano told ESPN's Tom Wheatley in 2003. "It's just somebody taking a salary, and you hope nobody ever asks you what you got back. You're unloading a contract, and you don't want to look like an idiot."

A salary you say? Pray tell, what salary would that be?

"We ended up giving them a buck," Devellano said.

Yup.

At the height of his power, Mike Smith sold off one of the biggest names to come through Winnipeg, literally, for an almighty dollar.

Draper, as already stated, went on to have a standout NHL career. Shortly after being dealt to Detroit, the Toronto native was assigned to the Adirondack Red Wings. Devellano recalled that this was the main purpose of the pick-up.

"Doug MacLean actually did that deal," Devellano told ESPN. "He was our assistant general manager at the time, and he was running our farm team at Adirondack. Doug knew Draper was a good minor-leaguer."

That in the AHL period only lasted 46 games. Draper then spent the rest of that season—and 16 others, in the locker room of the Joe Louis Arena. Though never a prolific scorer (the height of his output came in 2003–04 with 24 tallies), Draper became a true locker room leader and became just the fifth member of the Red Wings organization to play 1,000 games in the white and red. After retirement, Draper joined the Red Wings' front office staff as special assistant to the general manager.

It's fair to say that Draper exceeded all expectations that he faced in the 1989 NHL Entry draft; unfortunately, a true comparison of the trade cannot be broken down.

You see, no one knows what happened to that dollar. It could have just as easily ended up in a vending machine as it could have been laid down at a table at one of Winnipeg's casinos and ended up making Mike Smith a pile of cash.

Oh, and the rest of that 1989 draft class for the Jets? Picks included future Stanley Cup–winning coach Dan Bylsma and short-term sizzle player Evgeny Davydov.

68 Captain Tkrunch

There are polarizing personalities in any sport, in any league, and on any team. The players you love because of their talent and hate for one reason or another. For Winnipeg, that player was Keith Tkachuk.

Things didn't start off on the wrong foot with Tkachuk. Borne to the Jets out of a draft pick in the Dale Hawerchuk trade,

Tkachuk was well established as a strong prospect when he debuted late in the 1991–92 NHL season. Already, the young power forward had played in two World Junior Hockey Championships, at the Olympics with Team USA, and he also had an NCAA Finals appearance under his belt with Boston College. In a 17-game audition, Tkachuk tallied three goals and eight points.

One season later and still considered a rookie by NHL standards, Tkachuk counted 28 goals and 51 points, a phenomenal output; but his contributions were more than just on the scoresheet. Midway through this campaign, Tkachuk was given the "A" as assistant captain on his jersey. One season later, Tkachuk was instituted as the team's full captain, taking over for Dean Kennedy. The responsibility was one that Tkachuk embraced.

"I put a lot of pressure on myself, especially being captain," Tkachuk told Rich Nairn in the Jets "Action" program on April 5, 1995. "It really helped my confidence level putting the 'C' on my sweater; it picked up my game a lot, and I'm very happy wearing it. It shows a lot of confidence in me by management and the coaches by giving it to me at such a young age."

Indeed, Tkachuk did up the ante in his game. In 1993–94, Tkachuk tallied 41 times and one season later—the lockout-shortened 1994–95 campaign—he was over a point-per-game. That season, though, was the last on Tkachuk's contract, and boy did he take the time to make the new one worth his while.

Despite the Jets being declared on their way out of Winnipeg, Tkachuk put an absolute dagger in the heart of Winnipeg when he signed an offer sheet with the Chicago Blackhawks. Randy Sportak of the *Calgary Sun* later summed up the agreement.

"Tkachuk signed a front-loaded $17.2 million deal that gave him $6 million in the first year and roughly $3 million per season over the rest of the deal," Sportak wrote. "The Jets were on the verge of leaving for Phoenix and the Blackhawks were trying to take advantage of the club's weakness. Winnipeg matched the deal, but the organization had to put up with Tkachuk whining he was underpaid a few years later."

The offer from the Hawks was legitimate, and apparently was not a bargaining ploy by Tkachuk.

"We've been trying for a long time to acquire him and make our team better. We were frustrated, and found no other way to do it." Chicago GM Bob Pulford told the *Chicago Tribune*. "Obviously, he felt there was a good chance they wouldn't match it or he wouldn't have signed it."

Matching the offer for the good of the franchise was one thing; but Tkachuk quickly felt the slings and arrows of the Jets' faithful. During the first home game of the 1995–96 season, Tkachuk was thoroughly booed by fans in attendance during game introductions. With the controversy surrounding him, Tkachuk was stripped of his captaincy for all but the final game of the Winnipeg Jets' remaining season.

Give Tkachuk credit, though—he did everything he could to show that he was worth the exorbitant dollars as he reached the 50-goal mark for the first time in his career, which came in Winnipeg's the final regular season game. Tkachuk also hit what would end up being his career high in points with 98.

Tkachuk remained with the franchise in Phoenix for several years as its captain before being traded to St. Louis during the 2000–01 season. He later was sent to the Atlanta Thrashers by the Blues before coming back to St. Louis and closing out his career in 2009–10. Though he did not earn a Stanley Cup ring, Tkachuk did join the 500-goal and 1,000-point clubs before calling it quits.

69 See Bob Essensa's Mask in the Hockey Hall of Fame

As I discussed elsewhere, three Jets (so far) have gained entry into the Hockey Hall of Fame as Honoured Members; and while the old adage of "He'll only gain entry by buying a ticket" applies to some members of the team, other players are borderline.

Take for example Phil Housley and Keith Tkachuk. Both achieved milestone numbers during their playing days that would weigh in their favour, to go along with All-Star Game appearances and international hardware.

Other Jets had standout careers, no question, but won't gain entry into hockey's hallowed hall. Take, for example, Anders Hedberg and Ulf Nilsson—two WHA greats who had limited NHL success (where the Hall looks most, let's face facts).

Another player who enjoyed some success in his career, especially in Winnipeg, was Bob Essensa, or as Curt Keilback proclaimed on a nightly basis, "Esssssennnsaaaa." Truly, if there was a better name for Keilback's legendary calls, you'd have a hard time finding it.

Essensa was one of those long-range early goalies who didn't emerge in the NHL until years after he was originally picked. The Jets first selected the Toronto native in the third round of the 1983 NHL Entry Draft, and he didn't start a game in the NHL until 1988 following four years at Michigan State and one season in Moncton, the Jets' AHL affiliate. That first partial season was solid but not spectacular—he tallied a 6–8–3 record with a 3.70 GAA and a save percentage just under .900.

One season later, Essensa stood as one of the top netminding prospects in the NHL and proved that he was more than just hype by going 18–9–5 in 36 games. He was also the driving force behind the Jets' run to a seven-game series against the Edmonton Oilers in the 1990 playoffs. For all his work, Essensa was named to the NHL's All Rookie Team.

Even in those early days, Essensa wore what ended up being his trademark mask with the Jets. The lid was simple in design—white planes soaring through streams of blue red and white—but it just looked beautiful. Stacking it up against other designs that resonate with fans—Ed Staniowski's striped face shield or Nikolai Khabibulin's "fire-breathing wolf" classic—you'd have to give the nod to Essensa for the best designed mask in Jets 1.0 history.

So attractive was the design, in fact, that in the early '90s, one of the masks made its way into a display of top goalie masks that was featured at the Hockey Hall of Fame, sitting perched alongside other classics. Though the Hall regularly rotates its displays, Essensa's mask remains part of the archives of hockey's hallowed hall, and undoubtedly it will see the light of day once again.

Following that rookie season, Essensa counted three more full seasons in Winnipeg, including the 1992–93 campaign where he won a career high 33 games. In 1993–94, with the Jets having difficulties racking up W's, Essensa was traded to the Detroit Red Wings alongside Sergei Bautin for Tim Chevaldae and Dallas Drake.

Essensa went on to play for the Edmonton Oilers, Phoenix Coyotes, Vancouver Canucks, and Buffalo Sabres before retiring in 2002. One year later, Essensa was hired by the Boston Bruins as their goaltending coach, helping the team win the Stanley Cup in 2011.

When asked about how he wishes to be remembered in Winnipeg, the classy Essensa answered not that his performance on the ice was most important, but instead his dedication to the city.

"I hope people think of me as a decent goalie who was a good community guy. My wife and I tried to stay involved in the community while we were here. She was involved in the wives carnival over our time here. We tried to be as good to the community here as they were to us."

70 WHA vs. NHL

Comparing the Jets of the NHL to the team that practically owned the WHA would be criminal. Until the 2.0 team can become a dynasty that reels off three championships and an additional two finals appearances in the space of seven years (which we all hope will happen), the comparison can't justly be made.

What can be compared, however, is how the Jets would have performed in the NHL in a perfect scenario where they would not have lost any of their players and had the two leagues actually merged rather than the WHA being absorbed.

And what would the results have been? Curtis Walker has a rough idea. "I do, however, believe the Jets, particularly the 1975–76, 1976–77, and 1977–78 editions, were as good or better than most NHL teams," he said. "Depth and the lack of a farm system would have hurt the WHA teams over the course of the season. When the Jets ran into a rash of injuries in 1976–77, they had to call up two amateur players, whereas an NHL team would have been able to draw on professionals."

It's a similar theme to what we've heard before from ardent Jets fans who believe that their club was truly the best in North America, if not the world; but there is a little bit of history on Winnipeg's side to support the claim, coming in the form of exhibition games that were played between the WHA and NHL. The games, as Walker explained, were the result of a legal battle. "These games came about as a result of the settlement of the antitrust lawsuit launched by the WHA against the NHL," he said. "There was even a provision that mentioned the possibility of regular-season games between the two leagues."

After the first two seasons of WHA play, the teams began facing each other in the exhibition season, and the Jets were one of the two most-involved teams from the WHA in these games. The first came in 1974 when the Jets faced the Atlanta Flames, and unfortunately came up on the losing end of the contest, perhaps not surprising given the preparedness of the two participating teams. "The Jets had just begun camp and didn't have Bobby Hull available, whereas the Flames had been in camp for three weeks," Walker recounted.

The Jets' fortunes turned quickly, however, against their NHL counterparts. Though no games were played in 1975, the rivalry was reignited in 1976, and the Jets took part in two contests. First, they defeated the Pittsburgh Penguins 5–3 and later upended the St. Louis Blues 6–2. In 1977, the exhibition schedule grew exponentially, and the Jets turned in more dominating efforts over their NHL opponents, winning four of five games, including splitting two games with the Minnesota North Stars, sweeping a two-game set with the St. Louis Blues, and defeating the Detroit Red Wings.

As the WHA crumbled, however, and embarked on its final season, the tides turned in favour of NHL clubs. With some of their top players now gone to the NHL, the Jets turned in a 1–3–2 in the final year of the inter-league contests, defeating the North Stars, losing to the New York Rangers twice and Colorado Rockies once, and tying the Blues and North Stars. Similar numbers awaited the Jets when they arrived in the NHL the next year.

The true shame of these exhibition games was that the champions of both leagues didn't meet. The Montreal Canadiens, perpetual Stanley Cup holders during the 1970s, never participated in an NHL vs. WHA game, let alone had it been the Habs vs. the Jets. Walker added a bit of speculation to a question that will remain unanswered. "If the champions of the two leagues would have met in a best-of-seven series after the season," he said, "I think the Jets could have even given the Montreal Canadiens all they could handle."

71 Rub the Foot of Timothy Eaton's Statue

If there's any advantage that the MTS Centre has over the Winnipeg Arena, it's that the location in the middle of downtown Winnipeg means that the skywalk lets you walk from almost anywhere in the area from building to building without having to go outdoors. In the dead of winter, where temperatures with windchill can get down to -40 degrees Celsius, the less time you spend outside the better off you'll be.

Leading into any hockey arena, this is a huge luxury, one that no Winnipegger takes for granted (nor any visitor, for that matter); but the true treasure that comes with the skywalk is that your entry to the MTS Centre brings you on a walk through Winnipeg history. Along the way you see photos from the *Winnipeg Free Press* and other media, and quite possibly the most important artefact you'll ever see—the statue of Timothy Eaton.

Timothy Eaton was, of course, the man behind Eaton's, which has its own tie to hockey history. For most Canadians of a particular vintage who grew up reading *The Hockey Sweater* by Roch Carrier, it is "Monsieur Eaton" whose catalogue the protagonist's mother ordered the dreaded Toronto Maple Leafs jersey from instead of Maurice Richard's Montreal Canadiens sweater.

But Winnipeg's connection—and the reason why Eaton's statue stands in the MTS Centre—runs deeper than a mere hockey fable; the city was one of the biggest hubs for Eaton's during its decades-long stand as one of the top retailers in Canada.

As detailed in a "Winnipeg Downtown Places" blog entry, the story of Winnipeg's statue—one of two in existence, goes like this:

"Timothy's son and company president Sir John C. Eaton came from Toronto for the unveiling. The Winnipeg store was known as "J.C.'s Baby" as it was Sir John who was instrumental in having the store and mail order catalogue house built in Winnipeg. He even personally selected the site.

The ceremony was attended by 'thousands of employees' and began on the main floor at 8:00 AM, a half-hour before store opening. After the singing of O Canada, H. McGee, an Eaton's vice-president and its oldest-serving employee, made the presentation.

Eaton was in attendance but suffering from a severe cold or flu. His response read on his behalf:

"To me it is most gratifying....that the deeds of my father still live and will be perpetuated for all time by the erection of this magnificent memorial."

Now somewhere along the line, though unspecified as to when, rubbing the left foot of Timothy Eaton's statue became good luck, similar to rubbing the famed "Lucky Loonie" housed at the Hockey Hall of Fame. Today, there is a noticeable sheen on the outstretched foot of Monsieur Eaton as Winnipeggers gave it a continual buff job. It's still considered a good omen for anyone who passes by, just as it has for decades; but for a short time it looked as though Winnipeg was going to lose its beloved statue.

In 1999, after Eaton's closed, Sears brought the statue to Polo Park (coincidentally close to the Winnipeg Arena), and after an attempt by the once-competitor to resurrect the Eaton's brand fell flat, the Eaton family elected to move the statue to St. Mary's, Ontario, home of one of the first Eaton's stores. However, injunctions from the province that made the statue a heritage piece kept the statue in Winnipeg with a proviso from the family that it not be kept in storage and instead have a place of prominence in the city.

Not surprisingly, the most logical place became the MTS Centre, which now occupies the space of the famed downtown Eaton's location. The statue sits one floor up from its original location, greeting fans as they enter the new premier hockey rink in the city, and bringing good luck to those who touch it.

72 Join the Voices of the MTS Centre

"Crosby's Better!"

—Winnipeg Jets fans

If there is any rivalry that has captured the attention of the NHL landscape over the last 10 years, it's Alexander Ovechkin vs. Sidney Crosby. Before they were two of the best rookies the NHL had seen in years, Crosby and Ovechkin were on opposite sides of epic World Junior battles between Canada and Russia; but once the two first overall picks met on NHL ice, the league and media had a field day, proclaiming a new rivalry in hockey the likes of which had never been seen. We now had our Magic Johnson vs. Larry Bird.

Which only made opportunity for ridicule that much better.

Amid a 3–2 third period lead over the Washington Capitals on March 16, 2012, Winnipeg's packed house began one of the most unique chants ever heard in the NHL—"Crosby's Better!"

It was one of those surreal moments. Here was the opportunity where most crowds would chant "Go—insert home team name—Go!" or utilize the drawn out goalie taunt (think Homer Simpson chanting "Flaaaanderrrrrs"); but not Jets fans. They're smarter than that. Goalies are immune to this sort of thing since they hear it game after game.

Nah—instead you go for the biggest dog in the fight.

Over the course of the season, the Jets' faithful had turned a new trick, booing the star player on the opposing team. Often this was the highest scorer or the most famed defenceman.

But things escalated on this night. The chant of "Crosby's Better!" was different and caught the attention of media. Try as they might, broadcasters of the night's game couldn't help but acknowledge the chant, and it quickly became the focus of post-game talk.

Interestingly, the chant didn't bother OV at all.

"It's always nice when they talk about you and then get the chants. I love it. It's great for the league, it's great for us," Ovechkin told *Washington Times* reporter Stephen Whyno after the game. "Everybody thinks who's better, who's not. For me, it's nice atmosphere and I love that kind of stuff."

Dale Hunter, Caps' head coach at the time, provided more insight to the *Times*.

"Everybody's going to raise their game when the crowd's on you," the former intimidating defenceman said. "It's playoff hockey, and you expect it."

Though the "Crosby's Better!" chant is by far the most well known, it wasn't a one-time effort. Others followed, such as "Jordan's Better!" directed at Carolina Hurricanes forward Eric Staal, and "Silver Medal!" a shot taken at former Vezina Trophy winner Ryan Miller. "Refyousuck" is quite possibly the most recognizable and longest lasting, as blown calls ignite the boo birds in a whole new way. Gone are the days of "A rope! A tree! Hang the referee!" "Refyousuck" is much more succinct.

But those chants—including "Crosby's Better!"—weren't the first. Months before Ovechkin became the object of Jets fans' "affection," the Philadelphia Flyers paid a visit to the MTS Centre for a Saturday afternoon tilt against the Jets. The goalie for the day, as selected by benchboss Peter Laviolette was Sergei Bobrovsky—he was not who the Jets' faithful wanted to see.

They wanted Ilya Bryzgalov between the pipes.

Months earlier, when Phoenix was rumoured to be coming to Winnipeg, Bryzgalov was his outspoken self in the media, proclaiming if the Coyotes did make the move to Winnipeg, he wouldn't be coming with the team. Flash forward to that faithful afternoon, and Bryzgalov had changed his tune.

"I'm pretty sure good people, beautiful people live in Winnipeg. I'm pretty sure there's passionate fans. I didn't mean it. I don't want to offend anybody," Bryzgalov told the *Winnipeg Free Press* on November 18, one day prior to the Jets vs. Flyers game. "I sincerely apologize if I offended anybody, any fans in Canada or Winnipeg."

Yeah, like that was going to work.

The Jets feasted on the Flyers, and as the goals built up on the score sheet, the chants for Bryzgalov increased.

"We Want Ilya!" the fans beckoned. "We Want Ilya!" they repeated over and over.

By the time the score was 5–1, the chants were deafening; yet Laviolette didn't relent, and there sat Bryzgalov on the Phillly bench, decked out in a Flyers toque.

Final score—Winnipeg Jets 6, Philadelphia Flyers 4.

73 Weaving Winnipeg Hockey History

It's a fairly unique part of Winnipeg professional hockey that there are players who played for more than one franchise in the city. While many wait to see if Shane Doan will still come back to Winnipeg before he hangs up his skates (or charitably wonder if KHL All-Star Deron Quint will get another shot on North American shores) there are no 1.0'ers that also played for 2.0; but to have played for the Moose and Jets? There, we have quite a few players.

First to the 1.0 list:

Scott Arniel—A second-round pick of the Jets in the 1982 NHL Entry Draft, Arniel played five solid seasons in Winnipeg that included three seasons of at least 40 points. Arniel was sent to Buffalo in 1986 only to be reacquired in the Dale Hawerchuk trade. He spent only one season back in Winnipeg before being sent to Boston in the subsequent off-season. As his career wound down, he found himself in the IHL and was with the Moose for the club's first three seasons. Later, Arniel became coach of the Moose in the AHL.

Jason Doig—One of the players who debuted with the Jets in their final season in the NHL, Doig managed to get into 15 NHL games in 1995–96 while also spending time with AHL affiliate Springfield Falcons and his QMJHL club, the Granby Predateurs. Doig never really found a permanent spot in the NHL, as was evidenced by his return to Winnipeg in 2005–06 after being signed by the Vancouver Canucks and being assigned to the Moose.

Bobby Dollas—After a strong QMJHL career, Dollas was a first-round pick by the Jets in 1983. In his first season of pro hockey, Dollas played one game with the Jets. He also played (larger) parts of two other seasons in Winnipeg and spent a full season in Sherbrooke before moving over to the Quebec Nordiques. Dollas ended up having a fairly decent NHL career, but as his time wound down he found himself in the IHL with the Moose for eight games. It was during this time, by the way, that he scored his only goal as a member of the home team in Winnipeg.

Dallas Eakins—Originally a Washington Capitals draft pick, Eakins came to Winnipeg the first time after being signed away by the Jets in 1989. His first tenure with the franchise was mainly spent with the Moncton Hawks, but he did manage to get into 14 games with the big club in 1992–93 before the Florida Panthers took a chance on him. The Jets eventually re-acquired the now journeyman during the 1995–96 season, and he played two games with the club. As his career wound down, Eakins found a spot with the 2003–04 Manitoba Moose, and, like Dollas, scored his lone goal here as a member of a Winnipeg-based club.

Randy Gilhen—Like Eakins, Winnipegger Gilhen had two stints with the Jets. First, he was picked up by the Jets after being originally drafted by the Hartford Whalers and played parts of three seasons in Winnipeg before being traded to Pittsburgh where he won a Stanley Cup. Gilhen was later reacquired by Winnipeg in a trade for Stu Barnes with Florida and played out the remainder of his NHL career with the team before the franchise left. Gilhen then stayed on in Manitoba and played with the Moose for their first two IHL seasons.

Russ Romaniuk—Romaniuk was originally a second-round pick of the Jets in 1988 and played parts of four seasons in Winnipeg after finishing an NCAA career in North Dakota. The native Winnipegger was traded to the Philadelphia Flyers before the 1995–96 season, but returned to Winnipeg just one year later with the Moose. Here, Romaniuk played one full season and part of a second season with Manitoba, and later became a broadcaster for the club.

And for Jets 2.0, as of the end of the 2014–15 NHL season only two players came from the Moose (though with several players still active in the NHL, there may be more to come). They are:

Mark Flood—Originally drafted by the Montreal Canadiens, Flood bounced around the NHL and AHL with various franchises before being picked up by the Manitoba Moose and signed to an AHL contract in 2010–11. Flood played well enough in that single year that True North retained him when the Jets arrived. He spent that first season split between Winnipeg and St. John's, scoring his first NHL goal during this period. Flood later bounced between the AHL and KHL, where, as of the 2014–15 season, he still plays.

Jason Jaffray—Jaffray was a pick-up by Craig Heisinger after playing for multiple franchises in the ECHL and AHL. His first season with the Moose came in 2004–05 and he would remain with the franchise through the 2008–09 season, during which he was officially signed by the Vancouver Canucks but spent time travelling between the NHL and AHL. Jaffray ended up signing with the Calgary Flames for the 2009–10 season, only to return to Manitoba for its final campaign. Jaffray was picked up by the Jets and has since spent all his time in Winnipeg's system, including playing 13 games with the club in the 2011–12 inaugural season.

74 The Superstitious Randy Carlyle

Hockey players, for whatever reason, are the most superstitious folk you will ever meet. Once they find a routine and have some success with it, they'll stick to it for every waking moment of their careers.

Whether it's a certain pattern they follow in getting dressed for a game or, perhaps being the last player to leave the locker room, there are intricacies that if anyone outside a hockey rink practiced, they'd get an odd look. Could you imagine, for example, if the cubicle dweller beside you only picked up a phone call after three rings? Yep, it would seem odd and probably get on your nerves.

And as good as he was, and as important as he was to the Winnipeg Jets through the 1980s and '90s, Randy Carlyle was that superstitious personality.

Young fans today will only know of Randy Carlyle for his exploits behind the bench as a head coach for the Toronto Maple

Leafs and Stanley Cup–winning Anaheim Ducks, as well as, of course, in his various capacities with the Manitoba Moose both in their IHL and AHL days. But in the years before he entered the coaching ranks, Carlyle was a leader on the ice with the Winnipeg Jets.

Originally a Maple Leaf, Carlyle came to Winnipeg by way of a trade from the Pittsburgh Penguins. A helmetless warrior, Carlyle came to Winnipeg in 1984 and played the next 10 years in a Jets uniform. Along the way, the former Norris Trophy winner was both a captain and assistant captain with the Jets while providing a solid presence on the blueline. He had five consecutive seasons of at least 40 points while with the Jets and, as his career wound down, he became a true mentor to developing d-men. Toward the end of his career, Carlyle was a commissioner's selection to the NHL All-Star Game.

The superstitious one, Randy Carlyle, played several seasons for the Jets before coaching them.

After retirement, Carlyle remained with the Jets as an assistant coach, and when the team moved to Phoenix, Carlyle remained in Winnipeg, becoming assistant coach to new Manitoba Moose head coach Jean Perron. A disastrous stretch in the 1996–97 season led to Carlyle becoming the new lead, a position he held for several years, interrupted only by a short stint with the Washington Capitals as an assistant coach.

But it was during his playing days that the intricacies of Carlyle's superstitions were on display for his teammates. Carlyle developed two different habits with the Jets, the first coming during the '80s. As Laurie Boschman retold, Carlyle had the unusual insistence of being the fifth player onto the ice. This led to a unique situation one time when the team was ready to take the ice.

"I got caught in it," Boschman said. "It just so happened that I had to go out before him, and I didn't know that until one time when I had my skate blade cracked. Craig Heisinger was fixing my blade up and we all had to wait until that skate was finished before we could go out on the ice."

Later, Carlyle's superstitions took on a different feel. Luciano Borsato, who was with Carlyle for the majority of his final two seasons in the NHL, recalled that the first superstition had disappeared, but was replaced with a second, more dangerous tradition.

"Randy did stop and stand in the middle of the ice, around the hash-marks during warm-up," Borsato said. "You had to always keep your head up or you would run him over, and that did happen a couple of times!"

No matter whether one found the superstitions silly or not, the bottom line is they worked for Carlyle. By the time his career finished, Carlyle had played 1,000 games and cemented a legacy in the ranks of all-time great Jets.

75 Starting in the East

When the Jets returned to the NHL in 2011, there was a lot to look forward to, including first goals, the emergence of fan favourites, and eventually the first playoff series (hey, we were realistic—this was the Atlanta Thrashers coming to Winnipeg).

But more than anything, Jets fans were looking forward to renewed hostilities with the likes of the Edmonton Oilers and Chicago Blackhawks. Rivalries were what hockey was built on and sustained interest even in lean years. Ask yourself—would the late 1990s have been as exciting as they were if the Detroit Red Wings and Colorado Avalanche didn't have the bitter battles they did?

Unfortunately, the Jets and their fans had to wait to renew hostilities, as the team had to start in the Eastern Conference. Given that the sale was completed so late in May, there wasn't enough time for schedule makers to alter the arrangements that had started with planning for the Thrashers. As such, the Jets' first campaign showcased battles with the likes of the Philadelphia Flyers and the Carolina Hurricanes. And guess what? The Jets were fairly competitive. While they finished eight points out of the playoffs, they did so only because of a late-season collapse after they were effectively eliminated from postseason competition; but they more than handled themselves against the likes of Washington and Florida. Against Southeast opponents, the Jets went 14–6–4, a better record than any other team in the division.

Under normal circumstances, the Jets may have returned to the West for their second season of play, but this was 2012–13, when the NHL was in lockout mode for months. Some even feared that, like the 2004–05 campaign, the entire season would be lost. Fortunately though, cooler heads prevailed and a 48-game schedule was played. Again, the Jets were competitive with their Eastern Conference rivals, particularly those in their division. This time, the Jets finished only four points out of a playoff spot and second overall in the Southeast, leaving some fans to even hope that Winnipeg was now going to be a permanent fixture in the East. Heck, if the Winnipeg Blue Bombers could play in the CFL's Eastern Division, why couldn't the Jets do the same in the NHL?

Alas, it wasn't meant to be as finally, in season three, the Jets returned to the Western Conference where they belonged. The move was part of a full realignment by the NHL, where the Detroit Red Wings, long desiring to be part of the Eastern Conference, finally got their wish granted, joining the Columbus Blue Jackets in the move. The Jets found themselves in the west's ultra-competitive Central Division with the likes of the Chicago Blackhawks, Dallas Stars, and Colorado Avalanche. At long last, the Minnesota Wild were going to be the geographic rival that many sought to see develop; and although the first year in the West was forgettable (the Jets finished dead last in their division), the second year proved to be more promising, even though virtually every pundit in the league predicted similar peril.

Ultimately, the move to the West was logical, league wide. The new structure brought the number of divisions per conference down from three to two. The resulting intradivisional concentration meant less long-distance travel for road-weary players.

"I think overall it's going to be better for travel, especially for Western Conference teams," Bryan Little told KenoraOnline.com. "They won't have to fly over as many time zones. A lot of teams in our conference are just on the coast."

76 The Jets Once Drafted Phil Esposito

When you think of hockey legends, one thought comes to mind—what would have happened if they played on the same team?

From time to time we've seen this happen in the latter years of great careers—Guy Lafleur coming out of retirement to play alongside Marcel Dionne on Broadway, Wayne Gretzky going to St. Louis where he teamed with Brett Hull, Gordie Howe, and Dave Keon together in Hartford…

But how about Bobby Hull and Phil Esposito in Winnipeg?

There's no question that the Winnipeg Jets were among the most fortunate of the WHA teams—signing the Golden Jet away from the NHL was an almost immeasurable feather in their cap. Imagine for a moment what could have been if Espo had come to the River City, as well.

Esposito, of course, was one of the most prolific players of his era. Tallying more than 700 goals and nearly 1,600 points, Espo was the lynchpin of a Boston Bruins team that nearly took home two Stanley Cups with his leadership. He was also one of the featured players of the 1972 Summit Series.

And had the stars aligned properly, and perhaps if he was as adventurous as goalie Gerry Cheevers, Esposito might have come to Winnipeg.

Esposito was given the opportunity by way of the 1973 WHA Professional Draft, a rarely-remembered attempt by the Rebel League to take a second swing for the fences and pluck more NHL stars from the ranks of their squads. Sure, there wasn't much in terms of expectation that anything would result from it, but it was still a draft worth pursuing.

"The 1973 draft was much like the 1972 draft where the WHA parceled out rights to players under contract to teams in other leagues, not just the NHL, but in minor pro leagues," Winnipeg Jets historian Curtis Walker explained. "It was fully expected that many of the players would never suit up in the WHA, but they still did it anyways."

And so, the Jets claimed Esposito in the draft. No, Espo didn't end up coming to Winnipeg, though he did play one game of his hockey career as a member of the home team—that being as part of the Summit Series team that played at the Winnipeg Arena in the famous tie game between Canada and the Soviets that turned the eight-contest friendly into a tournament that would have a decided winner.

But this wasn't the only time that the Bruins legend was courted by the WHA. At one point, Vancouver Blazers owner Jim Pattison offered Esposito a multi-million dollar deal to leave the Bruins and come to the Rebel League. Espo turned him down for a smaller salary to stay with Boston. It's a decision, it seems, he may have regretted.

"I signed a contract in Boston for less money than I could have gotten from going to the WHA. I could have made millions doing that," Esposito told the *Toronto Sun*'s Steve Simmons. "And you know how they repaid me? Three weeks later, they traded me [to the New York Rangers]."

Although Esposito didn't come to Winnipeg in '73, two other players selected by Winnipeg at that draft table did (albeit not immediately). Gary Bromley played one year in Winnipeg—1977–78—helping the Jets to the Avco Cup that season as he split netminding duties with Joe Daley. The other was Dave Kryskow, also a member of the 1977–78 team.

The other players who were picked by the Jets in 1973 include Mike Bloom, Peter McDuffe, Steve Stirling, Pierre Plante, John Marks, Gene Carr, Billy Fairbairn, Chuck Lefley, Doug Horbul,

Neil Komadoski, Larry Carriere, Ted Irvine, Andre Dupont, Luc Simard, Andre Aubry, and Yvon Lambert. Some are familiar names, some aren't, but none, not even as a combined group, likely would have done as much for Winnipeg as Phil Esposito.

77 "Memories to Cheer"

As opposed to the "Hockey Rocks" recordings the Jets released in the 1990s, "Memories to Cheer" was a much more somber song.

Created in 1996 to toast the final moments of the Winnipeg Jets, the song, written by Rod Palson and sung by Danny Kramer, was laced with memory and heartbreak. The song was distributed on cassette with proceeds going to the Winnipeg Jets Goals for Kids Foundation.

It was a true project of love and easily the most tear-jerking ballad that anyone in Winnipeg ever heard. Below are the lyrics. Feel free to sing along.

In this, the final chapter of a love affair between a hockey team and its fans, this song is for all of us, here, in hockey's heartland.

You've shattered my dreams, you take my team,
Leave me with only a fear;
The flashbacks of highlights, too painful in hindsight,
When there's no team here to cheer.
Thinking back to the golden era,
Bobby shoots, he scores, he smiles;
Anders, Ulf, Sully, Shoe, and Joe
Daley lit up my life.

This cassette not only paid tribute to the Jets, but also raised money for Goals for Kids.

Luke was there, in the leap to glory,
Fergy, gave it hell;
At Portage and Main, we signed the first,
Mighty duck in the NHL.
But we can still dream of those great hockey teams,
That we'll always have here,
Flashbacks of highlights, while painful in hindsight,
We'll always have memories to cheer.
Teemu, a light, prominent, bright,
Fans of yours standing tough,
Keith, Alex, and Eddie O and Teppo.
Randy and Thomas, they've hung them up.
Remembering hat tricks, we look at the mavericks
That revelled in our very place

In the Hockey Hall, that belongs to us all,
That's why we'll, never lose faith.
But we can still dream of those great hockey teams,
That we'll always have here,
Flashbacks of highlights, while painful in hindsight,
We'll always have memories to cheer.

If you stood tall last summer, to help save our Jets, stand up now and take a bow; for you are a big part of the spirit of Manitoba; a spirit that showed the world what we're made of.

We stood up and fought, we wouldn't be bought,
In our hundred-and-twenty-fifth year;
Manitoba proud, came through clear and loud,
A memory forever we'll cheer.
Yeah we stood up and fought,
In our hundred-and-twenty-fifth year;
Manitoba proud, came through clear and loud,
A memory forever we'll cheer.
Manitoba's spirit, now one last time,
Let's hear it...yeah!
We'll always have memories to cheer.

78 The Flyers Almost Played in Winnipeg

If there's anything that the Winnipeg Jets' faithful watched most intently over the course of the 15-year absence from the NHL, it was the headlines that touted, at one point or another, that almost every team was rumoured to relocate to the MTS Centre.

Between the fall of 1996 and the spring of 2011, especially in the years leading up to the return, a bevy of teams were said to be considering Winnipeg as their new home rink; and yet the Atlanta Thrashers were ultimately announced to be the team on the move.

However, those clubs considering relocation weren't the first NHL team to inhabit Winnipeg. Heck, even the Jets' WHA franchise may not have been the first NHL squad to call the city home. Instead, that honour could have been bestowed on the Philadelphia Flyers…that is if the Winnipeg Arena had been just a wee bit bigger.

During the Flyers' inaugural season, their home—the famed Spectrum—had to undergo roof repairs, forcing the young club to hit the road for a number of games while repairs were made.

Amid the travels of the Flyers, Winnipeg Mayor Stephen Juba floated the idea of the orphaned team finding refuge in the Manitoba capital, and it got some interesting reception.

Flyers President Bill Putnam, in an interview with Kevin Boland that appeared in the *Winnipeg Free Press* on March 9, 1968, talked about the logistics that would need to be in place for his team to come to the River City.

"The things that depend on us playing there are conditions," he said. "First there's travelling and that's the main concern."

Along with ensuring opposition for this game in particular—the Los Angeles Kings—would sign off on the date, Putnam also didn't hold back when talking about finances. "I like the prospects of a full house in Winnipeg Arena. If the prices were right and the other factors fall in place, I'd be inclined to listen."

And what would those financials translate to for Winnipeg's fans of our national pastime? Get ready to cringe folks.

"I think about $3.50 for the best [seat] is a good price," Winnipeg Alderman and Winnipeg Enterprises Chair Mark Danzker told Boland in the same article. "People can afford that. It's usually the working man who stays home to watch the NHL games on Saturday night. He's the real fan; we'd like to give him the chance to see the action live and be able to take his wife."

That's right. For the price of a beer at the MTS Centre, father and child could have seen NHL hockey in Winnipeg in 1968.

Jack Kent Cooke, Kings owner, for his part didn't seem all that anxious about the prospect of playing hockey in Winnipeg in March, but ultimately, as he told the *Free Press*, the decision wasn't his to make. In recalling previous trips to Winnipeg, Cooke reflected that, "I still get a chill when I think about it. That's why I love it down here so much," and then relented, "But it's not my choice; the choice belongs to the Philadelphia people. If they say Winnipeg, it's Winnipeg. It's their home game, and their choice."

Unfortunately, the 9,000-seat Winnipeg Arena wasn't large enough for the Flyers to venture to the River City, especially in comparison to Le Colissee in Quebec, where Philly already had ownership of the minor league team in the 16,000-seat building.

After the announcement, *Free Press* columnist John Robertson encouraged Mayor Juba to not give up on his dream. On Saturday, March 16, 1968, Robertson opined:

"But if Mayor Steve Juba is really serious about getting National League hockey for Winnipeg, there is a way it *can* be done on a permanent basis, in the not too distant future.

"No, I haven't flipped my lid. But the NHL governors have made no secret of the fact that they are considering expansion to 18 teams before 1975. I agree that Winnipeg didn't have a chance in the first expansion, because, in the words of at least one NHL governor, Stafford Smythe, it was not a major league city.

"Well, a lot of things have happened since then. For one thing, the Pan Am Games has made all the world recognize Winnipeg as one of the most enthusiastic sports centres on the continent.

"But there is another equally important development that should enhance Winnipeg's chances even further. The NHL has found out, to its sorrow, that the size of a city doesn't necessarily dictate whether it can support big league hockey."

Though the NHL would wait, top-tier hockey, of course, soon came to Winnipeg—and Quebec—in the form of the World Hockey Association.

79 Have a Swig of Fan Brew

Winnipeg and beer—they go hand in hand. What else will warm the cockles of your heart on a night of -40 Celsius more than a pint of your favorite ale?

Winnipeg is so closely tied to the frothy adult beverage, in fact, that as the story goes, Labatt named its famed Blue brand after the CFL's Blue Bombers; but if you thought that the tie between Quebec's chief brewery and the home of Canada's largest Francophone community outside La Belle Province, then you haven't been introduced to the most unique brand that ever came out of a marketing mind.

Amid the 2011–12 first season of the Jets' return to the NHL, just about everyone had some sort of commemorative memento of the landmark return. Canada Post produced a stamp, the Mint struck special coins, and Budweiser, a subsidiary of Labatt, embarked on crafting a special beer.

Dubbed Fan Brew, the concoction was, on the surface, the same as any other beer that came from Budweiser's brewery. Except, one big difference—it had Winnipeg water—and lots of it—from areas across the city. As Budweiser outlined in a press release, water was collected from a variety of areas, including the MTS Centre and The Forks during the Jets' first weekend back in Winnipeg.

"The Winnipeg Jets Fan Brew is Budweiser's way of paying homage to Jets fans and celebrating the team's first season back on the ice," said Dan Chubey, district sales manager, Labatt Breweries of Canada, at the time of Fan Brew's introduction. "We are extremely proud of this brew and excited to share it with Winnipeggers and Jets fans alike. The Winnipeg Jets Fan Brew maintains the high quality and great taste Bud drinkers know and love along with some very special ingredients—the spirit, energy, and passion of Jets fans."

Of course, marketing being what it is, creating a special brew meant much more than just simply creating a beer with city water. Along with the appearance of packs of cans, framed pieces were created—and snapped up—that featured two cans mounted on a plaque.

But to top off the publicity, Budweiser and the Jets teamed up for one of the biggest toasts in the history of beer drinking. During the second intermission of the March 1, 2012, contest, the MTS Centre, *en masse*, saluted the new pride of Winnipeg with a toast. Some good came along with this, as Budweiser made a $25,000 donation to the General Council of Winnipeg Community Centres.

Now of course, while several Fan Brew cans were emptied and tossed in recycling bins, there are those ardent collectors who kept their 12-packs intact. Those are the same hardcores that purchased the commemorative first night program and never removed it from its plastic film package or even opened up a stamp book that contained those Jets images, including a reproduction of Nik Antropov's landmark first goal.

But of all the souvenirs created to commemorate that first season, none, perhaps, were more meaningful than a series of pucks available at the inaugural game that were autographed by members of the team. All proceeds were given to families of the victims of a plane crash that killed the entire Lokomotiv team of the KHL.

80 The Trials of Evander Kane

When the NHL returned to Winnipeg, some players were extremely excited for the rebirth and others were less than thrilled about the prospect of playing in the frozen hockey hotbed. Take for example, Ilya Bryzgalov's vocal opposition to the prospect of his Coyotes coming to Jetland.

But when the Thrashers came, there were few dissenters, vocally at least, about playing in the River City. Sure, we can all speculate that the confines of the 15,000-seat MTS Centre weren't going to be the most forgiving for a player, but most seemed happy with the idea of being heroes to Winnipeg, a city that has never, ever thumped its chest like Toronto or Vancouver. Ego, for the most part, is checked at the door in Winnipeg, and that could be why Evander Kane seemingly never got off on good footing with the Jets' faithful.

From the very beginning of No. 9's time in Winnipeg, Kane, a Thrasher pick in the number-four position of the 2009 NHL Entry Draft, almost immediately began rubbing fans the wrong way. Urban legend suggested that Kane had stiffed local restaurants on his food bill. Gary Lawless, *Winnipeg Free Press* columnist, talked about the rumours in 2012, after a sign in the crowd in a Jets vs. Senators game spoke to those accusations.

"Some wiseguy hears a rumour and takes a sign to a hockey game slandering Kane. Someone else takes a picture of the sign and puts it on Twitter and whoosh—the whole thing catches fire."

Evander Kane skates down the ice before Jets fans anxiously drove him out of town.

Lawless wrote. "Websites, Facebook pages, and Twitter accounts repeated rumour after rumour about Kane on Saturday with no evidence to support the claims. Posts became so inflammatory on the *Free Press* website Saturday night the comments section was shut down. Disgusting is only one way to describe it."

Further, Lawless didn't say Kane was innocent of all charges; just that there had been no conclusive evidence that Kane had legitimately dined-and-dashed. "Mistakes are to be expected but not invented. Accusations, such as walking out on a bill, need to be substantiated," Lawless wrote. "I'm the last guy you'll hear suggesting we give Kane a break. But he shouldn't be fair game to half-truths because he's becoming the most well-known guy in the city."

If this was the worst that Kane did, then all could have been forgiven and forgotten, but it wasn't.

Amid the 2012–13 lockout, Kane took to Twitter, flashing large stacks of greenbacks, something that didn't sit well virtually across the Twittersphere and irked league officials. Kane dismissed the backlash as not getting the joke he was sending to Floyd "Money" Mayweather. "I totally understand why some people maybe don't enjoy that tweet as much as others with what's going on," Kane told the *Free Press*' Ed Tait. "And maybe some people are more sensitive, and I totally get that. But, at the same time, it's funny to me how I throw something out there as a joke and then I get all these tweets, many of them which I don't pay much attention to."

Again, had the controversy ended there, Winnipeggers may have forgiven and forgotten, but Kane's seeming lack of maturity wore not only on the Jets' fan base, but also on his teammates. While a second money stack Tweet didn't impact as much as the first, Kane's actions in February 2015 seemed to be the final straw.

Before a game early in the month against the Vancouver Canucks, it was announced that Kane was going to be a healthy scratch for the night. In the subsequent days, it was revealed that Kane told management that he simply wasn't going to play in the game, curious if for no other reason than Kane being a Vancouver native.

As the days rolled on, it was first revealed that Kane showed up for team practice wearing a track suit, violating the team's dress code. What led to his refusal to play in the Vancouver game was treatment in the locker room, namely his suit being soaked either in a shower or an ice bath. Word later leaked that it was Dustin Byfuglien who committed the prank, something media assessed as the veteran exercising a measure of authority and trying to get Kane to fall in line with the club.

It was soon after this word leaked that Kane elected to have season-ending arm surgery, and just about every Manitoba hockey pundit assessed that his time in Winnipeg was done. Perhaps the truest sign from Jets fans that they were done with Kane was a souvenir jersey, bearing his nameplate and No. 9, was thrown on the ice following a Jets overtime loss to the Chicago Blackhawks at the end of the tumultuous week. The closure came just days following, as Kane, along with Zach Bogosian, was traded to the Buffalo Sabres in exchange for players, prospects, and a draft pick.

Though at press time nothing has been announced by the Jets, speculation has rained in from Jets followers that, official or not, the first visit by the Sabres to Winnipeg could become "Track Suit Day" at the MTS Centre. Tuxedo Night? Not quite, but equally as fun.

81 Kid Stuff

Ahh to be young again.

Back in the day, the Winnipeg Jets were larger than life superheroes. Sure, on the outside they may have seemed like your average 20 or 30 something, but on the ice they were transformed into these mega men, bravely battling with the pride of the symbol you wore on your chest on the line. They fought for you while you cheered them on, hoping one day to join them.

That era saw fan friendliness start to open up as the Jets were more than happy to do extra things for their youngest fans. If you were lucky, a Jet would come out to your school or local Y to give you a talk about being safe and playing fair, and if you asked really nicely at a game, a security guard would hand you a coveted puck from the warm-ups at the Winnipeg Arena.

But the height of excitement came with the opportunity to be members of the Junior Jets Fan Club. For any tyke in the 1980s and '90s, this seemed like the coolest thing ever—you got an official club card (which you immediately kept in your neon Velcro wallet) plus other swag that ranged from posters to pennants to other gimmicky goodness.

Yes, to borrow from Archie and Edith Bunker, those were the days...except when you compare them to the amazing efforts by the current Jets. You see, as good as the Jets were for children of a particular vintage, they're even better at connecting today. Being a young Jets fan today has all sorts of opportunities availing themselves to you.

Let's start on the even level of the kids club, or as it's known today—the Jets Cadets. As promised on the Jets' website during the 2014–15 season, young sons and daughters (legitimately young) received the following goodies:

- Your 2014–15 Official Member Pass
- Jets Cadets Lanyard with sleeve
- Mick E. Moose Jersey Lunch Bag
- Mick E. Moose Bobblehead Toothbrush Holder
- Jets Cadets Pencil Case
- Jets Cadets Official Member Dog Tag
- Mick E. Moose Oversized Souvenir Card
- Winnipeg Jets Toothbrush courtesy of Children's Dental World
- Membership Activation Card
- 10% discount on regular priced merchandise at all Jets Gear locations (with Member Card)

The Jr. Jets Fan Club was undoubtedly the best fan club in Winnipeg hockey history.

So far, kids of the modern day are winning out right? Okay, how about the visits? Yep, kids today get those, as well. During "I Love to Read Month," members of the Jets go to schools across Winnipeg and read to kids from the team-published book, *The Home Team*, answer kids' questions, and sign autographs. Other appearances happen throughout the year, including dedicated efforts to visit kids in hospital. Among those visits is a Christmas-time visit, one that Adam Lowry participated in during the 2014–15 season.

"Any time you can get into the community and make an impact, make a difference in someone's day, we want to take that opportunity," Lowry told the *Winnipeg Sun*. "I think you see here the atmosphere around this room and the difference these guys are making right now. You see the kids smiling, it's making their day. It's a special feeling. They go through a lot of hardships, so for us to be able to give back, it's awesome."

So player appearances and kids club are on even keels with the past, more or less; here's where older generations get hammered though:

- At each Jets home game, a child is chosen as the flag bearer for the team and skates with the club.
- Another opportunity presents itself to ride the Zamboni during intermission. This at times comes hot on the heels of a Timbits demo game between local clubs.
- Still another advantage for today's kinder—in 2014–15, in partnership with Duraco Windows, the Jets introduced a TV time-out game, whereby a kid takes shots at a "house." Break the window (or not) and the kid gets a game-used stick.

Now all of these factors play into the favour of today's generation; but for kids of the 1990s, there was one memorable experience for some, that no one will ever, EVER be able to match.

"I can remember Selanne playing street hockey," Barry Shenkarow said. "If we were playing Sunday afternoon or night, he was on the street after practice playing street hockey with kids."

82 Best of the Broadcasters—Don Wittman

There are legendary broadcasters across the hockey landscape. Foster Hewitt, Danny Gallivan, and Mike Emrick are among them.

Each team will lay claim to having its own favorites, and just like any other city, Winnipeg will boast about some of the play-by-play and color commentators who have taken their turns on the airwaves, telling the story of the action on the ice either by radio or television.

Winnipeg is not immune to arguments over the best names to ever sit behind a microphone and extol the virtues of a sports franchise. Between the likes of Ken "The Friar" Nicolson, Curt Keilback, and through to Dennis Beyak, there have been several great broadcasters in Jets history; but for all the debates that this chapter is sure to spark, there is one man that all can agree was one of not only the best play-by-play men in Jets history, but one of the greatest in Canada—Don Wittman.

Born in rural Saskatchewan, Witt, as he would come to be known, had a booming, commanding voice in the broadcast booth. Starting in the 1960s, Wittman was part of the CBC family and had moved to Winnipeg for regional coverage. When the Jets entered the NHL, it was Wittman who was the lead on their games.

One who remembers Witt in particular was Scott Oake. In 1975, Oake came to Winnipeg, where Wittman had spent so many years of his career doing local coverage. Witt was moving up to join the CBC's national team on a fulltime basis, with Oake taking over the regional duties. Now a member of the national broadcasts for CBC and Rogers Sportsnet, Oake talked about how Wittman mentored him in the days they were together for Canada's national broadcast.

"Don was an incredible influence in my career," Oake recalled. "Don and I established a close relationship. He was always very good with advice for me, his work ethic was second to none, and I've tried at times in my career to match it."

The work ethic Oake speaks of is that Witt was one of the most impressive voices CBC ever had. Not only did he cover hockey, but he was recognized as a top voice for the CFL and the Olympics, as well. It was Wittman who called Donovan Bailey's 1996 Olympic 100 Metre Dash among other legendary achievements by Canadians on the world stage.

"He was the best commentator at covering any event that went up and down a field of play, whether it's ice or grass, or around in a circle," Oake attested. "He had an incredible gift of association, and even if you watch now on the NHL classic channel the vicious battles between Calgary and Edmonton, it's Don's voice on them and he doesn't miss a thing. He's incredibly sharp.

"I have a picture in my house—an article that someone cut out of the paper and had framed—and there's a comment in there from me about Don. I said at the time that it's really sad, because with the Jets returning, he'd still be calling games. He'd be at the rink every night and would be calling games for *Hockey Night in Canada*, and he would be. It's very sad that he's not here to see the rebirth of the team."

Wittman was recognized countless times and sits in multiple halls of fame, including his 1997 induction to the Manitoba Hockey Hall of Fame; but there may be no bigger recognition paid to Don than the honour he received from True North Sports and Entertainment in 2004, when he was asked to emcee pregame ceremonies before the final hockey game at the Winnipeg Arena.

"I was really looking forward to it when they asked me if I would do it," Wittman said soon after the ceremony. "I've seen so much hockey in this building and the opportunity to relive some of those moments and see some of the players, that was all part of it."

Don Wittman passed away in 2008, but his memory lasts forever in the minds and ears of anyone who ever heard him call a Winnipeg Jets hockey game.

83 GST! GST!

While superstars like Teemu Selanne and Dale Hawerchuk may have driven ticket sales and have been the most common names on the back of jerseys, the Jets roleplayers have had as much fan interest. Names like Perry Turnbull, Shawn Cronin, and Bryan "Butsy" Erickson resonate with fans of that era because of their willingness to put out solid effort after solid effort, no matter how many games in a row they played and no matter how many minutes (as minimal as they were at times) they got on the ice.

For fans of the modern Winnipeg Jets, there are two players that fill that role—Jim Slater and Chris Thorburn.

Slater, as discussed elsewhere in the book, was an Atlanta Thrashers pick who debuted in 2005–06. Outside of two stints with the Wolves, he was a fixture with Atlanta and quickly endeared himself to fans.

Thorburn, meanwhile, was originally a selection of the Buffalo Sabres back in 2001 and cracked their lineup in 2005–06 for two games after toiling in the AHL. Thorburn soon gained the reputation for being a bruiser, and moved around to help teams gain more muscle. First with the Pittsburgh Penguins, who claimed Thorburn on waivers prior to the 2006–07 season, and then the Thrashers, who traded for him after that season.

While with the Thrashers, Thorburn was positioned with Slater and the two just blended so well. In talking about Slater, Thorburn is quick to dish out compliments about his linemate. "He's a guy you can depend on and isn't out of position too often," he said. "We just keep our game simple and that's where we've found that we've been successful."

When Slater and Thorburn arrived in Winnipeg, they found a third for their line—Tanner Glass. Glass was originally a draft pick of the Florida Panthers in 2003 and, after finishing his collegiate career with Dartmouth, joined the franchise. Though he spent his first seasons in Rochester, Glass soon broke the Panthers' lineup. Eventually, the Vancouver Canucks took interest in him and signed him for two years. In the summer of 2011, however, the Winnipeg Jets took a gamble and picked up Glass.

The trio were quickly put together, and the new line caught the attention of fans and media. Soon, they were christened the "GST Line," a recognition piece that is rarely bestowed in the NHL.

"In the first couple games of the inaugural season, I liked the energy that line brought," recalled Ezra Ginsburg of *Illegal Curve*,

The PST lines up for a faceoff during the 2014–15 preseason.

originator of the moniker. "I Tweeted out that I really needed to find a name for the line. It was pretty simple—take the first letters of their last names, and you get the G-S-T Line. It really took off when [co-worker] Dave Minuk started telling broadcasters like [TSN's] Dennis Beyak. He used it on television, and it really caught on."

Soon, shouts of "GST! GST!" were erupting in the MTS Centre as the trio plowed over opposing players. Glass' physicality, in particular, stood out as he was among the NHL leaders in hits that season. His stay in Winnipeg, however, was temporary, as at the end of the 2011–12 season, he was picked up by the Pittsburgh Penguins as a free agent.

"It's unfortunate that the line only stuck together for one year, but it was a lot of fun to watch those guys play together. They really seemed to feed well off each other," Ginsburg said.

Since that time, however, other iterations have arisen. Anthony Peluso, another bruiser, made his mark in the NHL in 2013–14, creating the PST Line. Since then, the GST has had an occasional revival with T.J. Galiardi joining Thorburn and Slater.

Ultimately, it is Chris Thorburn and Jim Slater who have created the mystique of their line, no matter who shifts in beside them, the duo have remained among the most popular Jets, thanks to their dedication to their craft.

"It's a great feeling. It's something that you're proud of," Thorburn said of the duo's popularity. "It's a matter of keeping it going and getting a couple more followers along the way. We take pride in the way our line plays. It's important for our team to have our line go when we were called and be able to gain momentum."

84 The 2014 Olympians

For all the woes the Jets had in the 2013–14 NHL season, one that saw them finish distantly out of a playoff spot in their first year in the Western Conference, there were still elements to celebrate for the squad, namely accomplishments on the international stage.

Winnipeg has always employed a strong mix of players from across a variety of hockey playing nations; thus, it's perhaps not that surprising that when the 2014 Winter Olympic rosters were announced that several Jets were included on the list. This was a group that was already fairly strong pared down from a larger group that included the likes of Andrew Ladd (Canada), Jacob Trouba, Dustin Byfuglien, and Zach Bogosian (USA), and others.

When the rosters were announced for each country, Jets fans waited with bated breath to find out who from their ranks would be the first roster Jets to be selected for the largest international competition to be held across shinny's landscape (World Juniors aside), and their hopes were answered with four participants:

USA—Blake Wheeler

Wheeler's inclusion was not surprising by any stretch; the surprise was only that the triumvirate of Jets' American D-men weren't picked.

Wheeler was in the midst of his best statistical season to date. He finished the campaign with 28 goals, far exceeding the previous best of 21 in his rookie season, and 69 points as he continued to edge toward being a point-per-game player.

Wheeler's selection was the third for his career to don the red, white, and blue. Previously, the Plymouth, Minnesota, native dressed for the World Junior tournament in 2006 and the Senior

Blake Wheeler (No. 26) and Michael Frolik (No. 67) were Jets forwards and Olympic heroes.

Men's in 2011. In all three cases, the U.S. finished outside the medals, the Olympic result coming down to a loss in the semi-finals.

"We were buzzing pretty well through the first four games. To be part of that was awesome," Wheeler told the CBC after returning to Winnipeg. "It was great to be part of that group. It was a great group of guys and it was an experience that, later down in life, I'll look back on and cherish."

Czech Republic—Ondrej Pavelec, Michael Frolik

Though no one would ever accuse the Czechs of being Winnipeg Europe, they outpaced other hockey nations for picking up Jets for their roster.

The more obvious choice was goaltender Ondrej Pavelec. Winnipeg's lead netminder was a consensus lock to make the squad long before the team made the announcement official, having already enjoyed a multitude of experience on the international stage. In Senior Men's competition, Pav counted two medals—a gold in 2010 and bronze in 2011—in addition to one World Junior tournament (2007) and a third Seniors (2013). At the Olympics, Pav came away with a 2–2 record.

Frolik, meanwhile, is one of the more decorated international stars in Jets' history (nevermind winning a Stanley Cup while with the Chicago Blackhawks). In total, Frolik, as of 2014, has five medals—all bronze—in his collection, including two from the Senior Men's (2011, 2012), one World Juniors (2005), and two U-18 Worlds (2004, 2006). Frolik played in three additional World Junior tourneys and one other U-18 tourney.

Unfortunately, like the U.S., Czech finished out of the medals, closing out the tournament in sixth place.

Finland—Olli Jokinen

The only Jet to come out of the Olympics with hardware, perhaps not surprisingly, was Olli Jokinen, who earned a bronze medal with the Finns (who included Jets 1.0 alumn Teemu Selanne in their ranks).

As prolific as Frolik's trophy case is with international awards, it pales in comparison to Joki's, who has 11 medals to his name. The group includes a World Junior gold (1998), a World Cup silver medal (2004), three silver (1998, 1999, 2014) and three bronze (2000, 2006 and 2008) at the Senior Men's, and three Olympic medals including two bronze (2010, 2014) and a silver (2006).

Across the various international competitions Jokinen has been in (which has been plenty due to consistently missing the NHL playoffs) has 85 points in 128 games.

With the 2018 Olympics, as of publish time in doubt, these four Jets may be the only active players in 2.0 history to ever crack the Olympic stage.

85 Pokey and the Bandit

Combinations in hockey are nothing new—linemates, defensive partners, and goalie tandems have been part of the NHL and other leagues for ages.

The last of the three, however, is fairly rare by today's standards. Sure, there are a few teams that have the "1" and "1a" format, but you're more likely to find a single goalie taking on the lion's share of games. Such was the case for the Jets, who had Ondrej Pavelec play in almost every game for their first two seasons, and even when his schedule was reduced in 2013–14, he still got into 70 per cent of the season's contests.

This wasn't always the case for the Jets. There were periods where goalies split season duties and were on equal footing with fans; and no tandem was as beloved in Winnipeg as Eldon Reddick and Daniel Berthiaume, better known as "Pokey and the Bandit." Reddick (Pokey) and Berthiaume (Bandit) filled the Jets' net for three seasons, starting in 1986–87. Preceded by the tandem of Dan Bouchard (retired) and Brian Hayward (traded for Steve Penney), Reddick and Berthiaume were two rookies when they were all but sworn in as the tandem in training camp, especially when Penney petered out very quickly.

Berthiaume was the more experienced of the two, having snuck into a playoff game the year prior. Though he lost that appearance, he turned aside 39 of 43 shots against him in a contest that stretched into overtime. This came hot on the heels of only having been drafted by the Jets in 1985 (third round, 60th overall) and having been named the MVP of the QMJHL that same year. Reddick, meanwhile, was an undrafted signee by the Jets in 1985, whose career encapsulated runs in the WHL (including a season with the Brandon Wheat Kings), IHL and AHL. It was in the IHL that Reddick shared the James Norris Memorial Trophy for lowest goals against average with Rick St. Croix.

In the duo's rookie season, they combined for 39 of the Jets' 40 wins, with Berthiaume putting up an 18–7–3 record and Reddick 21–21–4. Their efforts not only enthralled fans, but also led to the Jets making it to the playoffs and knocking off the defending Campbell Conference champion Calgary Flames in the first round, thanks to Berthiaume who took all four Jets victories in the 4–2 series win. Unfortunately, the next round's opponent was the Edmonton Oilers. Enough said.

In their second season, Pokey and the Bandit showed little sophomore jinx. Again, the tandem led the Jets to the postseason, primarily on the strength of Berthiaume's 22–19–7 record that went along with Reddick's tally of 9–13–3. Unfortunately, this second season saw the Jets face the Oilers in the first round, but it wasn't all bad news—Berthiaume did manage to get one win against Edmonton, the first of its kind for Winnipeg in the NHL.

The third and final season for Pokey and the Bandit, however, didn't go as successfully. Reddick dipped to 11–17–7 while Berthiaume only got into a handful of games and went 0–8–0 while spending a lot of time in the minor leagues. It quickly became apparent to Jets' management that the tandem wasn't going to lead Winnipeg to the promised land, especially with the emergence of Bob Essensa as the team's goalie of the future.

Unceremoniously, Reddick and Berthiaume were broken up. Reddick was traded to the Edmonton Oilers in September of 1989, and in a bitter twist was part of the Stanley Cup–winning team in 1990 (after they eliminated the Jets in the first round). Berthiaume, meanwhile, hung around the Jets a bit longer before being traded to the Minnesota North Stars amid the 1989–90 season as Stephane Beauregard and Rick Tabaracci emerged as Essensa's backups.

Berthiaume later returned to the Jets as part of a trade with the Boston Bruins but never saw game action.

Interestingly, both Reddick and Berthiaume's careers encapsulated rarities. Pokey spent some time playing in Germany and finally finished in the UHL, while Berthiaume went so far as to give roller hockey a shot before hanging up his skates, also in the UHL.

Ultimately, Pokey and the Bandit's two seasons between the pipes for the Jets were among the more fun ones for Winnipeg fans and showed management what a true tandem could do in net.

86 Dan Snyder

When the Atlanta Thrashers relocated to Winnipeg, there was little that was retained by True North outside of player personnel. New coaching and management staff was hired, a new colour scheme for the jerseys was found, even the team mascot, Thrash, was left behind.

But amid all the changes, one thing was retained and today remains a constant for the Jets—the Dan Snyder Memorial Award.

Snyder was an undrafted signee of the Thrashers back in 1999 after finishing his junior career with the Owen Sound Platers. He joined the Orlando Solar Bears of the IHL and won the Turner Cup with the club in the league's final season. After the league dissolved, Snyder joined the Chicago Wolves and spent the next two seasons travelling between their locker room and that of the Thrashers. Across parts of three seasons, Snyder played in 49 NHL games and registered 16 points.

Snyder's life came to an end six days after being in a car wreck with teammate Dany Heatley. Heatley was the driver in a single-car collision, hitting a brick pillar and fencing. Snyder's passing was a shock and devastating to those who knew him; but in the wake of his death numerous beneficiaries have come about, including a scholarship fund and a memorial foundation, which has benefited the construction of a sports complex in his hometown of Elmira, Ontario.

Snyder's legacy was also carried forward by the Wolves, who named their Man of the Year award in his honour, the OHL in naming their humanitarian award the Dan Snyder Memorial Trophy, and the Thrashers created the Dan Snyder Memorial Award, given to the player that, "best embodies perseverance, dedication, and hard work without reward or recognition, so that his team and teammates might succeed."

The award's continued legacy can be attributed to one man—Jets GM Kevin Cheveldayoff. Chevy was the general manager of the Chicago Wolves when Snyder played for the club. After Snyder's passing Cheveldayoff remained close with his family.

"I've known the Snyder family for a long time," Cheveldayoff told the *Winnipeg Free Press*. "They're special people that obviously went through a real tragic time. Their son was a real special person in my world because he embodied how you should play the game.

"He was a person that didn't get a lot of notoriety or recognition, who fought his way into the organization, earned his way up through the ranks and earned his way onto the NHL team. He was a character person. He played hard each and every night. He would be a player that would make the Winnipeg Jets fans very proud if he was on the Jets' team right now."

Snyder's father, Graham, asserted the closeness and was thankful for everything Chevy has done.

"He felt that he had a pretty close attachment with Dan and he shared with me that when he's looking at hockey players sometimes, he'll compare them to Dan and say, 'That guy's got a little bit of Dan Snyder in him,'" Snyder said in a *Winnipeg Free Press* interview. "That's always great to hear. Chevy was a big part of Dan's career with the Chicago Wolves, and we have some great memories from there."

Since the Dan Snyder Memorial Award was ported over to the Jets, four Jets have received the honour, including Mark Stuart (2012), Zach Redmond (2013), Bryan Little (2014), and Chris Thorburn (2015). Little also was the final recipient of the award while the Thrashers were in existence.

Snyder's No. 37 was retired by the Thrashers, and though Winnipeg hasn't followed suit officially yet, the Jets continue to honour him, as no player has worn Snyder's No. 37 to date.

87 The Popcorn Incident

"I'll never forget this as long as I live—we're playing in Winnipeg and we're winning the hockey game and some fan threw a box of popcorn on the ice. It stopped the game and gave Sather a chance to regroup his team."

—Barry Shenkarow, former Winnipeg Jets owner

Oh what could have been.

As discussed earlier, Dave Ellett's heroics during the 1990 playoffs put the hated Edmonton Oilers on the brink of elimination in the first round of the series. With the Jets up three games to two and at home, they seemed to be in the fast lane to finally shake the albatross. In Game 6, the Jets went into the first intermission down 3–0 on goals by Esa Tikkanen, Mark Messier, and Randy Gregg. To the delight of local fans though, the Jets slowly crawled back. First Mark Kumpel scored in the second, followed by Doug Smail and Doug Evans in the third to even up the game. Momentum was on their side.

But then came that fateful box of popcorn. For whatever reason, the Jets just couldn't overcome the shakeup of that fateful day. When that moment interrupted play, the Jets were seemingly on the way to victory; but everything stopped dead. Jari Kurri ended up putting home the game winner.

For those who bore witness to the events that unfolded, it was heartbreaking. So much potential was on the Jets side that season, but it all fell apart in Game 6, and the team just couldn't recover. Game 7 was to be played in Edmonton. The Oilers struck first with a Glenn Anderson marker, one that was equalized less than 30 seconds later by Thomas Steen, giving the Jets a glimmer of hope. But unfortunately, Steen's goal was going to be the last. With just over two minutes left in the period, Mark Lamb tallied. A scoreless second period put the Jets up against the ropes, with Tikkanen putting the Oilers up 3–1 just over five minutes into the final frame. A final tally, again by Kurri, put the game out of reach.

It was a killer moment for the Winnipeg faithful.

"The deciding game of that series, I remember, because it was like a dagger through the hearts of the team and its fans," longtime broadcaster Scott Oake said. "It's unfortunate that I remember a trying time more than a successful one, but at the time the Jets were playing in a division with the Oilers and the Calgary Flames and they were, some could argue, among the three best teams, if not *the* three best teams in the NHL, and the Jets just couldn't get past the Oilers or Flames.

"That was their big opportunity to do it. It didn't work, and it's unfortunate because I think or certainly thought at the time what might've been had they been able to get past the Oilers. It looked like they would, but they didn't."

For the next six years, the Jets languished in the standings. Three times they didn't make the playoffs. In 1991–92, the Jets again took a decided opening series advantage, this time having a 3–1 against the Vancouver Canucks; but just like in 1989–90, the Jets crumbled and lost in seven. It was a heartbreaking experience, but not nearly as hurtful as that 1989–90 playoff series, decided by a box of popcorn.

88 Chant "True North!" Outside of Winnipeg

Earlier, I discussed how there's no experience quite like taking part in the anthem when it is sung at the MTS Centre; but if you really want to have fun, try chanting "True North!" in a venue outside of Winnipeg. It's almost irritating to another home rink, and can surely throw the Jets' opposition off their game for the night; and it's something the NHL fanbase has had to see on several occasions.

Winnipeg Jets fans can be found across North America. Part of the reason for that, naturally, can be attributed to the affinity that the Jets built by simply returning to the NHL.

The good will that Mark Chipman and his associates brought to hockey simply cannot be ignored, and it gained the new Jets a cult following, the likes of which are rarely seen outside of the Original Six. Comparing those two sides is like apples and oranges—the Six have deep roots in almost every hockey venue simply because, for decades, they were the few clubs that were broadcast across the frozen landscape, while the Jets are so new that they have not established bitter rivals and instead have been able to gain admiration for their dedicated play.

This brings us to the second reason why you'll hear "True North!" shouted in every corner of the hockey globe—migration. Though Winnipeggers are a hearty breed, loyal to their city, they spread across North America almost unlike any other city's population. That cities like Toronto have been known to host "Winnipeg parties" chock full of proud ex-pat 'Peggers tells you all you need to know about how far and wide born and bred River City sons and daughters have gone.

Those who did leave Winnipeg proudly carried the banner of the Jets with them. During the absence of the Jets from the NHL, the familiar blue or white jerseys would often be seen in arenas across North America, proudly worn by Winnipeggers who remained faithful to the team they grew up with, not those of their adopted new homes.

The third reason, then? There is a strong group of Winnipeggers that travel across the map to see their beloved Jets in enemy territory. Known on Twitter as #jetsarmy, these group of road warriors travel across Canada and the U.S. to show just how dedicated they are, with their rally cries of "True North!" and "Go Jets Go" leading the way.

Though the ultimate stop comes in the previously discussed visits to Arizona, there are larger trips that are made, including full swings through the west coast to Anaheim, San Jose, and Los Angeles. Ted Wyman of the *Winnipeg Sun* talked about one particular road trip made in early 2015. "This should be fun. I'm heading to Arizona Wednesday morning to cover the Jets game against the Coyotes on Thursday. I'm hearing there are likely to be hundreds, if not thousands, of Jets fans at the game in Glendale and a similar number are expected to be on hand for the Teemu Selanne tribute on Sunday night at the Honda Center in Anaheim," Wyman said.

But it wasn't the only trip. In 2014, Subway sponsored a contest that would bring Winnipeggers through a similar California tour, while other independent trips have been assembled.

As a result of this movement, the two strongest words that anyone in any rink across the NHL—not just in Winnipeg—will ever hear are, "True North!"

89 Worst Seasons

As much as hockey fans love to celebrate the best of their team's performance on the ice, they like to forget the worst periods in franchise history; well, unless said slump results in a first overall draft pick, but I digress.

When you look through NHL record books, you're going to find a bevy of lists that tribute the best teams in NHL history; but there's also that curious eye that then goes over to the worst performances. And this, unfortunately, is where the Jets come into the mix.

Now the Jets' first NHL squad will never be confused with being a hockey heavyweight. Outside of the mid-1980s squads, the team was fairly solidly entrenched in the middle pack of the league, more often than not making the playoffs but never being a serious contender to vault past the Smythe or Norris Division play (namely because of their uber-power opposition).

There were however, six seasons in which the Jets didn't qualify for the playoffs, and among those you'll find horrible seasons of ineptitude.

The first season came in 1980–81. This, of course, was the season that led to Dale Hawerchuk being picked first overall in the following summer's NHL Entry Draft. How bad was the Jets' year you ask? They only mustered nine wins in 80 games. Yep, they didn't even make double digits. They also finished an astounding 42 points out of a playoff spot. Heck the Colorado Rockies, the fifth-ranked team in the Smythe Division, finished 25 points ahead of them.

Those nine precious victories were split evenly between three goalies: Markus Mattson, the protected netminder from the

WHA dispersal, Pierre Hamel, who only a season earlier sported a lofty-by-comparison 9–19–3 record, and Michel Dion, a moody netminder who earlier in the season quite literally walked away from the Quebec Nordiques. But the netminders' sorrowful performances were matched by the team's forwards. In the goal-rich 1980s, only one Jet—Morris Lukowich—broke the 30 goal barrier.

The 1980–81 season wasn't just a low for the Jets—it was a landmark level of ineptitude in the NHL. The Jets still hold the record for most consecutive games without a win: 30 (23 losses, 7 ties). By the narrowest of margins—one game—the Jets escaped the full-out humiliation of being the team with the lowest number of wins in NHL history. That dubious distinction belongs to the Washington Capitals with eight wins in 1974–75.

The Jets' other black mark comes from 1993–94. That season, the Jets finished 25 points out of a playoff spot and at the bottom of the Western Conference. Fans in Edmonton who were hurting and aching for the days of their dynasty were still able to have one gloating mark—they finished seven points ahead of Winnipeg.

Just how bad was the season? Like the 30-game winless skid that preceded it, the Jets went on a horrible streak of 19 games without a W. So bad was the performance on the ice that the Jets felt the need to create an advertising campaign to express how sorry they were. A commercial that aired locally thanked fans for sticking by the team through this dark period.

Now knock on wood this sort of ineptitude will never happen again for the Jets, but if it does happen, there are two precedents set in Winnipeg for just how bad a team can be; and hey, it's not like the preceding Thrashers, who made the playoffs only once in their history (and never won a single postseason contest), were that good, either.

90 The Dissection of the 1984–85 Jets

The Winnipeg Jets' general managers have made some trades that are puzzling and others that outraged fans; but none quite had the puzzlement of the deal that brought Ray Neufeld to Winnipeg.

Sure, Teemu Selanne's departure to Anaheim hurt like all heck, but when you see that the decision became whether it was he or American Keith Tkachuk that was going to continue on with the team to Phoenix, you understand why management made the decision they did. Dale Hawerchuk's trade was in part out of frustration with the Jets' management, so that too is not the team's fault (well, except for their choice in office employ).

But looking back at the trades the Jets made in the 1.0 years, none are as head-scratch inducing as the one that brought Ray Neufeld to town and sent Dave Babych to Hartford.

Babych, of course, was coming off one of his best seasons since being taken second overall in 1980. With the powerhouse team of 1984–85, Babych potted 62 points in 78 games.

The same amount of points, coincidentally, as Neufeld. So from the statistical view, the trade made sense right? If they scored equally they're equally as good, no?

Hardly.

Neufeld (a forward, vs. Babych, a defenceman) arrived in Winnipeg and finished the 1985–86 campaign with 25 goals. The next two seasons he couldn't crack the 20-tally plateau. Soon, he earned a dubious nickname: Stone Hands.

Now to be fair, Neufeld wasn't just any player—he was a *hometown* player. Born and bred in Winnipeg, Neufeld played his first two years of junior for the Flin Flon Bombers of the old WCHL.

He was also coming off three straight seasons of at least 25 goals and 55 points, so the Jets had good reason to try to snag him.

But ultimately, Neufeld was one of the trades that marked the not-so-careful dissolve of what had been a strong team in mid-1980s and became a symbol of expectations that the Jets weren't going to be able to meet. Other deals looked like this:

Brian Hayward—Steve Penney and Jan Ingman—Hayward was a bit more of a unique situation. Up until the 1984–85 season, he was merely a part-timer with the Jets, often biding his time in the AHL; but with the trade of Doug Soetaert, he was elevated to starting duties in Winnipeg and posted a 33–17–7 record in his first full season in the crease at the Winnipeg Arena. One year later, though, Hayward was sporting an unsavoury 13–28–5 run and was soon dealt to Montreal. There, he posted three straight seasons of above-.500 hockey playing in tandem with Patrick Roy. Penney, meanwhile, played only 15 times for the Jets over two seasons, compiling a 3–8–12 record, while Ingman never left the Swedish Elite League.

Paul MacLean—Brent Ashton—MacLean played seven seasons with the Jets and only once scored less than 30 goals. Heck, he hit the 40-goal mark three times and also thrice had over a point-per-game pace; yet the summer of 1988 saw the Jets swap MacLean for Brent Ashton, who by this point had already been on six different NHL teams. In his three years with the Jets, Ashton broke the 30-goal mark once. Early in the 1991–92 season, Ashton was sent to Boston for Petri Skriko.

Brian Mullen + 1 Draft Pick—2 Draft Picks—Mullen was another of the Jets' many 30-goal scorers in 1984–85. More importantly, in his five seasons with the club, he never went below 50 points, nor did he in his four subsequent seasons with the New York Rangers. Say what you will about draft picks, but trading away Mullen's production was not the best move management ever made.

Laurie Boschman—Bob Brooke—Boschman was a rugged player who, in eight seasons with the Jets, went over the 25-goal mark four times and over the 150-penalty minute milestone six times. He was still playing effective brawny hockey when he was swapped to the New Jersey Devils for Bob Brooke in 1990. What makes the trade worse is that Brooke never played for the Jets, as he retired that summer.

91 Jennifer Hanson and Stacey Nattrass

Throughout the Winnipeg Jets' history, there have been a variety of anthem singers, including major names from the recording industry like Burton Cummings; but ask any Jets fan who their favourite voices were and it will come down to two names: Jennifer Hanson and Stacey Nattrass.

Hanson came into her role as the anthem singer through Ralph James, an agent whose roster of stars now includes the likes of Nickelback and the Barenaked Ladies. Hanson was signed to James at the time, who approached her with the opportunity to sing at a Jets game. Pushing herself out of her comfort zone, Hanson agreed to take on the challenge.

"It's terrifying," she said. "It doesn't matter if you're totally famous; when you step out in front of 15,000 people, it's terrifying."

After that first outing, Hanson began to sing more often, sharing duties with Chantal Kreviazuk, but by 1993, Hanson took the lead. The rest was history. For the vast majority of games through the team's departure, Hanson was the singing voice of the Jets, belting out "O Canada" and the "Star Spangled Banner" before home games through the end of the Jets' tenure in

Winnipeg. Perhaps unlike most singers, she admits to making a couple of mistakes along the way.

"One time I lost my voice at the top of a note and everybody laughed. I just wanted to fall through the ice and die," she recalled. "But when you're a professional you just move on and pretend that nothing happened."

Despite those trip-ups, Hanson became a known entity in Winnipeg and that translated into her becoming an integral part of the team's presentation.

"People responded to, what I think didn't have much to do with my singing, but the tarty red dress I was wearing," she said. "I think it just became more that I was seen on a regular basis, so it was a thing like anyone else who's regularly seen somewhere—you like seeing the same guy selling beer and hot dogs. People like knowing what they're getting—that familiarity."

Familiarity is also what Stacey Nattrass has in Winnipeg today. Back in 1997, True North was looking for someone to take the mic at Moose games. At the time Nattrass was a University of Manitoba music student and jazz singer by night. The guys she regularly played with were approached asking if they knew anyone who would be a potential anthem singer. Soon, Nattrass was auditioning and quickly became the melodic voice of the Moose. When the Jets came back, True North remained loyal to her. "When it was announced that the NHL was returning I waited until midsummer to learn that True North wanted to keep me on as their anthem singer," she said. "I was, of course, so thrilled!"

Much like Hanson's continual appearances at Jets games bred familiarity, so too has it for Nattrass, who notes that she gets people coming to talk with her when she's out and about in her daily life.

"I do get recognized from time to time," she said. "It usually happens at the store or the gas station. Sometimes people have just said 'Go Jets Go!' when they pass me. Other times, a person will ask for a picture. It really is flattering and sweet to be noticed at all. People are really generous and often just take time to tell me they like the job I do or to ask if it throws me off when people yell 'True North.'"

92 Deron Quint and the Two Fastest NHL Goals

Without sounding down on the Winnipeg Jets, there were admittedly a few times that the club pulled out some fluke performances.

In some seasons when the Jets had trouble beating those "easy picking" teams—that is when they weren't those teams themselves—they seemed to excel against the tougher clubs, though undoubtedly a few of those games were truly flukes.

But the biggest fluke of all in Jets history had nothing to do with winning a game—it was more about one of the lower-profile players gaining one of the most unique NHL records—Deron Quint and his tie of the mark for the two fastest goals in a game.

Quint, you see, was a rookie during the 1995–96 team that was the Jets' last in Winnipeg. Quint was on the opening night roster and tallied an assist in his first game. He showed all the promise of having a great NHL career as he finished the season with 18 points in 51 games—very respectable for a freshman rearguard.

Quint's NHL career wouldn't quite fill the promise of that first season. Though he'd play in more than 450 NHL games, he shifted play through five clubs, totalling only 143 points. Instead of becoming a standout in the NHL, Quint became a solid European name whilst spending time in leagues across Europe, including the German, Italian, and Swiss Leagues before landing solidly in the KHL, where he was still active as of the 2014–15 season and was also an All-Star.

The record came against the hated Edmonton Oilers in December of 1995, against Joaquin Gage, a career minor leaguer who saw action in just 23 NHL games, going 4–12–1. The first came toward the end of a powerplay for the Jets, with Quint throwing a wristshot on net off a feed from Dallas Drake that got through traffic and initially looked like it was going to be credited to another rookie, Shane Doan; but replays showed that the puck went in off an Oiler stick.

Then the game made history.

In the ensuing faceoff, Quint took a pass from Alexei Zhamnov at his blue line and threw what looked like an innocent shot toward the boards. The puck took a funny bounce, and rather than Gage playing it behind the net as he had anticipated, the biscuit ended up in the yawning net.

The accomplishment tied a record that, surprisingly, has been accomplished on one other occasion. The first "two in four" trick was turned by Nels Stewart in 1931 while with the Montreal Maroons.

Here's the funny thing—if you look the video up on YouTube, Quint barely plays up the moment. Sure, unless he was the Rain Man of hockey, there's no way young Deron would've known he tied an age-old record, but his reaction made it seem like it was just another day at the office for the blueliner, rather than being a feat that, even without the time span, is unique for a defenseman.

As unique as the accomplishment was for Quint, it wasn't the only time a Jet hit an NHL standard for quick goals. In 1981, Doug Smail scored just five seconds into a game against the St. Louis Blues, a mark later tied by Bryan Trottier and Alexander Mogilny. Additionally, on February 29, 1980, fresh off his performance at the Miracle on Ice, Dave Christian established the NHL record for fastest goal to start a career, when he tallied just seven seconds into his inaugural game, a contest against the Vancouver Canucks.

Winnipeg also has a tie to a similarly-themed mark. The most celebrated of all speedy records belongs to Bill Mosienko, a former Winnipegger, who put together a hat trick in just 21 seconds. Mosienko, incidentally, still has a mural up in Winnipeg on the side of his namesake bowling alley in the city's north end. The depiction shows Mosienko in a reproduction of the famous shot of him holding the three pucks. Unfortunately, no such rendition exists of Deron Quint.

93 Taking Flight in the Maritimes

Think it takes a lot to have the privilege of sipping from Lord Stanley's Mug? Try getting your gloves on the Calder Cup. Just ask Mark Chipman.

Chipman, of course, cut his teeth with team ownership during the days of the Manitoba Moose. He knows the ropes of how things operate and the pitfalls that can happen, even as a team moves deep into the playoffs.

The reality Chipman faced with the Moose and every AHL team executive faces is that roster changes can happen any time, including during the playoffs. This can wreak havoc if both NHL and AHL clubs continue to stay off the golf course, and only once since the 1990s have both an NHL team and its AHL affiliate won their respective league championships—the 1994–95 season where the New Jersey Devils and Albany River Rats won the Stanley and Calder Cups, respectively.

Chipman and Co. experienced this hardship themselves. During the 2010–11 season, both the Moose and parent Vancouver Canucks were playing exceedingly well and both qualified for the

Ice Caps alum Adam Lowry skates past the faceoff circle.

playoffs. With Vancouver advancing all the way to the Stanley Cup Finals, the Moose were on high alert for call-ups which could throw their game off as they advanced into the second round, and stopped there, dead in their tracks.

That summer, Chipman reflected on the difficult journey for an AHL team.

"It's tough to win in the National Hockey League, but it's more difficult to win in the American League because of the uncertainty in your lineup and how deep your parent club is. We went to Game 7 in round two and lost in triple overtime. Had we got past that series, I don't know if we would've got much further," he said.

For the Winnipeg Jets' first affiliates, the St. John's Ice Caps, the playoffs were not a concern through the Jets' first three years, as the senior club didn't make the playoffs. This allowed the Ice Caps to bond as a team and take a serious run at the Calder, which they did in 2013–14, advancing all the way to the Finals.

There is a uniqueness to the Jets' AHL affiliate, the St. John's Ice Caps (as they were known through the 2014–15 hockey season)—True North owns the club.

Not many clubs have this system in place, and as a result they are not always in control of their partnerships. As NHL watchers check out the frenzy that is free agency, AHL fans will keep an eye on affiliation agreements to see which club's prospects, middle-of-the-road players and older veterans will be playing in front of them in the forthcoming season.

There is unquestionably a benefit for a budding talent to get his first crack at the pro game in St. John's. The Newfoundland and Labrador capital, like Winnipeg, felt the sting of losing its club. Back in 2004–05, St. John's was home to the Maple Leafs' affiliate, the last Maritime team in the AHL; but at the end of the season, Toronto pulled its affiliation, bringing the team to the Ontario capital for the 2005–06 season. Thus, when Chipman chose to place his team in St. John's, there was a huge roar of applause and appreciation from local hockey-starved fans who have sold out the Mile One Centre game after game.

As a result, a player like Adam Lowry, a 2011 Jets draft pick who spent two seasons on the Rock, gets a taste of what it's like to play in front of a rabid crowd, similar to what he'd see in Winnipeg.

"St. John's does a great job of preparing you for the next level," Lowry said. "Obviously the size of the rinks is different, but to play in front of a sold-out crowd every night at home and get treated like you do—the organization is first class—is great and gives a smooth transition."

Though the Jets control their roster now, this wasn't always the case, as the first Jets organization had several affiliates over the years, including another Maritime team—the Moncton Hawks. For seven seasons, the Jets and Hawks did business together after the team was abandoned by Calgary and Boston. In their history, the Hawks made the postseason four times, going all the way to the Calder Cup Finals in 1993–94, their last year in existence.

94 Sit in a Winnipeg Arena Chair

The destruction of the Winnipeg Arena wasn't an easy time for anyone involved. Fan, staff member, construction crew…

Oh that last one? Allow me to explain.

Whatever the Arena was constructed from should be used for airplanes and cars, because on the fateful day that the building was rigged up for the biggest implosion in Winnipeg history outside of the 2014 provincial government, the Arena was detonated but didn't fall. Sure, the outer brick and mortar collapsed as it was supposed to, but the metal framework of the Winnipeg Arena stayed intact. It took haulers to finally bring the Arena down to its final resting spot.

Truly, the Winnipeg Arena was a symbol of the strength of Winnipeg's hockey faithful, who persevered and refused to give up hope that the Jets would one day return to Winnipeg. The closing of the original building was emotional, and as was the case with so many stadiums of that vintage who met the wrecking ball, the Winnipeg Arena was gutted well before destruction day and parts were sold to the public.

Here's what differentiated the Arena from others—the sale only involved seats. Whereas the Montreal Forum sold off everything up to and including its hot dog rollers and the Boston Garden put its bricks up for sale with placards mounted for posterity, the Jets only sold the chairs—reds and blues—to the public. Where possible, the entire seat was put up for bids, but other cases only had the backs available. Some were old-fashioned wood, others had leather-covered cushions.

The sale went well with thousands of seats grabbed up as the only official offering by the club, though it wasn't a complete sell-out on first go. As such, the number of seats visible around Winnipeg today aren't as numerous as they are in other markets. Montreal Forum seats aren't hard to come by, but try to find a Winnipeg Arena chair these days.

Thus, the challenge—find a Winnipeg Arena seat to sit in. They aren't as plentiful as you might think.

Oh but don't think these seats are the only living remnants of the Winnipeg Arena, not by a longshot.

As one might expect, the day that the Winnipeg Arena came down wasn't just a day of distant mourning for the citizens of Winnipeg—it became a rescue day. Once the Arena was clear of the destruction crew, fans began scouting the area for bricks and other pieces of the building to rescue as souvenirs. Spaces in the chain link enclosure that kept the public secure when the implosion went off were now just wide enough for fans to break through and secure their piece of Winnipeg hockey history. Other fans were known to have gone dumpster diving, picking up other discarded items from the old barn such as glass panels from out of town scoreboards.

Other fans chose the more, shall we say, "sane-itary" method to getting their memories in. During their last year-and-a-half of play in the Winnipeg Arena, the Manitoba Moose wore commemorative patches on their jerseys, and, of course, the seasonal souvenirs like pocket schedules, media guides, and ticket stubs still make for fun eBay pickups.

95 Don Baizley

Winnipeg's work in the NHL has been seen in more areas than just on the ice. From team ownership to the broadcast booth, the heartland of hockey has produced some of the greatest to ply their trade around the sport; and there may be no individual who has made more of an impact with so many players across so many teams than Don Baizley.

Baizley was more than just your average player agent—he was a true builder of the sport of hockey. So revered was Baizley by his peers that, as the story goes, in the pursuit of bringing Paul Kariya under his wing, Michael Barnett once said that if the then prospect didn't sign with him, he hoped he would go to Baizley. Kariya would indeed become a client of Baizley's, along with the likes of Joe Sakic and Theoren Fleury.

But Baizley's biggest influence came in his relations with European players. In later years, he represented Saku Koivu and Peter Forsberg, but before that he was influential as one of the first agents to explore bringing Swedish and Finnish stars to the NHL and WHA. It's perhaps not surprising that Baizley, who called Winnipeg home after being born in Kenora, was instrumental in bringing European players to the Jets. That pathway began in the WHA days, when Baizley was still a young buck. Part of his mission was to bring Anders Hedberg and Ulf Nilsson to Winnipeg. At the first meeting with the European superstars, Baizley wasn't, shall we say, at his presentable best. Having lost his luggage during a flight to Stockholm, Baizley was somewhat unkempt, as Hedberg recalled.

"It was the first and only time in my life I ever saw him unshaved," Hedberg told the *Globe and Mail*. "He didn't look like a sophisticated lawyer from a big law firm in Winnipeg at the time. But obviously he made a hell of an impression on us. We had our girlfriends at the time with us and there was no question that he was going to represent us."

There was still an obstacle, though—being among the first Europeans to come to North America, there was a definite fish-out-of-water sense, along with some ill feelings from some in and around the NHL who didn't like the idea of import players taking jobs from local boys. Baizley, however, helped Hedberg and Nilsson settle into North American life.

"I can't imagine how we would have managed without Don," Hedberg said. "He allowed us into his and [his wife] Lesley's social network, which was so warm and so genuine and so interesting. We were new immigrants and they just opened their arms and allowed us to be part of their circle."

Later, Baizley represented Teemu Selanne in his journey to Winnipeg and beyond. Selanne, upon hearing the news of Baizley's passing in 2013, recounted how close the two were in an interview with the *Winnipeg Sun*. "Don was a very special person. He was not only a great agent for me—he was my 'American Dad,' great friend, mentor, and supporter during my career," Selanne stated. "Don will always have a special place in my heart."

At the heart of everything Don Baizley did was his passion for the game, and his influence has led to a local movement headed by former CJOB broadcaster Vic Grant. Among those supporting Grant's movement is Steve Dryden of TSN. In talking about the movement in an editorial on the station's website, Dryden described Baizley as such:

"Baizley was an original thinker whose counsel was sought by people at all levels of hockey—on and off the ice and on both sides of the management-labour divide.

"He conducted himself professionally and personally with the utmost integrity. He was regarded as the most respected man in hockey, and he used his position and powers of persuasion, not just for the betterment of his players, but for the sport."

96 Heading Outdoors

One of the traditions that almost every Manitoba boy and girl will take part in is getting out on a frozen pond and playing a pick-up game, regardless of how far below zero Celsius the temperature drops.

The tradition is as old as the game itself, and is a huge reason why the province has become known as one of the hotbeds for the game. While full-contact league play requires helmets, padding, and the whole nine yards, pond hockey is simple—a few sticks, pairs of skates, a puck, and a designated goal (if a net isn't available) is all you need in order to get a game going.

When outdoor games were first popularized in the NCAA and NHL just after the start of the new millennium, Manitobans began to ask when it would be Winnipeg's turn to host such a game. With Canad Inns Stadium a suitable size for a game and its successor, Investors Group Field being built, the whispers and speculation grew that a game could feasibly take place. Sure, the dead of winter wasn't going to be the best time, nor would the NHL's showcase date of New Year's Day for the Winter Classic due to the inhuman temperatures; but with schedules going into April, the possibilities were certainly there.

Fuelling the speculation that an outdoor game, be it the Heritage Classic or another branded opportunity, were outdoor practices that the Moose and later the Jets began indulging in; and if you haven't been to one of those practices, they're quite a sight to see. Exhaust barrels out of players' mouths and noses while bits of frost form on their facial hair. Truly, these players are getting a taste of what so many of us grew up doing.

But more than just being an opportunity for the Jets to get outside and enjoy some fresh winter air, the outdoor practices have become one of the most anticipated events on the calendar for fans. Though the team from time to time will open up the doors to the MTS Centre or IcePlex for Jets faithful to watch the players go through their daily drills, this becomes one of the biggest outdoor festival days on Winnipeg's social calendar, drawing fans outdoors for the chance to get up close and personal with their beloved Jets.

The tradition probably met its biggest challenge in 2014. This was one of the harshest winters on record in Winnipeg, dating back to the late 1800s and early 1900s; but that didn't stop hundreds of fans from coming to The Forks and seeing the team first practice then play an intra-squad scrimmage game on the frozen waters of the Red and Assiniboine River, where a makeshift rink with boards that weren't more than a foot high met the Jets. Fans lined the areas around the boards and benches, even grabbed spots on nearby railway tracks to take in all the action. The day also included kids getting the opportunity to skate alongside their heroes in the scrim game.

"It's a great thing," Andrew Ladd told Kirk Penton of the *Winnipeg Sun*. "The train tracks in the background and everybody out here, it's cool. It would be nicer if it was a little warmer, but the guys are having fun just playing a little game of shinny."

But the outdoor skates were a mere tease for what has become anticipation for a full-out game to take place. Original reports had the game set to take place during the 2015–16 season; but then scheduling conflicts arose. As Gary Lawless of the *Winnipeg Free Press* reported in January 2015, the NHL and the would-be hosts of the game—the Winnipeg Football Club (aka the Bombers)—couldn't come to a mutually-agreed upon date.

"The NHL wanted to play the game in late December, while the football club was pushing for a February date," Lawless reported on January 20. "The Bombers didn't want the game played so close to the Grey Cup, while February doesn't work for the NHL due to its All-Star Game and other soon-to-be announced outdoor games."

And so, initial planning that had commenced in 2013 and seemed like such a sure thing was set aside, with the hope of a game happening instead in 2016–17.

No matter when the game happens, it will assuredly be the biggest event in Winnipeg hockey history, and will give everyone in the Manitoba capital, with the eyes of the hockey world on them, the opportunity to say in one united voice, "Cold enough for ya?"

97 The Patience of Kevin Cheveldayoff

Winnipeg hockey fans are among the most passionate in hockey, which can be a very good thing and a very bad thing.

Passionate fans don't just love the game—they love winning, at times with such vigor that they'll push as hard as possible for their team to pull out a victory. These aren't just armchair quarterbacks or fantasy league general managers—as far as they're concerned they *are* NHL general managers. Listen to any call-in sports show in Winnipeg and you'll get a lesson on what this line should have done, which goalie should have played, or which combination of defencemen would have worked best.

But the biggest sound of a dissatisfied fan will boil down to the lineup that is fielded game-in and game-out. As fans ached for swaps to be announced at the NHL Trade Deadline, at the NHL Entry Draft and throughout every season and off-season, there was one man who was standing in opposition to the pleas of the masses—Kevin Cheveldayoff.

Kevin Cheveldayoff was very familiar to Winnipeg's hockey nuts when he was named the new Jets general manager in advance of the 2011–12 NHL Entry Draft. A former member of the Brandon Wheat Kings, Chevy endured a career-ending injury before ever playing in the NHL; but he soon entered the management ranks, first with the Utah Grizzlies and then with the Chicago Wolves, a continual rival of the Manitoba Moose.

If there's anything that Chevy was able to do better than any GM in the minor leagues, it was win. Between the Grizzlies and Wolves, Chevy earned two Turner Cup and two Calder Cup championships, making him attractive to any NHL team; and that opportunity came with the Chicago Blackhawks. Again, Cheveldayoff was a winner, as the Hawks claimed the Stanley Cup in Chevy's first year as assistant general manager.

So when Cheveldayoff was named the GM of the Jets, he was arriving with the resume that every team would want; but he was entering an environment that was infamous for rushing prospects into the NHL. Names like Evander Kane and Zach Bogosian had been pushed into the big league right out of the junior ranks. That wasn't going to be the case with Chevy, who didn't rush any of the first round picks through 2014 into the NHL.

He also quickly gained the reputation for hitting the stop button on NHL Trade Deadline Day. Rather than panic and make a wild deal, Chevy was more prone to grab players like Grant Clitsome off the waiver wire. Free-agent signings at the beginning of the open buying period were also methodical—rather than get the biggest fish swimming in the bowl, Chevy built his team carefully, picking up the likes of Mathieu Perreault.

That didn't mean, though, that when needed Cheveldayoff didn't do what was best for his team, as head coach Paul Maurice told Gary Lawless of the *Winnipeg Free Press* in 2015. "We had a conversation on a Saturday before I took the job about the way this was going to go. The plan. He's been true to his word," Maurice said. "Twice now we've been in a bit of trouble, we had all our D going down and he brings in Jay Harrison and now Evander goes down and is done for the season and that's a hole we couldn't fill. Without hitting the panic button, when we've needed help, our management group has given us all we could ask for."

With each passing season, the Jets seemed to inch closer to the promised land of the playoffs. And when they did make it, it was because of the patience shown by Keven Cheveldayoff.

98 Exhibitions in Winnipeg

In the "in between" years, Winnipeggers had more than just the Manitoba Moose to whet their appetites for premier-level hockey. Though the AHL and IHL sustained the interest and were the primary reason why the NHL seriously considered a proposal to return to the Manitoba capital, there were other considerations.

After a couple years' wait, the NHL began to tour through Winnipeg on a nearly annual basis as exhibition games were staged at the Winnipeg Arena and later the MTS Centre. In total, eight games were played on the two rinks, and more often than not they had a tie to local hockey.

The first three games were contests of the Vancouver Canucks, who were the Moose's parent club for two of the three games (the first, in 2000, was while the Moose were still in the IHL). Played at the Winnipeg Arena, the games featured the Canucks against the Minnesota Wild twice (2000, 2003) and Edmonton Oilers once (2002). The next three were those of the Phoenix Coyotes. In consecutive years starting in 2006, the Yotes returned to Winnipeg, squaring off with Canadian opponents each time—the Oilers (2006), the Toronto Maple Leafs (2007), and the Calgary Flames (2008). Those games were followed up by the Tampa Bay Lightning playing "host" to the Oilers (2009) and Chicago Blackhawks (2010), the last of which may have been the most popular of all the contests—the team featured three hometown boys, including Jonathan Toews, Patrick Sharp, and Duncan Keith.

Having NHL players take to the ice on the home rink was a treat for a number of Winnipeggers. Yes, the squads didn't feature all the big names a club had to offer, what with this being a warm-up period for some and a proving ground for others as rosters had yet to be trimmed for the season; but the opportunity to see the likes of Henrik Sedin, Steven Stamkos, and Mats Sundin drew decent numbers overall.

The display wasn't, of course, favourable to everyone in Winnipeg. Sell-out arenas weren't the order of the day—they were a rarity. Some contests barely got past the 10,000-ticket plateu in attendance. This drew the cynicism from longtime journalist Tim Campbell of the *Winnipeg Free Press*. Prior to the 2009 contest between the Oilers and Lightning, Campbell wrote a scathing editorial about the NHL's now annual parade of shinny that came through the MTS Centre. Part of his write-up focused directly on the sufferings of the former team that dwelled in the city.

"The previous three, in fact," Campbell wrote, "were a golden-goose scenario for the Phoenix Coyotes, who daringly parachuted into their old hometown to extract bags of cash from Manitobans pining for their old league and an in-person glimpse of Wayne Gretzky. The Coyotes, actually clever enough to bring in the Toronto Maple Leafs as their opponents once, made a bundle more than they would have holding preseason games at home, which goes some way to explaining why their fate is today in the hands of a bankruptcy judge."

But was there a hidden agenda by the NHL? Yes, the teams could choose out-of-town locations for their hosted exhibition games, but the NHL had final say. So, one then has to wonder if there was a bit of site investigation into Winnipeg, especially with five consecutive years of games. Darren Ford believed so.

"Definitely a gauge. 100%," he said. "Not that the revenue didn't hurt, but they did their research meticulously. As did I. Ticket pricing models were my forte, and the Oilers had been gracious in divulging their classified financials to True North, as the next smallest market, to work from."

99 Ties to the Moose

Uprooting any sports team and moving it, no matter what the level, often means that personnel changes will come. It's inevitable.

As demonstrated earlier with the Winnipeg Jets and Craig Heisinger's decision to remain in Winnipeg, some staff will stay back in the original city. Others will join the team in their new location. It's not an easy decision to make, and usually one that doesn't come immediately.

In purchasing the Atlanta Thrashers, True North had its own staffing decisions to make—do they put forward offers to the existing Thrashers personnel? Do they start from scratch, putting out "wanted" ads to the sporting world, knowing that countless professionals would be knocking at their door? Nope—they kept the vast majority of their Manitoba Moose staff in place. From Heisinger and head coach Claude Noel, to front office staff like marketing and PR departments, the look and feel of the Jets very much mirrored that of the AHL franchise.

Mark Chipman was one of the men behind this retention. "It's vital. [It's] one of the reasons we were able to do this," he said in the summer of 2011. "When we first presented in 2007, the way I positioned it to the executive committee is that we were a plug-and-play operation. We had all the assets needed. We had a building, we had a group of roughly 100 people that are running the hockey team now that are a hockey-based business. Literally, when we concluded the [2010–11] season, it was the same group we have. We couldn't have done it, we wouldn't have done it, if we didn't have a very mature organization."

But the loyalty to the Moose didn't stop there. Either immediately or over the course of their first few seasons, former players became part of the Winnipeg Jets' staff. They include:

Wade Flaherty (Goaltending Coach)—In the NHL, Flaherty was a well-travelled netminder who spent time with the Sharks, Islanders, Lightning, Panthers, and Predators, and though he tended the net for numerous AHL clubs as well he had one of the longest and most productive stretches of his career in Manitoba. The Jack A. Butterfield Award winner as playoff MVP in 2004, Flaherty was a dependable netminder and mentor for the Moose, going 62–36–9 during three seasons while helping guide prospects like Alex Auld and Corey Schneider in their development. Flaherty's last season in North America came with the Rockford IceHogs and he went on to play in Asian League Ice Hockey before joining the Chicago Blackhawks as a developmental coach and later the Jets in 2011.

Mike Keane (Assistant, Player Development)—It seemed a guarantee that Keane, a native Winnipegger, would eventually find his way onto the Jets' staff. Retiring from pro hockey with the Moose in 2009–10, Keane holds the unique distinction of being a Stanley Cup champion with three teams—the Montreal Canadiens, the Colorado Avalanche, and the Dallas Stars. Keane also was a captain in Montreal among other NHL accolades. He later signed on with the Vancouver Canucks and, after sitting out the NHL lockout season, joined the Moose in 2005–06 and spent the last five seasons of his career in Winnipeg. Keane's No. 12 jersey was the only one retired by the Moose, and the banner still hangs in the MTS Centre today.

Jason King (Assistant Coach, St. John's Ice Caps)—When the Jets returned, one of the players they brought back to the organization was King. Originally a Vancouver Canucks draft pick, King spent his first two professional seasons bouncing between the Moose and parent Canucks. By the time the 2004–05 NHL lockout was complete, King was shown to be not in the future plans of the Canucks, and after spending the 2006–07 in the Swedish Elite League, King was dealt to Anaheim where he played one season before returning to Europe to play in Germany. He was brought back to North American shores by the Jets but never made the NHL squad and retired partway through the 2012–13 season. When TNSE relocated their affiliate to Winnipeg, King remained with the Ice Caps.

Jimmy Roy (Coordinator of Player Development)—A long-serving member of the Manitoba Moose, Jimmy Roy played nine seasons in Winnipeg, including four years in the IHL and five in the AHL. Originally a Dallas Stars draft pick (1994), Roy came to the Moose in their second season after a tour of duty with the Canadian national team. Roy was a true grinder on the ice, eclipsing 100 penalty minutes in eight of his nine seasons. Roy was among the leaders of the Moose as an assistant captain, with his inarguable career highlight coming in 2006 when he was named captain of the Canadian team at the Manitoba-hosted AHL All-Star Classic.

100 Years of Manitoba Hockey

Through all the ups and downs and the presence and the absence of top-tier professional hockey, the joy of the sport has remained permanently etched in the fabric that makes up the province of Manitoba.

For a province that sees more days below zero Celsius (or Fahrenheit for that matter) than just about anywhere else on the planet, it's not hard to understand the connection between its citizens and the sport. From the Stanley Cup–winning days of the Winnipeg Victorias and Olympic champion Winnipeg Falcons to the modern days in the NHL, Manitoba has maintained a solid foundation of being part of the landscape of Canada's favourite sport.

For more than 100 years, the sport has driven youth activity in the province and adult adulation; so it was no surprise that when Hockey Manitoba set forth to produce a unique celebration for its centennial, that they looked to the future of organized hockey in the province, first by doing a unique program whereby kids were given free sticks by the organization. A series of outdoor games was also planned that began in December 2014 and carried forward to one of the coldest days on the calendar—a chilled mid-February day in 2015. Most would have seen kids playing outdoors and called their sons or daughters back home. But it was Hockey Manitoba Executive Director Peter Woods who summed it up best when he told the *Winnipeg Sun*'s Jim Bender that, "We were blessed with some good weather, a little chilly maybe, but okay."

For one coach, it was an opportunity to share the experience he had as a child with the kids he now had under his charge. "It's

Winnipeg's Stanley Cup Champions

While the Jets have yet to bring a Stanley Cup home to Winnipeg, there was a team that did accomplish this feat—twice.

Back in the days when the Cup was a championship more akin to what you'd see in MMA than a traditional sports trophy, the Winnipeg Victorias claimed the Dominion Hockey Challenge Cup (as it was named by Lord Stanley of Preston) on two occasions—first in 1896 and then in 1901. The second reign by the Victorias even extended into 1902 as they fought off multiple challenges.

Among those who played for these teams were future Hall of Fame members Dan Bain and Jack Marshall.

a big thing. They don't get to play outside like we did when we were kids. It'll be a change for them," Cory Usipiuk told the *Sun*. "They're learning they have to double up [clothing] like we did when we were kids to protect certain parts that are exposed."

These events may have been organized to commemorate and honour 100 years of the province's governing body for organized hockey, but the true celebration was that of a spirit that exists in Manitoba that is unparalleled. It was a staunch reminder that when a community comes together, anything is possible, even the rise of a new era of professional hockey. The Winnipeg Jets may have been born again by opportunity, but it was the spirit of Manitoba that brought professional hockey back to its capital, back to its biggest arena, and back to its people.

Acknowledgments

Thank you to the following people as part of this major project:

My loving wife, Elana, for her support and understanding as I spent many nights at the MTS Centre prepping this book.... My parents, in-laws, family, and friends who understood my need to continually talk hockey at every gathering, and at very least humoured my passion.... True North Sports and Entertainment for providing a cub Internet reporter the chance to first gain access to the team's locker room so many years ago (I won't say how many).... Triumph Books who believed in this project (and put up with my deadline shifting).... Dave Babych for writing an amazing foreword.... the players and personalities who took the time to talk with me and give me so much material to write about.

This book would not have been possible without the support of many individuals who either provided themselves for interviews or helped arrange others, or provided background information or photography. These individuals are recognized in the sources portion of the book.

Sources

Books

Hull, Brett and Allen, Kevin. *Brett: His Own Story*. Triumph Books, 2003.

Silver, Jim. *Thin Ice: Money, Politics, and the Demise of an NHL Franchise.* Fernwood Publishing, 1996.

Newspapers/Magazines/Agencies

Associated Press
Chicago Tribune
Edmonton Sun
Globe and Mail
Jets—The Official Magazine of the Winnipeg Jets
Jet Stream
Jewish Post and News
Kenora Daily Miner and News
Los Angeles Times
Metro Winnipeg
National Post
Ryerson Review of Journalism
The Hockey News
Toronto Sun
Washington Times
Winnipeg Free Press
Winnipeg Men Magazine
Winnipeg Sun

Websites

blackhawkslegends.blogspot.ca
cbc.ca
coyotes.nhl.com
espn.com
Facebook.com
hhof.com
hockeyadventure.com
jets.nhl.com
jetzaviation.com
kenoraline.com
Lastwordonsports.com
mnhockeyclub.com
nhl.com
ourhistory.canadiens.com
rivercitysportsblog.com
slam.canoe.ca
stadiumjourney.com
usahockeymagazine.com
winnipegbusstories.com
winnipegdowntownplaces.blogspot.ca
winnipegwhiteout.com

Broadcast Media

TSN
24 Hours Winnipeg

Other

Budweiser Canada (commercial)
Frykas, Randy *White Noise* Nüman Films (2011) (documentary)
Labatt Breweries (press release)
Manitoba Entertainment Complex (government presentation document)
Palson, Rod "Memories to Cheer" 1996 (song)

Interviews

Personalities interviewed for this book include:

Alex Steen
Alexandre Burrows
Anders Hedberg
Andrew Ladd
Andrew Paterson
Barry Shenkarow
Bob Essensa
Bob Irving
Brent Hawryluk
Bryan Little
Chris Thorburn
Corey Schneider
Curtis Walker
Dale Sawchuk
Dallas Eakins
Darren Ford
Dave Babych
David Perron
Dustin Byfuglien
Ezra Ginsburg
Gary Bettman
Jannik Hansen
Jennifer Hanson
Jim Slater
Joe Daley
John Ferguson
Jonathan Toews
Jordan Farber
Kris King
Laurie Boschman
Luciano Borsato
Matthew Janzen
Michael Hutchinson
Pat Elynuik
Paul Maurice
PK Subban
Robert Brown
Ryan Reeves
Scott Campbell
Scott Oake
Scott Taylor
Shane Doan
Stacey Nattrass
Teemu Selanne
Thomas Steen
Travis Zajac

Thank you to the following individuals and organizations for their assistance in setting up interviews:

Scott Brown (Winnipeg Jets/True North Sports and Entertainment)
Alfred de Vera (Vancouver Canucks)
Greg Oliver
Kalen Qually (Winnipeg Jets/True North Sports and Entertainment)
Rich Nairn (Phoenix Coyotes)
Kevin Shea
Carrie Shenkarow

Thank you also to Ezra Ginsburg, Michael Remis, Andrew Paterson, Michael Coodin, David Wolodarsky, Jets Hockey Forum members, and TSN1290 Radio listeners for their input on the creation of this list.

Photos

Thank you to the following individuals and organizations for their assistance with photography:

Steve Feldman
True North Sports and Entertainment